KEN FRANK'S

COOKBOOK

by KEN FRANK with Dewey Gram

SIMON & SCHUSTER

NEW YORK LONDON TORONTO
SYDNEY TOKYO SINGAPORE

Simon & Schuster
Simon & Schuster Building
Rockefeller Center
1230 Avenue of the Americas
New York, New York 10020

Copyright © 1992 by Ken Frank and Dewey Gram

Designed by Laurie Jewell
Manufactured in the United States of America

10   9   8   7   6   5   4   3   2   1

Library of Congress Cataloging-in-Publication Data

Frank, Ken, 1955–
[Toque cookbook]
Ken Frank's La Toque cookbook / Ken Frank with Dewey Gram.
p.   cm.
Includes index.
1. Cookery, French. 2. Toque (Restaurant) I. Gram, Dewey.
II. Title. III. Title: Toque cookbook.
TX719.F792   1992
641.5'09794'94—dc20   91-41343
                                                       CIP

ISBN 0-671-50617-X

To Nancy and Daniel
WLY?

Acknowledgments

I have long felt that cooking is truly the world's oldest profession. Everything I have learned comes from those who cooked before me. To acknowledge everyone who has contributed in some way to this book would be impossible. I have been encouraged and helped by Dewey; my agent, Kathy Robbins; and my editors, Carole Lalli and Kerri Conan—who are all possessed with endless patience. I have learned along the way from fellow cooks, family, friends, students, customers, and even dishwashers. But I have learned the most from a few truly great chefs. They love to cook, they love to eat, they love to teach, and they share recipes that pretenders would keep secret. Thank you all.

K.F.

The Project got its start, in good L.A. fashion, in a hairdresser's chair. Nancy (Ken's wife) cut my hair for years before I ever met Ken. Her raves about Ken's gifts with food whetted my appetite, and her clever matchmaking got us together.

Writing Ken's book with him—which turned out to be a far more demanding process than it looked—also turned out to be the most gratifying writing assignment I've ever had. I had the joy of learning a life skill from a master. As we wrote the recipes, I participated as one of the student-testers in Ken's cooking classes for over a year. It opened a room in the palace of life's pleasures where I feast gratefully today.

Special thanks also to my own wife, Nancy Hunt, and to the forebearing friends who invited us to dinner during this project. I went overnight from being a culinary illiterate to that most dangerous of creatures, a self-appointed food critic with a little knowledge and the craving to pontificate. I hereby apologize. I couldn't help myself. I hope the book makes up for it.

D.G.

Contents

Introduction

I am a lucky guy. Cooking is the love of my life, and there's nothing I'd rather be doing. Like a professional athlete or musician, I'm getting paid to do what I really enjoy. My restaurant, La Toque, is known in Los Angeles purely and simply for its great food.

La toque means the chef's hat. So La Toque, you might guess, is a chef's restaurant. That means the setting, the food, the cooking, and the style of service all spring from one person—the chef. That's me. And this book, you'll soon see, is my book. It's my personal, rather particular, and sometimes quirky statement of how to do great cooking.

Abandon old habits and preconceptions. This is one man's version of the right way to do it. Right at least by the lights of my seventeen years' experience in the heat of L.A.'s best restaurant kitchens. Right because I've made my reputation cooking great food to order for a small audience.

Since this is my book, it comes complete with my fanaticisms. This is how I taught myself to cook. I'll try not to pull any punches. You want unequaled cooking and eating experiences? Follow me. I'll lure you along with proddings, directives, exhortations. Trust me, it is a path to pure pleasure.

I've gotten a lot of praise and attention (too much even for my ears). But the skills, secrets, and palate that prompted such flowery acclaim are the guts of this book. Pull up a chair, let me share with you. Hey, I didn't get to where I am being bashful.

THE PERSON

The cooking bug bit me when I was just a kid, though I only realized what hit me much later. It sneaked up on me when I was helping with backyard barbecues. It creeped up unnoticed when my grandfather, also a self-taught cook, let me make the flapjacks for breakfast and showed me how to pull saltwater taffy.

Who knows why, but Howard Johnson's became a mecca for me. I used to watch the chefs in their tall white hats moving back and forth in the kitchen, and I remember wondering, What are they up to? I wish I could be in there too.

In seventh grade I made my first investment in the restaurant business.

Bought one share of Howard Johnson's stock and held it, excited when it split. When I ate them out of any possible profits by downing three dinners on all-you-can-eat fried-fish night, I thought, That's okay, I'm an owner.

Then I had the ultimate stroke of good fortune. My family moved to France for a year when I was fifteen, and we lived in a tiny fishing village called Yvoire on Lake Geneva. French public school and French girls took most of my time, but I really fell in love with French food. The lunches local women prepared in the school cafeteria were incredible. Richly flavored country food—stews, roasts, sausages, farm-fresh vegetables and cheeses—better food than I had ever known. These women could have made a fortune running a restaurant in the United States. It was an eye opener for me.

Then came another stroke of luck. I got the summer job that changed my life. My best friend, the youngest son of a ten-child French family, helped me get a job in a village restaurant. I washed dishes fourteen hours a day, seven days a week. Within a couple of weeks, eager beaver that I was, I got to be the kitchen gofer. I spent the rest of the summer making mountains of french fries, following the chef around and cleaning up after him—and absorbing all I could about French food.

I was hooked. There was no turning back.

The first thing I did back in the United States was figure out how to make the money to get right back to France. I got a weekend job cooking hamburgers at a nearby ski resort and was back in Yvoire the next summer, smelling and eating and cooking that indescribable food. I began to realize I could make my living this way.

THE PROFESSIONAL

The next winter in Pasadena, I parlayed my limited skills but fluent French into a job at a French restaurant with a real French chef, Ernest Didier. He took me under his wing. From there I went on to jobs in nine different fancy restaurants in the L.A. area until I was anointed head chef at La Guillotine at age twenty-one.

It was with my first mentor, Ernest Didier, however, that I made up my mind to become a great chef. In good adolescent fashion, I determined to become the American Paul Bocuse.

By the time I surfaced as head chef at La Guillotine in 1977, I had the temerity to write my own menu. And I got away with it—people liked my dishes. I realized I could keep doing my own thing. That jolt of confidence crystallized my chef's philosophy: I wanted to cook only at the very highest level, which means cooking to order for only a few people. Everything exactly my way, my hands on every dish. It is the style I still use at La Toque: cooking carefully for just a handful of people at a time.

That's what this cookbook is all about—great recipes on the scale of home cooking. Recipes that are great because they are born of the great traditions, brought up to date, and made useful to the home cook. Spontaneous, accommodating to the seasons, and relatively fast.

With practice, there is a great cook in everybody. That's the message of this book. It's a teaching book, meant to supply not just great recipes but all the experience and hints and shortcuts I've learned myself.

But don't mistake this for a "chef's" book, full of fancy recipes you need a professional kitchen to pull off. I call for a minimum of special equipment, other than good pans and knives. I don't believe in filling the kitchen with expensive gadgets. My idea of special chef's equipment runs more toward the plastic squeeze bottle of water I keep handy for thinning sauces.

The book *is* organized as a chef thinks, however, from prep work to presentation. When a chef walks into the kitchen to cook, he starts by putting everything in a certain order in his mind. Hence the organization of these recipes. They proceed from the laying out of ingredients through logical cooking sequences to the timely coming together of the completed dish.

This is a direct, practical style: It cuts right to the heart of what needs to be done. Follow my steps; stay with my sequences. After just a few of these recipes, you'll see the method to my madness— —you'll start to think like a chef.

The key is practice. That's how you learn to trust yourself.

I do use some chef's terminology in the book. It's because they are the best, most descriptive words and expressions for what they refer to. They shouldn't be a secret. They bespeak aspects of a professional kitchen that are relevant, that should be demystified and made accessible to the home cook.

Mise en place is the one French phrase I've left untranslated throughout the book, because there is no good English equivalent. It means thinking of what you need, organizing the steps in your mind, getting all your ingredients ready— laid out, organized, peeled, cut, mixed. It can be anything from trimming the meat and filleting the fish to making a mousse and chilling it. It includes chopping garlic, shallots, and herbs; peeling and blanching vegetables; making a dough or a filling; setting up a garnish; and making stocks and reductions.

Essentially, *mise en place* is doing whatever you can ahead of time so you can focus on the most important steps at the last minute. It is at the core of any good professional kitchen. It's the only way I manage to cook to order. Without *mise en place,* I'd be dead. *Mise en place* is part of thinking like a chef and cooking like a chef. Whether you're in the home or professional kitchen, the same thinking applies. Good cooks have good habits.

To deglaze a pan means to add liquid, usually wine, to a still very hot pan to loosen and dissolve the drippings and incorporate their flavor into a sauce.

Verify the seasoning is the single most important exhortation in the book. It means taste it, think about it, adjust it, taste it again—until it's right. Don't just give a cursory check, be sure of the flavor. Getting used to verifying the seasoning is important to cooking well. Learn to trust your palate.

THE FANATIC

Let me talk for a minute about why I like to do certain things certain ways. I am a little fanatical—in matters like turning vegetables, chopping shallots by hand and never in the food processor, making sure the diced vegetables for the seafood soup are pretty little dice, religiously skimming and carefully reducing my stock.

I'm not going to insist on traditionalist dogma like putting the head of the fish at the left of the plate—something an older, classically trained French chef does instinctively. I'm talking about details as a level of caring about what goes into a dish. I turn vegetables all to a similar size so they'll cook evenly. But they also look better and better express the idea that every little thing is as good as can be.

For instance, shallots chopped by hand taste better. In a food processor, shallots exude juice, which instantly oxidizes and ruins their flavor. By hand you can chop them perfectly evenly and fine, and most importantly without juicing them.

Another example: If you want perfect sauce, you have to start with perfect stock. All professional kitchens use stock—you can even buy stocks (at the Stock Market, of course), but they are invariably mediocre. As long as you're going to take the time to make stock, you might as well make it perfect. It doesn't take any longer or cost any more. The key to great stock is going back again and again to skim away all the impurities and fat—it simply makes it taste better. And it's more healthful. And once you've made a great stock, you'll have it ready to use on a moment's notice from the freezer.

Aesthetics are a big motivator for me: haphazard looks will diminish an otherwise perfect dish. With practice, doing things right takes no longer.

I think of the way my friend Sato, a sushi master, does things. The food at his sushi bar is always a little bit better. One day I saw him very carefully cutting an impossibly long paper-thin ribbon of daikon and shredding it with his knife. Shredded daikon is a standard garnish on a plate of sashimi. There's a great little machine that shreds daikon. I asked him why he was doing it by hand. He said that to the sushi master the shredded daikon represents his soul on your plate. The machine has no soul.

Ultimately soul is at the core of cooking really great food. And it's what sharing really great food with others is all about.

SUBSTITUTIONS, ALTERNATIVES

On the other hand, there are times I want people to take liberties, make substitutions, trust their own instincts. My recipe may call for two whole chickens. You can always use chicken breasts instead of cutting and boning your own chicken.

If you want to leave out some of the butter, if you want to mix and match sauces and fish, try it. If you want to add to or subtract from a salad, go ahead. It will usually work.

No, you don't have to fillet your own fish. You can buy fish already prepared. I like to buy whole fish because fish on ice and in the round stays much fresher. Once it's cut, handled and exposed to air, it begins to spoil and lose its fresh edge. If you want your fishmonger to cut your fish for you, the thing to remember is to buy it just before you are going to cook it.

EQUIPMENT

Knives Knives are the right place to start thinking about kitchen equipment. A few good knives are really essential. For the home cook, hardened stainless steel is a great choice. The good news is that you don't need as many as some people pretend they do.

MUST HAVES
A good ten-inch chef's knife
A good utility knife

A good but not expensive paring knife
A serrated bread knife
A sharpening steel

A **boning knife,** if you do a lot of butchering and filleting. Other specialized knives—cleavers, slicing knives, etc.

A **chef's knife** will last a home cook a lifetime and a chef ten years. There are times when only a large chef's knife will do—a big, long, heavy knife. Times when chopping with a small knife is just frustration. Trying to chop the knuckle off a chicken leg just doesn't work with a little knife. And a good sharp chef's knife does a pretty good job of slicing too. I tend to like a small chef's knife—10 inches. It's more versatile and easier to handle. It's rare that you really need a giant size.

You'll use the **utility knife** the most. It should be comfortable to hold in your hand, and should be quality steel that will hold a keen edge. At 7 or 8 inches it's the knife you'll spend the most time with, and it should be a good knife.

The **paring knife** shouldn't be expensive because, the way I use them, they are almost disposable—they only last a year or two. The blade gets sharpened almost to nothing fairly quickly. They are easily lost.

You'll need a **serrated knife** primarily if you're going to be baking. Try cutting a delicate genoise into thin layers without one. It never needs to be sharpened and need not be expensive.

If you've bought good knives you're going to want to keep them sharp. A **sharpening steel** will not sharpen a dull knife, but it will keep a sharp knife sharp if used frequently. A steel doesn't actually sharpen; what it does is straighten and clean the edge. Using a steel to keep your knives sharp is smarter than letting them get dull and having them ground regularly, which wears the blade down.

Buy a **boning knife** only if you do a lot of butchering and filleting. It takes a lot of practice to use one well. If you don't use it often and are not used to it, it's not going to do you any more good than a utility or paring knife. It's really a single-usage knife. If you're going to go in deep and carve around a bone in a lamb saddle, then you'll need one. I haven't kept a boning knife at my station for five years. I borrow one when I need one. It's just not an essential knife.

There are a number of good knife brands available and there is no perfect knife to recommend. When I go shopping for a knife, I pick it up and feel it and hold it in my hand. You want a knife with balance, one that gives you the gut feeling you're going to like it.

Pots and Pans You also don't need a lot of pots and pans, and not all of them need be expensive, but a few of them do.

Copper is a nice way to go if you want to display them and don't mind polishing them and don't mind the weight. Traditional thick copper pans with cast-iron handles are unbelievably heavy and hard to handle. Then again, nothing looks better, and the heat transmission properties of copper are legendary.

Recently, modern metal sandwiches have become my favorite. Although slightly expensive, stainless-clad pans are ideal. They have an aluminum core that distributes heat very evenly, and a thin layer of stainless on the cooking surface. It is the thin layer of stainless that is the key. It is scratch-resistant, somewhat nonstick, and does not discolor food. Its most endearing feature to a chef is the strength the stainless gives to the aluminum, which keeps the bottoms flat and the handles tight. The single most frustrating thing to a chef is an aluminum sauté pan with a bowed bottom and floppy handle. A chef's nightmare. Try reducing a sauce without burning the edges when the pan won't sit straight.

Any pan that I would buy has an ovenproof handle. A pan is worthless if it can't go in the oven. The handles are brass, aluminum, or iron, but always metal.

You'll also need:

■ One **very large pot,** 12 quarts or more for making stock and soups and for cooking lobsters and pasta.

■ A few **saucepans,** large, medium, and small.

■ At least two good **stainless-clad sauté pans** with tight-fitting lids. These will be the pans you'll probably end up using the most. The 10-inch sauté pan is the workhorse of professional kitchens. You use it for everything from poaching fish to sautéing and roasting, to small sauces à la minute (to order), to making delicate crêpes. A restaurant kitchen will have racks of them.

Machines and Tools In the last ten years, food processors have helped revolutionize home cooking in America. I do not, however, believe in making extensive use of the numerous gadgets that can be attached to these machines. Unless one is slicing or grating an incredibly large amount of something, they are simply a waste of time. By the time you get the attachment set up and your carrot perfectly aligned, you could have sliced two carrots by hand. But for making mousses and purées, pesto, mayonnaise, and any number of pastry items, a **food processor** is simply indispensable.

The home baking revolution would not have been possible without the **5-quart mixer.** It is the home-sized version of the baker's mixer that is the heart of every professional bakery. The whip, the paddle, and the dough hook are all essential and allow you to bake virtually everything at home. Your mom's egg beater is obsolete. I find it hard to believe that the basics of pastry were invented before these machines, that people made doughs, buttercreams, and meringues by hand. It's amazing.

I don't use very many hand kitchen tools—I'm not big on gadgets—but there are two cheap handy things I depend on:

I use the hand-held **shredder** the most. It's a coarse grater, flat, about 3½ by 6 inches, with a handle. I use it every day to grate potatoes for rosti potatoes with caviar and to grate small amounts of cheese, and I have found it to be the ideal grater for fresh white truffles. It is a supermarket item, too inexpensive to be found in trendy cookware shops.

I also use **fish tweezers.** These are literally giant tweezers with half-inch-wide tips. I first found them a dozen years ago in sushi bars and had to buy them at a hardware store in Little Tokyo. They have now been widely discovered and are available in most cookware shops. They are not expensive and they are ideal for plucking the pin bones from filleted fish or from a side of smoked salmon before you slice it.

S A L T

Let me close with some salty wisdom. Salt is an important and severely misunderstood element in cooking. Learning to use it properly is one of the biggest culinary steps forward you can make.

First off, you don't use salt for its salty taste. That's the myth. The proper function of salt is to tie together, balance, and bring out other flavors. You want to keep adding salt, tasting as you go, until all the flavors have been maximized, but not until the salt becomes a distinct flavor in itself.

Since the real function is to glorify the other flavors, an undersalted dish is just as wrong as an oversalted dish. Don't undersalt with the reasoning that salt can be added later; salt added from a shaker just isn't the same. Once on the plate, it's too late; the food hasn't cooked with the salt.

One of the big differences between a professional kitchen and a home kitchen is the salt shaker. Chefs don't keep shakers at their station; they have little bowls of salt. With a shaker it's hard to get a feel for how much salt you're adding. It takes a little practice, but with a pinch in your fingertips, you can sense exactly what you've got.

Practicing, developing the senses, acquiring the sensitivities that I talk about in this book are what being a good cook is all about. I want to transfer the traits found in a professional chef to you who cook at home. Great food is a joy and a gift, both to cook and to eat. If you have half as much fun as I do cooking these recipes, you're in for a great time.

Soups

Onion Soup with Roquefort

SERVES 4

There must be a thousand variations of French onion soup. This one, while undoubtedly not the original, is definitely *an* original—a two-hundred-year-old recipe from the mountainous Roquefort region in south-central France. I learned it from a Roquefort Association lawyer, whose sole mission is to travel the world defending the purity of the Roquefort trade name. This wonderful soup contains—along with real Roquefort cheese, of course—a splash of Armagnac brandy ready to burst from under the crust of croutons and cheeses at the first bite.

2 medium onions

2 tablespoons unsalted butter

6 ounces genuine Roquefort cheese

2 tablespoons flour

4 cups chicken stock or water

⅓ cup heavy cream

Salt and freshly ground white pepper

1 baguette

6 ounces Gruyère cheese, grated

4 teaspoons Armagnac

Special Equipment 4 ovenproof soup bowls

1. Halve and thinly slice the onions. Melt the butter in a cast-iron pot and sauté the slices, stirring frequently, until deep golden brown.

2. When the onions are caramelized, add half of the Roquefort and all the flour. Cook, stirring constantly, for 1 more minute.

3. Add the chicken stock and cream. Season with salt and pepper. Bring to a boil, then reduce to a simmer and cook for 25 to 30 minutes.

4. Thinly slice the baguette and toast for croutons. Grate the Gruyère and crumble the remaining 3 ounces of Roquefort.

5. When ready to serve, preheat the broiler.

6. Verify the seasoning of the soup—soups will always need adjusting at the last minute. Ladle into the ovenproof bowls. Float a teaspoon of Armagnac on the surface of each bowl of soup and cover with the croutons. Sprinkle with the Gruyère and crumbled Roquefort.

7. Place the bowls of soup under the broiler until a bubbly, golden-brown crust forms. It will take a couple of minutes. Serve.

Wild Mushroom Soup

This is a smooth, creamy version of mushroom soup that smells truly wonderful. It is to standard mushroom soup (bland, bland, bland) as foie gras is to chopped liver. Wild mushrooms are considered new and exotic, but the truth is there are ancient fungi growing wild in the hills all over America.

1 large onion

2 pounds fresh wild mushrooms (see Note)

4 tablespoons (½ stick) unsalted butter

Salt and freshly ground pepper

1 cup heavy cream

1. Thinly slice the onion. Rinse and slice the mushrooms.

2. In a large cast-iron pot, heat the butter over moderate heat until it just begins to turn golden brown. Add the onion and mushrooms. Cook over moderate heat, stirring frequently, at least 4 to 5 minutes, or until all the water exuded from the mushrooms is cooked away and the onion just begins to brown.

3. Deglaze the pot with 2 quarts water, stirring well with a wooden spoon and scraping the bottom to loosen any crust. Season with salt and pepper. Add the cream.

4. Bring the soup to a boil, then reduce to a simmer and cook partially covered for 30 minutes.

5. Purée, using a blender, food processor, or hand-held soup mixer. Strain through a fine strainer. Verify the seasoning. Serve.

Note Wild mushrooms are more interesting and flavorful, but almost any mushroom makes good soup.

Chilled Cream of Cucumber Soup with Curry

S E R V E S   4

A lively cool soup for a summer's day. Served hot, this has plenty of kick. But cold, the contrast between the spicy curry and the chilled cucumber is an invigorating surprise.

1 medium onion

4 tablespoons (½ stick) unsalted butter

2 hothouse cucumbers

2 tablespoons curry powder

Cayenne pepper

Salt

1 cup heavy cream, chilled

¼ cup crème fraîche (page 55) or sour cream

4 teaspoons chutney

Crushed red chilies (optional)

1. Thinly slice the onion. Sauté it in a cast-iron pot with the butter until golden brown.

2. Halve the cucumbers lengthwise and thinly slice. Add them to the pot when the onion is brown. Moisten with 1 cup water. Add the curry powder, a pinch of cayenne, and salt to taste. Bring to a boil, then reduce to a simmer and cook partially covered for 15 minutes.

3. Remove the soup from the heat and allow it to cool to room temperature. Purée, using a blender, food processor, or hand-held soup mixer.

4. Strain through a medium strainer —not a fine one—we want a soup with body. Add the cream. Refrigerate until cold. Verify the seasoning—the salt and the spice. It will take more seasoning cold than hot.

5. Ladle the soup into 4 chilled bowls. Garnish with a zigzag of crème fraîche squeezed from a plastic squeeze bottle. Top each serving with a teaspoon of chutney. (For the truly adventurous, sprinkle with crushed red chilies.) Serve.

Clam and Mussel Chowder

An American classic—one good enough to be French! What I've done is simply use the things I like in a chowder. I add mussels because the mussel juice has such terrific flavor—much more intense than just clam juice. I add chopped tomato: I like tomato in chowder but not tomato paste, not red chowder. And I add the seafood at the last minute instead of simmering it for 30 minutes, which just toughens it. The idea is to get the seafood at the peak of tenderness and flavor.

2 dozen mussels

2 dozen littleneck clams

½ cup dry white wine

1 carrot

1 onion

2 ribs celery

1 leek

3 tablespoons unsalted butter

3 tablespoons flour

3 cups heavy cream

Freshly ground white pepper

1 large white rose (long white) potato

2 red, ripe tomatoes

1. Thoroughly clean the mussels and clams and discard any that are more than a little open. Place them in a pot with the white wine and 1½ cups water, cover tightly, and bring to a boil. Steam the seafood for 4 to 5 minutes or until all the shells are open wide.

2. Remove the mussels and clams and allow to cool enough to pull the meat from the shells. Strain the juice from the pan to eliminate any sand or small pieces of shell. Reserve the juice and meat separately.

3. Peel and cut the carrot into pretty ½-inch dice. Dice the onion and celery similarly. Thoroughly rinse the leek, split the white part in half lengthwise, and cut into ½-inch sections.

4. Gently sweat the diced vegetables in the butter in a new pan for 3 to 4 minutes until tender. Add the flour and cook, stirring constantly, for 2 more minutes. Do not allow the flour or vegetables to brown.

5. While stirring, add the strained seafood broth and the cream. Bring to a boil, then reduce to a gentle simmer. Season with white pepper. The broth will add enough salt.

6. Peel and cut the potato into ½-inch dice, add to the simmering soup, and cook 25 minutes.

7. In the meantime, quickly roast the tomatoes over an open flame, charring the skins and then flaking them off under cold running water. Core and halve the tomatoes, then squeeze them in your hand to remove all juice and seeds. Chop the remaining meat into ½-inch dice.

8. After the potatoes have cooked 25 minutes, add the mussels, clams, and diced tomatoes and simmer 5 minutes more. Verify the seasoning and serve.

Roasted Garlic Soup

The first time I made this was for a garlic festival in Los Angeles, where the real point is garlic overkill. This recipe turned out much milder than I expected and quite delicious. Roasting the garlic is the key. It takes the harsh edge off, yet leaves the soup reeking with wonderful garlickiness. And for this recipe, you don't even need to peel your garlic.

3 heads garlic (heads, not cloves)

2 large russet potatoes, peeled and sliced

1 large onion

1 leek

4 tablespoons olive oil

2 quarts chicken stock or water

3 or 4 cloves elephant garlic

1 red bell pepper for garnish

1 cup heavy cream

Salt and freshly ground pepper

1. Preheat the oven to 350°F.

2. Roast the heads of garlic, whole and unpeeled, in the oven for 45 minutes. The paper will be dark brown but the pulp should be soft and golden brown. Flake off any loose burned paper. Reserve.

3. Peel and slice the potatoes. Slice the onion and the white of the leek. Sauté the onion and leek in 2 tablespoons of the oil in a large kettle until soft but not brown. Add the whole roasted garlic heads, sliced potatoes, and chicken stock and simmer partially covered for 1 hour.

4. In the meantime, cut the cloves of elephant garlic into thin slices to make "garlic chips" for the garnish. Fry the slices in the remaining 2 tablespoons oil for about 2 minutes until golden brown. Drain on a towel and reserve. Cut the red bell pepper into a pretty julienne and reserve as well.

5. Just before the soup is done, add the cream. Purée, using a blender, food processor, or hand-held soup mixer, and strain. Season with salt and pepper.

6. Pour the soup into 8 bowls and sprinkle with the red bell pepper and garlic chips. Serve.

Lobster Spinach Soup

In my kitchen there have been only a couple of accidents that became great successes. Although people just love this soup, I have to admit it was just a fluke. Six or seven years ago, in a hurry to get ready for lunch, I asked the dishwasher to add chicken stock to a spinach soup in progress. Maybe it was my faulty Spanish, but he very carefully added lobster stock to the soup. When I realized what had happened, I figured it couldn't be bad. I went ahead and finished the soup, tasted it, and, hey, it wasn't bad. We proudly served Lobster Spinach Soup for the first time; it has since become a signature dish for me, and I don't know anybody else who does it.

1 medium onion

4 large russet potatoes

6 bunches fresh spinach

2 lobster tails, cooked

4 tablespoons (½ stick) unsalted butter

2 quarts Lobster Fumet (page 29)

Salt and freshly ground pepper

2 cups heavy cream

1. Peel and thinly slice the onion and potatoes. Rinse and stem the spinach. Dice the lobster tails.

2. Sauté the onion in the butter in a large pot until it just begins to brown. Add the lobster stock and potatoes. Season with salt and pepper. Bring to a boil, then reduce to a simmer and cook, partly covered, for 30 minutes. The potatoes must be very soft to give a luxurious, creamy texture to the soup.

3. Stir in the spinach and continue to cook for 2 more minutes. (Adding the spinach at the end keeps the soup a nice green color.) Remove from the heat, add the cream, and purée, using a blender, food processor, or hand-held soup mixer.

4. Verify the seasoning. Add the diced lobster and serve.

Cream of Fennel Soup

SERVES 6

Though it's utterly easy to make, this is a very hearty and satisfying soup. The licorice taste of the fennel—a big rustic flavor—is both unmistakable and subtle at once. While fennel grows like a weed in the hills of California and is found in all the stores there, in most places in America it is neglected, a wallflower—though a captivating one if only given a chance. If you can't find it locally, this recipe makes a fine cream of celery or cream of asparagus soup—just leave out the Pernod.

1 medium onion

4 tablespoons (½ stick) unsalted butter

4 bulbs fennel

Salt and freshly ground white pepper

1 cup heavy cream

Splash of Pernod (optional)

1. Thinly slice the onion. Melt the butter in a large cast-iron pot over moderate heat, add the onion slices, and cook until they just begin to brown.

2. Cut the tops from the fennel bulbs, saving some of the leafy greens for garnish later. Thinly slice the fennel. Add it to the pot and sauté with the onion until the fennel becomes slightly tender and translucent.

3. Season with salt and white pepper. Add enough water to come 1 inch above the level of the vegetables.

4. Add the cream, cover, and bring to a boil. Then reduce to a simmer and cook partially covered for 30 minutes.

5. Purée the soup, using a blender, food processor, or hand-held soup mixer. Strain the soup to achieve a smooth consistency.

6. Verify the seasoning and stir in a capful of Pernod if desired. Ladle the soup into 6 warm bowls and lay a pretty, delicate sprig of fennel green on top of each as garnish. Serve.

Spicy Seafood Soup with Shrimp Dumplings

This is a modern blending of a rich, saffron-flavored Provençal fish soup and a spicy Thai soup with dumplings. I like it HOT and served with good garlicky croutons. You should be able to smell this soup at a hundred yards. This is not as hard to make as it looks—it can be set up in advance. And it's a spectacular soup.

½ cup finely diced onion

½ cup finely diced carrot

½ cup finely diced fennel

½ cup finely diced celery

¼ cup finely diced red bell pepper

¼ cup peeled, seeded, diced tomato

3 cloves garlic, finely chopped

1 heaping tablespoon chopped mixed fresh herbs (basil, tarragon, and parsley)

¼ cup good olive oil

2½ quarts Lobster Fumet (page 29)

18 threads saffron

Salt

Cayenne pepper

4 fresh large shrimp, shelled and deveined

4 fresh large sea scallops, tendon removed

1. Cut the onion, carrot, fennel, celery, and bell pepper into pretty ¼-inch dice. Peel, seed, and dice the tomato and put it aside until later. Chop the garlic. Chop the mixed herbs.

2. In a large pot, sauté the diced vegetables in the olive oil for 3 or 4 minutes or until tender but not brown. Stir in the garlic and sauté 30 seconds more.

3. Add the lobster stock, saffron, some salt, and a pinch of cayenne to the vegetables. Bring to a boil, reduce to a simmer, and cook, uncovered, for 30 minutes so that the liquid reduces by a few cups while cooking.

4. Verify the seasoning. If serving immediately, go to the next step. If not, let the soup cool and reheat before proceeding.

5. When ready to serve, add the diced tomato to the soup and bring it back to a simmer.

6. With a chef's knife, finely chop the raw shrimp and scallops together until smooth. Season with salt.

7. Form this mixture into little football-shaped dumplings, using 2 teaspoons. Poach the dumplings in the barely simmering soup for a couple of minutes.

8. Carefully remove the dumplings with a slotted spoon and divide them among 8 warm soup bowls. Fill the bowls with soup, sprinkle with the chopped herbs, and serve.

Ken Frank's La Toque Cookbook

28

Lobster Fumet

MAKES 3 QUARTS

As much as I love lobster, I don't have the patience to dig out and savor every tiny shred of meat buried in the head and legs. I have a great love for lobster heads, however, and save every one to use in lobster fumet— this concentrated lobster stock is a fundamental part of my cooking. I use it in soups, sauces, and pastas—it's a really good versatile tool, and we always have it on hand at La Toque. This same basic recipe can be used to make any shellfish stock—crab, shrimp, or crayfish—but lobster is my favorite.

1 carrot

1 onion

3 ribs celery

1 head garlic

3 or 4 freshly cooked lobster heads

¼ cup oil for cooking

¾ cup brandy

1½ cups tomato paste

1 tablespoon chopped tarragon

1. Peel and dice the carrot. Dice the onion and celery. Cut the head of garlic crosswise in half. With a heavy chef's knife, cut each lobster head into 3 or 4 pieces.

2. In a stockpot, sauté the vegetables in the cooking oil for a few minutes until they are tender and just beginning to brown. Add the garlic and the lobster and continue to cook for 3 to 4 more minutes, stirring with a wooden spoon and breaking up the lobster into tiny pieces.

3. Deglaze the pan with the brandy and flambé, allowing the alcohol to burn off. Add 3 quarts water, the tomato paste, and the tarragon. Bring to a boil, then simmer, uncovered, for 1 hour.

4. Strain the stock through a fine strainer and allow to cool before refrigerating or freezing for future use. It will keep up to 4 days in the refrigerator, indefinitely in the freezer.

If your lobster is a pregnant female (you'll be able to tell by the dark green egg sack running down the center of the tail), remove the roe, mix it well in a splash of water or wine to loosen the individual eggs, and use it to flavor and color the sauce. Added just before the final reduction, the dark green eggs will immediately transform to a thousand bright orange dots lighting up the sauce.

Fresh Tomato Soup with Sweet Basil

SERVES 6

I've loved tomato soups since I was 3 or 4 years old. This one, which can be served as a hot antidote to a chilly day or as a spicy-cold, refreshing appetizer, is an especially flavorful, tomatoey soup. It is made according to my philosophy of soups: using the original fresh vegetables—no stock—with cream, butter, and the proper fresh seasonings. A chiffonade of basil makes a natural and subtle garnish. For more pizzazz, stir in a spoonful of pesto.

1 medium onion

2 tablespoons unsalted butter

12 red, ripe tomatoes (plum are good here)

1 small head garlic

Salt and freshly ground pepper

1 cup heavy cream

1 bunch fresh sweet basil

¼ cup crème fraîche (page 55) or sour cream if serving cold

1. Slice the onion. Melt the butter in a large heavy pot and sauté the slices until they just begin to brown.

2. Quarter the tomatoes and add them—skin, seeds, cores, and all—to the pot.

3. Crush the entire head of garlic by giving it a good whack with the flat of a cleaver, loosening the cloves and slightly cracking their skins. Add the garlic, skins and all, to the pot.

4. Add enough water to come 1 inch above the level of the tomatoes. Season with salt and pepper. Add the cream.

5. Bring the soup to a boil, then reduce to a healthy simmer and cook partially covered for 20 to 25 minutes.

6. Purée the soup well, using a blender, food processor, or hand-held soup mixer. Strain the soup, pushing through as much of the pulp as possible, to obtain a smooth, thick cream.

Tip for Straining

The tool of choice for pushing the maximum amount of juice and pulp through a strainer or china cap, normally a tedious job, is a small ladle. Try it—you'll be pleased at how efficiently the rounded bottom of the ladle does the job.

TO SERVE HOT

7. Verify the salt and pepper seasoning. Make a chiffonade of very finely julienned basil leaves. Ladle the soup into 6

warm soup bowls and sprinkle with the basil. Serve.

T O   S E R V E   C O L D

7. Allow the soup to cool to room temperature, then place it in the refrigerator to chill for at least 2 hours.

8. When cold, verify the seasoning. It will require more salt and pepper than when served hot. Make a chiffonade of very finely julienned basil leaves.

9. Whisk the crème fraîche to loosen its consistency slightly and pour it into a plastic squeeze bottle.

10. Ladle the soup into 6 chilled bowls. Squeeze a zigzag pattern of crème fraîche across the top as garnish. Sprinkle the surface with the basil. Serve.

Salads

Hot Eel Salad

SERVES 4

Don't turn the page yet! ... It's only the *idea* of eel that's scary, certainly not the taste. Chances are you'll love this salad. The eel has a slightly sweet, smoky taste, though it's not smoked but slowly braised, a technique I learned from a sushi master in Santa Monica. The smokiness works wonderfully well with the nuttiness of the sesame oil and the cold, crunchy, peppery watercress. It's an exceptionally well-balanced medley of flavors.

8 small conger eels (cleaned, gutted, boned, and frozen)

⅓ cup soy sauce

2 tablespoons sugar

1 head red leaf lettuce

1 Belgian endive

2 bunches watercress

2 packages enoki mushrooms

VINAIGRETTE

1 teaspoon Dijon mustard

1 teaspoon Pommery mustard (whole-grain)

1 teaspoon soy sauce

2 tablespoons rice wine vinegar

6 tablespoons sesame oil

MISE EN PLACE

1. *To cook the eels:* Using a plastic scouring pad, or a sponge and coarse salt, scrub the skin of the frozen eels to remove the slippery coating. Lay the eels in a large shallow pan with 1⅓ cups water, the soy sauce, and the sugar. Bring to a boil, cover (aluminum foil will do), reduce to a simmer, and cook for 20 to 30 minutes. Remove the eels from the liquid and reserve. (They will keep 4 to 5 days in the refrigerator.)

2. *To make the vinaigrette:* Place both mustards, the soy sauce, and 1 tablespoon of the vinegar in a mixing bowl. Whisk well. While whisking, add the sesame oil in a thread. Whisk in the remaining tablespoon of vinegar.

ASSEMBLY AND SERVING

3. Tear off the large, pretty outside leaves of the red leaf lettuce, rinse, dry, and arrange as beds on 4 salad plates.

4. Slice the endive on the bias into ¼-inch strips and place it in a mixing bowl.

5. Rinse and dry the watercress and remove just the largest fibrous stems. Add to the mixing bowl.

6. Trim the enoki stems just above the base and add them to the bowl.

7. Lay the eels on a well-buttered sheet of aluminum foil. Place them under the broiler or in a very hot oven or toaster oven and toast for about 2 minutes or until piping hot. Cut each eel into thirds—2-inch pieces.

8. Toss the salad with the vinaigrette and arrange it on the beds of red leaf lettuce. Top each salad with 6 pieces of eel. Serve.

Asparagus with Red Bell Pepper Vinaigrette

SERVES 4

This dish is a real crowd pleaser and incredibly simple. Roast the red bell pepper over an open flame, flake off the charred skin, and *voilà!*—roasted, nutty pepper meat becomes the savory foil for juicy tender asparagus tips. It's a dramatic presentation—a red against a yellow vinaigrette with bright green vegetables lying in between.

1 red bell pepper

24 jumbo asparagus (or more if smaller)

POMMERY MUSTARD AND SHERRY WINE VINEGAR VINAIGRETTE

1 tablespoon sherry wine vinegar

1 tablespoon Pommery mustard (whole-grain)

½ teaspoon Dijon mustard

Salt and freshly ground white pepper

⅓ cup peanut oil (or your favorite salad oil)

1. Put a generously salted large pot of water on to boil.

2. Roast the red pepper by placing it directly on the full gas flame and turning it every minute or so until the skin is black and blistered all over. Rinse off the charred skin under cold running water and remove the core and seeds, leaving the sweet red pepper meat. From the longest part of the pepper, cut 4 long, narrow (¼-inch) strips for garnish. Reserve separately from the rest of the pepper.

3. Holding each uncut asparagus spear at the tip and using a vegetable peeler, peel the whole length except the top couple of inches. Break off the top tender 6 or 7 inches of the spear at the point where it snaps easily. Tie the spears into 4 bundles, using a piece of string at each end.

4. Immerse the bundles in the boiling water and cook 4 to 5 minutes until tender—a slice taken off the bottom should no longer have a slightly bitter, raw taste. Remove the bundles from the water and plunge them into an ice bath to cool, stopping the cooking and setting the bright green color. When the asparagus is cool, remove the bundles to a towel to drain.

MAKING THE VINAIGRETTE

5. Whisk together the sherry wine vinegar, both mustards, and the salt and pepper in a mixing bowl. While whisking, add the oil in a thread. As the oil emulsifies, the dressing will become smooth and creamy. Verify the seasoning—mustards and vinegars vary in strength and character. Reserve.

6. Purée the roasted pepper in a blender until smooth, then add just under

half of the vinaigrette to the blender and mix again. Reserve the other half of the vinaigrette.

ASSEMBLY AND SERVING

7. Mirror half of each of 4 plates with the red vinaigrette (from the blender) and the other half with the yellow vinaigrette.

8. Wrap one of the garnish strips of red pepper around each still-tied bundle of asparagus. Place the bundles on the plates. Carefully snip and remove the strings—the bundles will be held in place by the pretty red pepper strips. Serve.

What if the vinaigrette breaks?

Ugly! Gone the creamy emulsion, instead, floating oil slicks. Don't despair, there is always a way. Here are three quick savers:

—Try a vigorous whisking of a very small amount starting at the edge of the bowl, then slowly incorporate the rest.

—If you've made a largish amount, sometimes you can pour the separated oil off the top, rewhisk the remaining mustards and vinegar, and when it emulsifies, add back the oil in a thread.

—Start a new batch in a clean bowl. After you've added some of the new oil in a thread, then add the broken vinaigrette in a thread. Once that is all incorporated, add the rest of the new oil. You'll have made a double batch, but it will keep.

Avocado, Tomato, and Mushroom Salad

SERVES 4

This simple chopped salad is perennially popular at La Toque. Its success rests on vine-ripened tomatoes and perfectly ripe avocados, attractively and uniformly diced. The smooth, creamy avocados and freshly cut mushrooms are a good texture contrast.

---

12 silver-dollar-size fresh mushrooms

2 large red, ripe tomatoes

2 avocados

8 large, pretty butterhead lettuce leaves

1 recipe Pommery Mustard and Sherry Wine Vinaigrette (page 36)

---

1. Remove the mushroom stems and cut the caps into ½-inch dice. Seed the tomatoes. Pit and peel the avocados. Cut the tomatoes and avocados into the same-size dice.

2. Rinse and dry the lettuce leaves. Cut out the stem from the bottom of each leaf and arrange 2 leaves as a bed on each of 4 chilled plates.

3. Toss the diced tomatoes, mushrooms, and avocados with the vinaigrette. Mound atop the 4 lettuce beds. Serve.

Salads
■
37

Endive Salad with Roasted Hazelnuts

SERVES 4

Endive salads made with walnuts or walnut oil are good but common fare. The ideal endive salad, however, is made with roasted hazelnuts. Nothing can match the magical power of the roasted hazelnut. I am talking about an addictive substance. Although hazelnuts (a.k.a. filberts) are safe as long as they are raw, once roasted, they are impossible to resist. And they are an expensive habit: You'll eat them endlessly, and you'll find it challenging to roast them to perfection without burning them at least half the time.

½ cup hazelnuts (filberts)

5 or 6 Belgian endives

I recipe Pommery Mustard and Sherry Wine Vinegar Vinaigrette (page 36)

2 red, ripe tomatoes

---

1. Preheat the oven to 350°F.
2. Roast the hazelnuts on a baking sheet for 10 to 12 minutes or until medium golden brown, shaking the sheet every couple of minutes to ensure even coloring and to prevent burning. (A toaster oven is ideal for small amounts.) Allow the nuts to cool slightly and flake off the skins. Coarsely chop the peeled hazelnuts. Reserve.
3. Break off and set aside 20 large pretty endive leaves. Slice the remaining endives on the bias into ¾-inch lengths. Toss the sliced endives with the hazelnuts and the vinaigrette.
4. Make a 5-pointed endive star on each of 4 plates. Spoon one-quarter of the salad in the center of each star.
5. Core and halve the tomatoes. Cut each half into 5 wedges and place the wedges between the points of the endive stars. Serve.

Roasting Hazelnuts

Though it may seem simple, this is a delicate task. The critical point comes after about 10 minutes, when the hazelnuts can go from raw to perfect to scorched beyond use in little more than a minute. Use a timer, shake the pan several times, don't leave the room. At the restaurant, I hold the record for this high-risk job, incinerating 3 big pans of hazelnuts in succession.

Avocado, Crab, and Cucumber Salad

S E R V E S   4

The crab and avocado combination is borrowed from the "California roll," found in American sushi bars. This is a very Japanese salad—but no raw fish!—rather, a tumble of other mysterious Oriental ingredients in a light, healthy, high-spirited salad full of palate surprises.

---

1 hothouse cucumber

1 piece *yama-imo* (Japanese potato; see Note)

1 small piece *takuwan* (pickled daikon)

1 ripe avocado

2 teaspoons soy sauce

¼ cup rice wine vinegar

¼ teaspoon finely chopped or grated fresh ginger

2 packages *kaiware* (daikon radish sprouts)

4 heaping teaspoons *tobiko* (flying fish roe)

8 to 12 ounces fresh-cooked crab meat

---

1. Slice 6 to 8 inches of the unpeeled cucumber into thin circles. Stacking 6 or 8 slices at a time, cut them into matchstick julienne.

2. Peel 4 inches of the *yama-imo* and julienne the same as the cucumber.

3. Cut a 2-inch piece of *takuwan* in half lengthwise. Cut into paper-thin half circles.

4. Cut the avocado in half. Cut each half into 6 wedges. Peel the skin from each slice.

5. Place the soy sauce, rice wine vinegar, and fresh ginger in a mixing bowl. Add the cucumber, *yama-imo*, and *takuwan* and toss well. Arrange 3 avocado wedges in a triangle on each of 4 plates.

6. Cut the roots off the radish sprouts, then cut the sprouts in half. Add them to the bowl along with half the *tobiko*. Toss gently. Place a mound of the salad in the center of each avocado triangle.

7. Crumble or shred the crab meat on top of the salads and garnish the top with the remaining bright red *tobiko*. Serve.

Note If you can't find *yama-imo*, leave it out. If you can't find *kaiware*, use fresh daikon, thinly julienned. If you can't find *tobiko*, use *masago* (lake smelt roe) or even salmon caviar.

Crab Salad Chinoise

SERVES 4

This light and refreshing cold salad—a medley of blanched, tender vegetable juliennes with fresh crab meat and my favorite tarragon cream vinaigrette—has simple but irresistible flavors and surprising texture contrasts. And it's versatile—use crayfish tails, lobster, or shrimp, or even poached, shredded chicken in place of the crab.

CREAMY TARRAGON DRESSING

1 tablespoon Pommery mustard (whole-grain)

1 teaspoon chopped fresh tarragon

Juice of ½ lemon

1 teaspoon sherry wine vinegar

Salt and freshly ground white pepper

2 tablespoons extra-virgin olive oil

⅔ cup heavy cream

8 ounces snow peas

1 carrot

2 ribs celery

1 Belgian endive

1 fresh-cooked Dungeness crab (see Note)

2 red, ripe tomatoes

1. *To make the dressing* (best prepared 3 or 4 hours ahead): Whisk together the mustard, tarragon, lemon juice, vinegar, salt, and pepper in a mixing bowl. While whisking, add the olive oil in a thread. Whisk in the cream. Verify the seasoning. Let stand at room temperature for 3 or 4 hours for the flavors to develop. The cream will ripen (sour) slightly.

2. Put a large pot of salted water on to boil.

3. Pull the strings from the snow peas and cut them lengthwise in half, making long green ribbons.

4. Peel the carrot, cut into 3-inch lengths, and slice each length into thin ribbons approximately the same size and shape as the snow peas.

5. Using a vegetable peeler, peel the strings off the outside of the celery. Cut into 3-inch lengths and again slice into thin ribbons.

6. Cut the endive on the bias into narrow slices, starting from the top.

7. Carefully clean all the meat from the claws, legs, and body of the crab. (Reserve the shells for making a bisque some other day—freeze them until you have enough.)

COOKING AND SERVING

8. Prepare an ice bath in a mixing bowl for chilling the vegetables once they are blanched.

9. In a wire basket, plunge the snow peas into the boiling water and blanch for no more than 30 to 45 seconds—they should still be slightly firm. Remove imme-

diately and chill in the ice bath, stopping the cooking to set the bright color.

10. Repeat the same process with the celery, blanching 30 to 45 seconds and chilling. Do the same with the carrot, which, however, will take 2 to 3 minutes to blanch and become tender.

11. When all three vegetables are chilled, spin or blot them dry in a towel.

12. Core and cut each tomato into 8 wedges. Dip one end of each wedge into the vinaigrette and place 4 on each of 4 plates like the points of a compass.

13. Toss the vegetables and the crab with the vinaigrette. Place a mound of the salad in the center of each plate. Serve.

Note If you can't find Dungeness crab, 8 ounces of another type of fresh crab meat will do.

Hot Spinach and Foie Gras

SERVES 4

Once every restaurant fancy enough to have a maître d' and a captain had a hot spinach salad flambé with bacon ends. This is so much better. Instead of the bacon, use sautéed medallions of foie gras set off by a sauce of sweet/tart sherry wine vinegar, shallots, and pink peppercorns.

4 bunches fresh spinach

Salt

2 tablespoons pink peppercorns

8 ounces fresh raw foie gras (see Note)

3 plump shallots

Freshly ground white pepper

3 fluid ounces bacon fat

1½ teaspoons sherry wine vinegar

20 Belgian endive leaves

1. Carefully rinse, stem, and dry the spinach. Place it in a large stainless steel mixing bowl. Lightly sprinkle with salt and the pink peppercorns. Reserve.

2. Slice the foie gras into ¼-inch-thick medallions. Thinly slice the shallots.

3. Heat a large sauté pan—dry—over high heat. Season the foie gras slices with salt and white pepper. When the sauté pan is very hot, quickly sear the foie gras slices no more than 15 seconds on each side,

about as fast as you can put them in the pan and turn them over. Do not overcook! Reserve.

4. Add the bacon fat and sliced shallots to the pan and cook, stirring frequently, over moderate heat until the shallots are golden brown.

5. Remove the pan from heat. Carefully deglaze it with the vinegar, standing back lest the hot oil splatter.

6. Pour this hot shallot dressing over the spinach in the mixing bowl. Cover the bowl with a lid, place it over moderate heat, and shake it back and forth for about 15 seconds to ensure even wilting. The spinach should be just wilted but not thoroughly cooked.

7. Make a 5-pointed endive star on each of 4 warm plates. Place the wilted spinach at the center of each endive star, top with the seared foie gras, and serve immediately.

Note If you must use canned foie gras, do not cook it at all. Simply cut it into matchstick julienne and sprinkle it on the finished salads.

Marinated Chanterelle Salad

S E R V E S   4

Very fresh, plump, turgid chanterelles just sautéed have an al dente texture that's just terrific. Buy the ones that are so fresh and firm they sound like a watermelon when you tap on them. This dish can be served as a salad course or as a garnish to a pâté. Marinate it overnight to allow the full flavor to develop.

1 bulb fresh fennel

1 small red onion

1½ pounds small, firm, fresh chanterelle mushrooms

3 fluid ounces extra-virgin olive oil

Juice of 1 lemon

Pinch of ground coriander (optional)

Salt and freshly ground white pepper

1. Cut the top off the fennel bulb, saving the leafy greens for garnish. Cut the bulb itself into ¼-inch dice.

2. Cut the red onion into ¼-inch dice.

3. Brush the dirt off the chanterelles with a towel—avoid rinsing if possible. Cut into ¼-inch slices.

4. Heat 2 tablespoons of the olive oil in a medium sauté pan until hot. Add the fennel and onion and cook until tender and

beginning to turn golden brown. Remove from the heat and set aside.

5. In a second sauté pan, heat the remaining ¼ cup olive oil until quite hot but not yet smoking. Add the sliced chanterelles and sauté for just a minute until the exuded water is cooked away. They should remain al dente.

6. Combine the chanterelles with the onion and fennel. Season with lemon juice to taste, coriander, salt, and pepper, and let cool to room temperature. Allow to marinate in the refrigerator overnight if possible.

7. Place the leafy fennel tops in a wreath around the edge of each of 4 salad plates. Arrange the salad in the middle and serve.

Baby Leeks with Tomato and Olive Oil

SERVES 4

This is a simple, rustic dish but with surprising flavors. It's not the kind of thing your guests will have had twice a week at home, although in France baby leeks are a common garden vegetable and are often served like tomatoes or asparagus, cold, in just a vinaigrette. In a break with tradition, this is a gutsy tomato, herb, and olive oil sauce that works wonderfully with the sweetness of the leeks.

12 to 18 baby leeks

2 quarts chicken stock or water

Salt

1 tablespoon chopped mixed fresh herbs (basil, chive, tarragon, rosemary, thyme—any 2 or better 3)

2 or 3 red, ripe tomatoes (such as plum tomatoes, chosen for flavor not appearance)

2 teaspoons tomato paste

⅓ cup extra-virgin olive oil

1 tablespoon sherry wine vinegar

Freshly ground white pepper

MISE EN PLACE

1. Trim the roots from the leeks. Cut off the dark green tops an inch or so above the Y, saving a few of the largest, prettiest

tops for making chevron garnishes later. Thoroughly rinse the leeks under cold running water to remove all mud and sand.

2. Place the leeks in a saucepan, cover with the chicken stock, and season with a sprinkle of salt. Bring to a boil, then reduce to a simmer and cook for 20 minutes.

3. Remove the cooked leeks from the stock and allow to cool to room temperature. The leeks will keep refrigerated for a couple of days.

4. chop 1 tablespoon mixed fresh herbs. Reserve.

5. *To make the sauce* (best if done 2 hours or more ahead): Quickly roast the tomatoes over an open flame, charring the skins and then flaking them off under cold running water. Core and halve the tomatoes, then squeeze them in your hand to remove all juice and seeds.

6. Reserve one-third of the tomato meat and place the other two-thirds in a food processor with the tomato paste. Purée 30 seconds while adding the olive oil in a thread.

7. Add the vinegar and chopped herbs. Season with salt and pepper. Mix with another short burst.

8. Finely chop the remaining tomato meat and stir it into the sauce by hand. Set aside, allowing the flavors to develop for at least a couple of hours if not overnight.

SERVING

9. Prepare an ice bath in a small bowl. In a small saucepan with a few inches of boiling water, dip the raw green leek tops for literally just 2 seconds, then immediately chill in the ice bath. The blanching and chilling will tenderize them and set the vivid green color.

10. Cut the naturally folded leek greens on the bias in ¼-inch strips. Unfold to make chevrons.

11. Arrange 5 chevrons around the edge of each of 4 plates as if the points of a star. Mirror the center of the plates with tomato sauce. Top with baby leeks. Serve.

Panaché
au Roquefort

SERVES 4

I was never part of the sprouts-in-everything craze of the seventies, but I'll have to admit this salad comes right out of it. The trick is combining crisp bean sprouts, fresh mushrooms, and crumbled Roquefort cheese—a magical contrast. Don't even think of putting bottled creamy Roquefort or blue cheese dressing on this salad—it's an American abomination you will never find in a French restaurant. Fresh Roquefort cheese served with the sherry-wine-vinegar vinaigrette is a much different animal, I promise you. Simple as can be—a terrific confidence builder—this *panaché* has been an amazing hit from the first day I made it.

1 head red leaf lettuce

2 bunches watercress

8 silver-dollar-size fresh mushrooms

4 ounces bean sprouts

1 recipe Pommery Mustard and Sherry Wine Vinegar Vinaigrette (page 36)

4 small red, ripe tomatoes

4 ounces Roquefort cheese

ASSEMBLING THE SALAD

1. Rinse and dry the red leaf lettuce and watercress. Make a bed on each of 4 salad plates with the large outer leaves of leaf lettuce.

2. Remove the large fibrous stems from the watercress. Slice the mushrooms.

3. In a salad bowl, toss the watercress, bean sprouts, and mushroom caps with the vinaigrette. Arrange atop each bed of lettuce.

4. Core and quarter the tomatoes and arrange them around the salads. Crumble the Roquefort over the top. Serve.

Three Duck Salad

SERVES 4

This very sophisticated, elegant salad is one of the best I do. It is a great start for a multicourse extravaganza, but a larger serving can be a very hearty satisfying meal in itself.

Make this with delicate haricots verts, rather than the more common big green beans. The introduction of haricots verts into American cuisine has greatly enriched our salads. They are the elite of the vegetable kingdom—the best and smallest are from the Loire Valley, Kenya, and Senegal, and there are good ones from Guatemala, too. They are now widely available in our markets and are even easy to grow yourself!

1 pound haricots verts (French green beans)

1 small red bell pepper

1 duck leg from Duck Confit (page 146)

8 thin slices smoked duck breast

4 quarter-inch-thick slices of fresh raw duck foie gras (grade A)

Salt and freshly ground pepper

1 small clove garlic

1 tablespoon balsamic vinegar

3 tablespoons extra-virgin olive oil

1 tablespoon chopped mixed fresh herbs (basil, chive, tarragon, rosemary, thyme—any 2 or better 3)

1 small red onion

2 red, ripe tomatoes

Ken Frank's
La Toque
Cookbook

■

46

MISE EN PLACE

1. Put a large pot of salted water on to boil. Snap the ends off the beans, removing any strings. Cook in the boiling water until tender but not mushy. Chill in an ice bath to stop the cooking and set the pretty green color. Drain and reserve.

2. Roast the red bell pepper over an open flame, rinse away the charred skin, remove the core and seeds, julienne, and reserve.

3. Remove the meat from the duck leg, discarding all skin and fat, and carefully shred the meat. Cut the sliced duck breast into a very fine julienne. Cut 4 slices of foie gras and season with salt and pepper. Reserve all three separately.

COOKING AND SERVING

4. Using a garlic press, press the garlic into a mixing bowl. Add the vinegar, olive oil, and chopped herbs. Mix and season with salt and pepper.

5. Cut 2 thin slices from the center of the red onion, cut them in half, and separate into slivers. Add the onion, haricots verts, red pepper, and shredded duck leg to the bowl. Toss and verify the seasoning.

6. Divide this mixture among 4 plates. Cut each tomato into 8 wedges and surround each salad with 4 tomato wedges. Sprinkle the julienned duck breast over the top.

7. Heat a small frying pan until *very* hot. Quickly sear the seasoned slices of foie gras, about 20 seconds on each side. They should be dark brown and crisp on the outside, just barely pink and meltingly tender on the inside.

8. Top each salad with a piece of hot foie gras and serve immediately.

Toasted Salmon Skin Salad

S E R V E S   4

Sushi aficionados will already know the virtues of salmon skin. For those who don't, eating is believing. Toasted, it has a delicious crunchy flavor. Combined with the spicy radish sprouts and zingy ginger, it makes a salad that is highly flavored and refreshingly light at the same time. This is a great, versatile salad—you can add almost any combination of seafoods.

Oil for cooking

16 inches salmon skin, scaled (see Note)

1 cooked lobster tail (nice optional touch)

4 packages *kaiware* (daikon radish sprouts)

¼ cup julienned pink pickled ginger

½ cup julienned Japanese cucumber

3 tablespoons *masago* (lake smelt roe)

D R E S S I N G

1 teaspoon Pommery mustard (whole-grain)

¼ cup sesame oil

2 tablespoons rice wine vinegar

Splash of soy sauce

1. Preheat the broiler to high.

2. Put a little cooking oil on a baking sheet. Cut the salmon skin into four 4-inch strips and place on the baking sheet, skin side up. Toast in the hot oven for about 10 minutes until the skin is bubbly, brown, and crisp.

3. *To make the dressing:* In a salad bowl, whisk together the mustard, sesame oil, vinegar, and soy sauce.

4. Slice 4 medallions of lobster tail and reserve. Cut the remaining lobster into small pieces. Toss the chopped lobster, radish sprouts, ginger, cucumber, and all but a tablespoon of the *masago* in the dressing. Arrange on 4 plates.

5. Cut the crisp salmon skin into ½-inch-wide strips with a sharp chef's knife. Arrange the strips around each salad like the spokes of a wheel. Top each salad with a medallion of lobster and a dollop of *masago*. Serve.

Note Next time you are skinning a salmon fillet (be sure to scale it first), leave ⅛ inch meat on the skin. Save the skin in the freezer until you make the salad.

Forestière Salad

SERVES 4

In traditional French cooking, *forestière* means anything with wild forest mushrooms. This is a very simple salad, made all in one bowl—my favorite green salad. The lettuces and mushrooms will vary with the seasons, but I always make a "mesclun" blend. That's a traditional French mix of lettuces that always includes a curly endive, two or three leaf lettuces, and fresh herbs such as chervil and chives. Use oyster and shiitake mushrooms, which are widely available year round. Depending on the season, you can add chanterelles, cèpes, morels, or virtually any other edible wild mushroom.

3 quarts mixed fresh greens

3 cups assorted fresh mushrooms

1 baguette

1/4 cup olive oil, plus more for the croutons

Freshly grated Parmesan cheese

Salt and freshly ground pepper

3 cloves garlic, finely chopped

2 tablespoons finely chopped shallots

2 tablespoons chopped mixed fresh herbs (basil, chives, tarragon, rosemary, thyme—any 2 or better 3)

1/2 cup crème fraîche (page 55)

1/4 cup balsamic vinegar

MISE EN PLACE

1. Rinse and dry the greens and tear them into small pieces. Clean and slice the mushrooms.

2. Preheat the oven to 450°F.

3. Cut 16 thin slices of French bread. Brush with a little olive oil and sprinkle with Parmesan. Toast these croutons on a baking sheet until light golden brown. Reserve.

COOKING AND SERVING

4. Sauté the sliced mushrooms in 1/4 cup olive oil with salt and pepper until golden brown. Add the garlic, shallots, and herbs and sauté 30 seconds more.

5. Transfer the hot mushrooms to a large salad bowl. Mix with the crème fraîche and balsamic vinegar. Season with salt and pepper and verify the seasoning.

6. Add the greens and toss with the mushrooms. Divide among 4 plates, surround with croutons, and serve.

Warm Roast Beef and Potato Salad

This is simple French country food, the kind of thing the French would have for *souper*—a light dinner when they've had a heavy lunch. It's an ideal summer salad and an excellent way to use a leftover hunk of roast beef. You can use filet mignon, but to be perfectly honest, top sirloin is one of the tastiest pieces of meat on the whole animal and is perfect here.

Salt and freshly ground pepper

1 pound top sirloin

Oil for cooking

4 medium long white potatoes

1 small red onion

1 red bell pepper

1 bunch chives

8 large, pretty leaves butterhead lettuce

2/3 cup crème fraîche (page 55)

1 tablespoon Pommery mustard (whole-grain)

2 teaspoons sherry wine vinegar

MISE EN PLACE (MAY BE DONE A DAY AHEAD)

1. Preheat the oven to 450°F.
2. Generously salt and pepper the beef. Heat a little oil in a sauté pan until hot and sear all sides of the roast over high heat. Place in the oven to cook for 20 minutes, turning once. The meat should be rare. (Plunge a skewer or the tines of a fork into the center of the roast, wait 5 seconds, remove, and immediately touch the tip to your lower lip; if it is slightly warm, the meat will be rare.) Remove the meat from the oven and allow it to rest.
3. Put the potatoes in a pan of salted cold water, bring to a boil, then reduce to a simmer and cook until tender, approximately 20 minutes.

Souper

Souper is French for supper—often soup, salad, sausages, and freshly baked bread, and always cheese. The soup is sometimes thickened with finely grated Gruyère. Sometimes it includes a green salad with crème fraîche dressing, and roasted sausage with piping hot french fries dumped right out of the fryer into the salad.

COOKING AND SERVING

4. Julienne the red onion. Core, seed, and julienne the red bell pepper. Finely mince the chives.
5. Peel the potatoes and cut them into 1/2-inch cubes. Dice the roast beef into 1/2-inch cubes.
6. Make pretty beds of the lettuce on 4 plates.

7. In a large sauté pan, bring the crème fraîche, potatoes, onion, and red pepper to a boil. Add the mustard, vinegar, chives, salt, and pepper. Verify the seasoning. Add the diced roast beef and toss until warm. Do not cook further—it will toughen the beef.

8. Spoon the mixture onto the lettuce beds and serve.

Endive, Asparagus, and Foie Gras Salad

SERVES 4

Not an inexpensive salad but one of my best. Foie gras tastes remarkably good combined with sweet, soft asparagus, crisp, slightly bitter endive, and this mustardy vinaigrette. (Foie gras, like any liver, tastes good with things sharply flavored.) If you know how to cook it properly—and getting it just right is not easy—use fresh, raw foie gras. There are also a number of excellent "mic-uit" foie gras (cooked slightly pink, which is just right) that come vacuum-packed, have to be refrigerated, and have a shelf life of 6 to 8 weeks. Next down the line, "bloc" is much better than "mousse" of "pâté." And between duck and goose, I prefer duck as being a little more flavorful.

6 ounces foie gras

Salt and freshly ground white pepper

20 finger-size asparagus

3 Belgian endives

I recipe Pommery Mustard and Sherry Wine Vinegar Vinaigrette (see page 36)

Special Equipment Small (4 by 2 inches) rectangular baking dish

1. *To make the terrine de foie gras:* (If starting with precooked foie gras, skip to the next step; if starting with raw foie gras, allow it to come to room temperature and soften.) Preheat the oven to 300°F. Sprinkle the softened foie gras with salt and white pepper and put it in a small rectangular baking dish, perhaps 4 by 2 inches. Pack it tightly into all the corners, cover with aluminum foil, and bake for 15 minutes. Remove it from the oven and transfer it immediately to the refrigerator. Refrigerate for 3 or 4 hours or until hard. (This will keep for 3 or 4 days refrigerated.)

2. Heat a large pot of generously salted water to a boil. Holding each uncut asparagus spear by the tip and using a vegetable peeler, peel the whole length except the top 1½ inches. Trim the spears to 5 inches, saving the bottoms for soup. Tie the spears into 4 or 5 bundles and cook in the boiling water 4 or 5 minutes, until tender. Shock in an ice bath or rinse under cold water to stop the cooking and set the bright-green color. Reserve.

ASSEMBLY AND SERVING

3. Break off 20 pretty endive leaves. Trim the bottoms, leaving 3-inch points and saving the ends to mix in the rest of the salad.

4. Make a 5-pointed endive star on each of 4 plates. Dip the tips of the asparagus in the vinaigrette and arrange them between the endive points, making a sunburst.

5. Cut the remaining endive into ½-inch lengths and toss with the remaining vinaigrette. Carefully mound this salad in the center of the plates.

6. Remove the foie gras from the refrigerator and unmold. Using a very sharp knife dipped in hot water, cut the foie gras into thin slices. Cover the top of each salad with the slivers of foie gras and serve.

Appetizers

Rosti Potatoes with Caviar

SERVES 4

This is the kind of thing you can eat until you're sick and still want more. It's a variation of a Savoyard peasant dish that my friend's mother used to make for us at lunchtime during my summers in France. I loved her food. During the school year, three peasant women cooked our lunches in the cafeteria, and I got so I couldn't go without them. I was sixteen and eating about twice what I do now. I gained 40 pounds in one year. About three months before I was scheduled to go home, I realized I would starve in America. I had become addicted to French food. The prospect of returning to hamburgers had me grief-stricken. I *had* to learn to cook French food. . . .

¼ cup crème fraîche (see box at right)

Juice of ¼ fresh lemon

I heaping teaspoon chopped fresh chives

2 or 3 turns freshly ground white pepper

2 medium russet potatoes

½ cup peanut oil

4 ounces caviar (or more or less to taste or to fit your budget)

1. A couple hours ahead, mix together the crème fraîche, lemon juice, chives, and pepper in a small bowl. Let rest for 2 hours at room temperature to allow crème fraîche to rethicken.

2. Scrub the potatoes—they needn't be peeled—and grate them on the coarsest side of your cheese grater. Form the shredded potatoes into 4 patties—loosely, don't press them—about ½ inch thick, the size of a homemade hamburger. Do this right away, otherwise the shredded potatoes will blacken.

3. Heat ⅛ inch peanut oil in a sauté pan over moderate heat so that a test shred of potato sizzles. Using a spatula, carefully place the 4 patties in the hot oil and fry them—never using more than a moderate flame—until they are golden brown on both sides. It should take 2 to 2½ minutes per side. Remove the patties and blot the excess grease on a paper towel.

4. Top each potato patty with the crème fraîche, top that with caviar, and serve immediately.

5. Return to the kitchen and make a second batch.

Making Crème Fraîche

Stir together 1 part fresh buttermilk and 4 parts heavy cream. Let it sit and cure for 8 hours at room temperature, then refrigerate overnight to allow it to thicken. The crème fraîche will then keep for 10 days to 2 weeks in the refrigerator.

Substitutions: If you haven't time to make crème fraîche, use Devon cream or sour cream.

Santa Barbara Shrimp with Mustard

SERVES 4

The rich, creamy mustard sauce served over these shrimp can be served with baby lobster tails, other kinds of shrimp, and almost any kind of fish, or add a little stock and try it with veal, chicken, or rabbit. But it's a sauce made in heaven for sweet, tender Santa Barbara shrimp, also known as spot prawns, which have a succulent texture unlike any other shrimp. They are absolutely perishable and must be bought perfectly fresh and kept packed in ice until ready to cook. They are also quite expensive, because of their rising popularity in the last half dozen years, but believe me, they are worth the price.

24 large fresh Santa Barbara shrimp (spot prawns; see Note)

2 tablespoons unsalted butter

2 tablespoons minced shallots

½ cup dry white wine

¾ cup heavy cream

2 tablespoons Pommery mustard (whole-grain)

1 tablespoon minced fresh chives

Special Equipment 4 ovenproof soup plates

1. Preheat the oven to 350°F.

2. Carefully peel the shrimp. (If the shrimp came with heads, freeze the heads for a tasty bisque at a later time, for Seafood Ravioli (page 162), or for Lobster Fumet (page 29).

3. Heat 1 tablespoon of the butter in a sauté pan over maximum heat until it just begins to brown. Add the shrimp and sauté, turning frequently, for about 1 minute, until they just begin to get firm. *Santa Barbara shrimp cook almost instantly—do not overcook.*

4. Remove the pan from the heat. Saving the pan and its drippings, transfer the shrimp to 4 ovenproof soup plates and reserve.

5. Place the pan back over the heat, add the shallots, sweat for 30 seconds, and deglaze the pan with the white wine. Add the cream and mustard and reduce over high heat until slightly thickened.

6. Place the plates with the shrimp in the oven to heat for just 1 minute.

7. Remove the sauce from the heat. Finish by whisking in the remaining tablespoon of butter and the chopped chives. Pour the sauce over the hot shrimp and serve.

Note If you cannot find Santa Barbara shrimp, substitute the best jumbo shrimp you can find.

Ken Frank's La Toque Cookbook

■

56

Scallops with Curry and Caviar

SERVES 4

What's neat about this recipe is the technique of sifting together the flour and curry powder for dredging the scallops. The curry thus applied offsets the sweetness of the scallops with a bit of spiciness, at the same time lending them a dramatic yellow-orange color. To pleasantly complicate the tastes, we gently sizzle the scallops in butter to achieve a nutty flavor, then punctuate with a rich burst of caviar.

1 heaping tablespoon finely minced shallot

½ cup dry white wine

Squeeze of lemon juice

Salt and freshly ground white pepper

1 tablespoon heavy cream

12 tablespoons (1½ sticks) unsalted butter, softened, plus 2 tablespoons more for sautéing

3 tablespoons flour

2 tablespoons curry powder

20 sea scallops

1 ounce (at least) good caviar

1. Place the shallot, white wine, and lemon juice, a pinch of salt, a few turns of white pepper, and the cream in a saucepan and reduce until only a few tablespoons remain.

2. Off the heat, swirl in the softened 12 tablespoons butter, bit by bit, to make *beurre blanc.* Verify the seasoning: It should be slightly citric and undersalted because you'll be adding caviar later. Reserve in a warm place.

3. Sift together the flour and curry powder. Remove the tough tendon from the side of each scallop. Dredge the scallops in the curry flour, patting off the excess.

4. Heat 2 tablespoons butter in a sauté pan over low to moderate heat until the butter just begins to brown. Add the scallops. Cook over moderate heat 1 to 1½ minutes on each side, allowing the scallops and butter to brown but never to burn.

5. Remove the pan from the heat and allow the scallops to rest in the pan to gently finish cooking.

6. In the meantime, mirror the sauce on 4 warm plates. Arrange 5 scallops on each plate. Top each scallop with a few grains of caviar or as much as you'd like. Serve.

Sautéed Potatoes with Truffles

S E R V E S   2

If, God forbid, I were a vegetarian, this is what I would live on—during the truffle season, of course. I love potatoes, and while the Rosti Potatoes with Caviar (page 55) are delicious to the point of decadence, this is better still. It is so simple and so good, really the ultimate vegetable to serve with meat. It will transform a great steak into the meal of the year.

2 russet potatoes

Peanut oil

4 tablespoons (½ stick) unsalted butter

Salt

1 small fresh truffle (must be fresh)

1. Preheat the oven to 450°F.
2. Peel the potatoes and cut them into ½-inch cubes. Rinse thoroughly under cold running water. Drain and blot completely dry with a towel.
3. Meanwhile heat ½ inch of peanut oil in a large ovenproof sauté pan until very hot but not yet smoking. Carefully add the diced potatoes, which must be very dry or the oil will spit and burn you.
4. After 30 seconds or so, give the pan a little shake to loosen the potatoes, then place the pan in the oven. Cook the potatoes for another 7 or 8 minutes, stirring or shaking from time to time to ensure even cooking.
5. By now the potatoes should be a rich golden brown. Remove them from the oven and empty them into a strainer, draining off all the oil.
6. Add the butter and return the potatoes to the still-hot pan; toss as the butter melts. Sprinkle lightly with salt and smother with freshly grated truffle. Toss again—the potatoes will absorb an unbelievable amount of butter and truffle flavor. Serve at once.

Note When grating the truffle, rub it just lightly on the shredder. This more delicate shred of truffle will yield a lot more flavor.

Oysters with Curry and Cucumber

SERVES 4

Oysters and curry are such a magical combination that people who swear they can't stomach oysters often end up converts after trying this dish. It's a fast, one-pan recipe (5 minutes once the oysters are shucked and cucumbers cut) and startlingly pretty with julienned red rose petals sprinkled atop the vivid yellow-orange curry.

½ large hothouse cucumber

24 oysters in shells

1 tablespoon minced shallot

¾ cup dry white wine

¾ cup heavy cream

2 tablespoons curry powder

1 tablespoon unsalted butter, softened

1 red rose (see Note), petals julienned

MISE EN PLACE

1. Peel the cucumber. Using a tiny melon baller, scoop out pearl-size balls from the meaty outside of the cucumber, not from the seedy core. If you don't have a melon baller, the second choice is to make "turned" ovals, and a perfectly acceptable third choice is to cut the cucumber meat into matchstick julienne.

2. Shuck the oysters, reserving the juice. Strain the juice and save it for the sauce.

COOKING AND SERVING

3. In a saucepan over high heat, combine the shallot, white wine, cream, curry powder, and oyster juice. Don't add salt; the oyster juice has plenty. Reduce the sauce until it just begins to thicken—no more than 3 or 4 minutes. Just at that point, add the oysters and cucumber pearls and cook only 30 seconds more, just barely warming them.

4. Off the heat, swirl in the butter. Verify the seasoning. Spoon into 4 warm soup plates and sprinkle julienned red rose petals across the yellow curry sauce. (The petals don't taste, they're just pretty.) Serve.

Note Use a flower from your garden if you can—roses from the florist are usually sprayed with pesticide.

Artichokes Stuffed with Snails and Basil

SERVES 4

Ever tasted the true grassy flavor of French Burgundy snails? Probably not if you've eaten them only the standard way—in garlic butter. Here the tomato-basil-artichoke combination in a light *beurre blanc* brings out the taste of the actual snail, and it is delicious.

4 artichokes

3 lemons

Salt

1 tablespoon finely minced shallot

8 fresh mushrooms

1 red, ripe tomato

2 dozen good French "Burgundy" snails

10 tablespoons unsalted butter

Freshly ground white pepper

¾ cup dry white wine

6 fresh basil leaves

1. "Turn" and cook the artichokes (see box at the right).
2. Preheat the oven to 350°F.
3. Finely mince 1 tablespoon shallot and quarter the mushrooms. Reserve.
4. Quickly roast the tomato over an open flame, charring the skin and then flaking it off under cold running water. Core

Turning and Cooking the Artichokes

1. For 4 artichokes, squeeze the juice of 2 lemons in a large pot of generously salted cold water and drop the lemon halves into the pot. Reserve.

2. Break the stem from the bottom of the artichoke. Holding the artichoke upside down in one hand and a sharp paring knife in the other, trim away all the green exterior of each leaf, leaving just the white flesh, turning the artichoke as you go. This is called "turning" the artichoke.

3. Once you've trimmed away a couple of layers of leaves, turn the choke on its side and cut the whole top off, leaving a trimmed heart about an inch tall. Trim the bottom flat with a knife so the choke will stand level.

4. Immediately rub the entire surface of the heart with a lemon half and plunge it into the cold salted lemon water to prevent blackening. Repeat with the remaining artichokes.

5. Cover the pot, bring it to a boil, reduce to a simmer, and cook for 15 to 20 minutes. The artichokes are done when the feel of an inserted knife is tender but not mushy.

6. When the artichokes are done, remove the pan from the heat and add a tray of ice to the cooking water. Reserve the artichokes in their own liquor. (They will keep nicely in this way for 3 or 4 days.)

and halve the tomato, then squeeze it in your hand to remove all juice and seeds. Finely chop the remaining meat.

5. Thoroughly rinse the snails under cold running water. Drain in a colander, squeezing them gently with the back of your hand to remove extra water.

6. Pull or spoon all the hair from the artichoke hearts, creating a shallow cup with a lip of cut leaves. Place a tiny dab of butter inside each heart, using ½ tablespoon of butter for all 4 hearts, and place the hearts in a buttered baking dish. Heat in the oven for 5 or 6 minutes.

7. Heat 1 tablespoon of the remaining butter in a sauté pan. Add the mushrooms and sauté over moderate heat until they just begin to turn golden brown.

8. Add the snails and continue to sauté 1 minute more. Add the shallot and tomato. Season with salt and white pepper.

9. Deglaze the pan with the white wine and reduce until only a couple of spoonfuls of liquid are left. Remove the pan from the heat. Swirl in the remaining 8 tablespoons butter, bit by bit.

10. Quickly julienne the basil and add it to the sauce. Verify the seasoning—you may want to add salt, pepper, or a few drops of lemon juice.

11. Remove the artichoke hearts from the oven. Arrange one on each of 4 plates. Fill with snails and sauce. Serve.

Duck Liver Mousse with Calvados

SERVES 8

This is great finger food—tiny, rich portions of classic duck liver mousse whipped with apples and Calvados, spread on freshly toasted brioche, and served with a crunchy fennel rémoulade.

MOUSSE

1½ Granny Smith apples

6 tablespoons (¾ stick) unsalted butter

1 shot Calvados (2 tablespoons)

½ medium onion

9 ounces duck and/or chicken livers

Salt and freshly ground white pepper

¼ cup crème fraîche (page 55) or heavy cream

⅓ cup hazelnuts (filberts) or 1 fresh truffle, finely chopped

1 bulb fresh fennel

¼ cup Pommery Mustard and Sherry Wine Vinegar Vinaigrette (page 36)

8 slices brioche or other good bread, toasted

MAKING THE MOUSSE

1. Peel the apples and cut them into ¼-inch dice. Cook in 1 tablespoon of the butter in a small sauté pan until golden

brown. Deglaze with the Calvados and flambé. Reserve.

2. Thinly slice the onion and cook the slices in a large sauté pan with 1 tablespoon of the remaining butter until dark golden brown.

3. Add the duck or chicken livers (any combination will do) and sauté 1½ to 2 minutes until medium rare—no more. Cut one open to check: the livers must remain pink inside. Season with salt and white pepper.

4. Put the livers and onion in a food processor and purée 30 seconds. Add the remaining 4 tablespoons butter and purée 30 seconds more. Add the crème fraîche and purée another 30 seconds. Verify the seasoning. Add the diced apple and stir it in with one very short burst.

5. Transfer the mousse to a Pyrex or stainless-steel bowl and chill in the refrigerator 3 to 4 hours.

SERVING

6. Roast the hazelnuts at 350°F. for 10 minutes until golden brown. Peel and coarsely chop. Reserve.

7. Slice the fennel bulb into paper-thin ribbons, reserving enough of the leafy greens for 1 teaspoon when finely chopped. Toss the fennel bulb with the vinaigrette. Finely chop the fennel greens and season the fennel ribbons with the greens, salt, and pepper.

8. With an ice cream scoop or spoon, scoop out enough chilled liver mousse to fashion a ball half again as large as a golf ball. Shape the mousse into 8 balls.

9. Roll the liver balls in chopped hazelnuts, or in finely chopped truffle, if using.

10. Place one ball in the center of each of 8 plates and surround it with the fennel rémoulade. Serve with toasted brioche or other good bread.

Snails with Port and Green Peppercorns

SERVES 4

This is one of my favorite sauces, an example of how contrasts can absolutely make a dish—in this case the hotness of the green peppercorns perfectly balances the sweet richness of the port. Cooked in this hearty sauce, the Burgundy snails swell up juicy and plump. Attack this dish as a Frenchman would: fork in one hand, plenty of bread in the other.

2 dozen extra-large Burgundy snails, fresh or canned

8 silver-dollar-size fresh mushrooms

1 tablespoon finely minced shallot

4 tablespoons (½ stick) unsalted butter

3 fluid ounces vintage port

1 teaspoon green peppercorns

1 cup Veal Stock (page 109)

Salt

1. If using fresh snails, clean and blanch them. If using canned snails, drain them, squeeze out all the excess liquid with your hand, and rinse them thoroughly under cold water.

2. Remove the stems from the mushrooms and quarter the caps. Finely mince the shallot.

3. Sauté the mushroom caps in 1 tablespoon of the butter in a 12-inch sauté pan over moderate heat until they begin to turn golden brown. Add the snails and sauté 30 seconds more, then add the shallot and sweat until tender.

4. Deglaze the pan with the port and add the green peppercorns, crushing them slightly with your fingers. Reduce the liquid until the pan is almost dry. Add the veal stock and reduce by about one-third or until the sauce just begins to thicken.

5. Remove the pan from the heat, and swirl in the remaining 3 tablespoons butter, bit by bit. Verify the salt seasoning and the balance of port to green peppercorn. Spoon into 4 soup plates and serve.

Note The port and green peppercorn sauce is not a sauce I would serve with seafood, though in truth the snail is phylogenetically closer to fish than it is to meat. It's a mollusk, like oysters and clams. Indeed, the cheap snails used by many restaurants are not authentic brown or Burgundy land snails but sea snails from Taiwan.

Tuna Tartare

S E R V E S   4

An ideal initial sushi experience. Raw tuna, you may be surprised to find, tastes better than the same fish cooked. It's by no means strong or fishy but subtle, with a meaty flavor similar to raw beef. I learned this beautiful presentation from Sato, my favorite sushi master. It's a distinctly Japanese dish that fits nonetheless gracefully into a French menu.

I hothouse cucumber

I green onion

¼ teaspoon grated fresh ginger

8 ounces very fresh tuna (see Note)

2 teaspoons soy sauce

4 quail eggs

I teaspoon sesame seeds, toasted

1. Cut the cucumber into 4 tulip-shaped cups, each about 2 inches tall. Save a segment of the cucumber to make butterflies for garnish.

2. Using only the green tops, mince the green onion as finely as possible.

3. Peel and grate or finely chop ¼ teaspoon fresh ginger. (Remember, a little ginger goes a long way.)

4. Dice the tuna into delicate ¼-inch cubes and toss in a bowl with the minced green onion, ginger, and soy sauce. Fill the cucumber tulips with the diced tuna.

5. Make a slight depression in each tuna mound for a raw quail egg yolk (just the yolk—discard the white). Sprinkle the sesame seeds over the tuna.

6. Cut the cucumber butterflies and place them atop the tuna. Serve.

Note It is important always to cut sushi or sashimi at just the last second. It oxidizes and looses its fresh taste if cut ahead of time.

Cut cucumber cup.

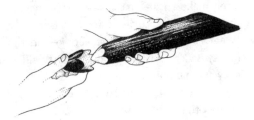

Finished tulip with cubed tuna.

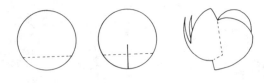

Making cucumber butterfly.

Stuffed Morel Mushrooms

SERVES 4

For an inveterate fan like me, morels have a frustratingly short season. They are good in so many things—salads, stuffings, sauces. But here the morel is itself the center of the dish. Morels are large, hollow cones, which makes the temptation to stuff them irresistible. They are earthy and strong-flavored, so I wanted something hardy and robust, like sausage, to stand up to them. A really rich Cognac sauce marries it all.

2 to 4 shoulder pork chops (about ¾ pound meat) or 1 pound boneless pork butt

¼ teaspoon ground allspice

Salt and freshly ground white pepper

2 bunches fresh spinach

2 tablespoons unsalted butter

1 clove garlic, unpeeled

8 large or 16 medium fresh morel mushrooms

¼ cup Cognac

¾ cup Veal Stock (page 109)

2 tablespoons crème fraîche (page 55) or heavy cream

Special Equipment
Meat grinder
Pastry bag with small (¼-inch) round tip
4 ovenproof plates

MAKING THE SAUSAGE STUFFING (MAY BE DONE A DAY AHEAD)

1. Cut all the meat and fat from the pork chops and grind it in a meat grinder, using the finest disk.

2. Season the meat with the allspice, a scant ½ teaspoon salt, and a few turns of white pepper. Reserve.

3. Rinse and stem the spinach. Flash-cook it in a tightly covered saucepan over high heat with 1 tablespoon of the butter, a light sprinkle of salt, and the garlic clove slightly crushed to break the skin. The spinach will cook in its own juices in no more than 2 minutes.

4. Remove and discard the garlic clove. Finely chop one-quarter of the cooked spinach, reserving the rest in the covered pan to garnish the plates.

5. Using a wooden spoon, stir the chopped spinach into the sausage stuffing, mixing well and adding a spoonful of water to loosen the mixture and facilitate stuffing the mushrooms. Reserve.

COOKING AND SERVING

6. Preheat the oven to 450°F.

7. Gently brush any dirt from the mushrooms—rinse only if muddy. Trim the bottoms of the stems if they are dirty or ragged.

8. Fit the pastry bag with the ¼-inch tip and fill the bag with the sausage. Pipe the sausage into the morels through the hollow stems.

9. Heat the remaining tablespoon of butter in an ovenproof sauté pan until the butter begins to sizzle. Add the morels and

sauté over high heat for 1 minute, shaking the pan from time to time to lightly brown the mushrooms all over. Place the pan in the oven and cook 5 to 6 minutes more, shaking the pan halfway through to cook the mushrooms evenly on all sides.

10. Remove the pan from the oven and place it over moderate heat. Immediately deglaze and flambé with the Cognac. Add the veal stock and crème fraîche and reduce until the sauce is slightly thickened.

11. While the sauce is reducing, arrange the remaining spinach in the center of 4 ovenproof plates and warm it in the oven.

12. Remove the mushrooms from the sauce. Slice them lengthwise in half and arrange in a star on the beds of spinach. Nap with the sauce and devour.

Santa Barbara Shrimp with Fennel

S E R V E S   4

One of the best and simplest ways to serve sea bass is to grill it with sweet fennel—a combination so popular in the Mediterranean it's almost a cliché. Here I do delectable Santa Barbara shrimp in that Mediterranean-inspired manner, using fennel in the stuffing and a splash of Pernod in the sauce. I can't rave about Santa Barbara shrimp enough, especially for this kind of subtly aromatic dish. They cook in just seconds, they are not chewy like other shrimp but meltingly delicate in the mouth, and they are incredibly sweet-tasting.

2 bunches fresh spinach

14 tablespoons (1¾ sticks) unsalted butter, slightly softened

Salt

8 silver-dollar-size fresh mushrooms

1 bulb fennel

Freshly ground white pepper

24 fresh Santa Barbara shrimp (spot prawns; (see Note)

1 tablespoon finely minced shallot

5 fluid ounces dry white wine

1 tablespoon heavy cream

3 tablespoons Pernod or Ricard

1. Rinse and stem the spinach. Put it in a tightly covered saucepan with 1 tablespoon of the butter and a light sprinkle of salt and flash-cook it over high heat for about 2 minutes so that it steams in its own juice. Reserve.

2. Very finely dice both the mushrooms and the fennel, saving a few of the leafy green fennel tops for a delicate garnish.

3. Stir-fry the diced fennel and mushrooms in 2 tablespoons of the remaining butter over moderate heat until they begin to turn golden brown. Finely chop the cooked spinach and add it to the mixture. Season with salt and white pepper. Reserve.

4. Peel the shrimp and butterfly them, making a slit partway through the underside.

5. Melt about a tablespoon of the remaining butter and brush a baking sheet with it. Arrange the shrimp, open side up, on the baking sheet. Top each shrimp with a spoonful of the fennel stuffing and reserve the prepared shrimp in the refrigerator.

6. Preheat the oven to a blistering 500°F.

7. Mince the shallot, and place it, white wine, and the cream in a saucepan. Reduce over moderate heat until all but a few tablespoons of liquid remain.

8. Off the heat, swirl in the remaining 10 tablespoons slightly softened butter, bit by bit. Season with salt, white pepper, and 1 tablespoon of the Pernod. Reserve.

9. Bake the stuffed shrimp in the preheated oven for approximately 2 minutes until the tails begin to curl up and the shrimp are slightly firm to the touch and no longer translucent. Remove the shrimp from the oven, sprinkle lightly with the remaining Pernod, and flambé.

10. Mirror the Pernod *beurre blanc* on 4 warm plates. On each plate arrange 6 shrimp with the tails at the center. Garnish with the leafy fennel sprigs. Serve.

Note If you cannot find Santa Barbara shrimp, substitute the best jumbo shrimp you can find.

Braised Endive and Asparagus with Sauternes

SERVES 4

Another marvelous contrast—the sour of the braised endives with the sweet of the smooth Sauternes and cream sauce. This is a terrific cold-weather appetizer—it's served hot, and endives are always available. Belgian endives are traditionally forced in France and Belgium in peat boxes in caves (they don't need the sun to grow), hence their white color; the pointed shoots are snipped off before they grow into what we call curly endive. They used to go out of season in the summer, but now we can get them from New Zealand, where the reversed seasons make them available to us all year round.

2 plump Belgian endives

10 tablespoons unsalted butter

16 extra-large asparagus

1 tablespoon finely minced shallot

¾ cup Sauternes

¼ cup heavy cream

Salt and freshly ground white pepper

MISE EN PLACE

1. Preheat the oven to 450°F. Put a large pot of generously salted water on to boil. Prepare an ice bath.

2. Cut the endives in half lengthwise.

Heat a heaping tablespoon of the butter in an ovenproof sauté pan until it just begins to brown. Add the 4 endive halves, cut side down, and allow to sizzle 1 minute. Cover tightly and bake in the oven 15 to 20 minutes or until well done. Reserve in a warm place.

3. While the endives are baking, break off the fibrous bottoms of the asparagus at the point where they snap easily. Peel the tender tops, except for the top 2 inches, with a vegetable peeler. Tie the asparagus into 2 or 3 small bundles (to prevent rolling and breaking) and cook in the boiling salted water until tender, approximately 5 minutes. Chill immediately in an ice bath to stop the cooking and to preserve the bright green color. Untie and reserve.

MAKING THE SAUCE AND SERVING

4. Place a still-warm endive half, the cut and browned side up, on each of 4 warm plates, and spread it like a fan.

5. Put the asparagus in a clean sauté pan with 1 tablespoon water. Cover tightly and heat over a low flame for about 2 minutes.

6. Remove the warm asparagus from the pan and place 2 spears on either side of each endive fan. Add the shallot to the pan with 1 tablesoon of the butter and sweat over low heat until tender. Deglaze the pan with the Sauternes and reduce by two-thirds. Add the cream and reduce until the sauce begins to thicken. Swirl in the remaining 8 tablespoons butter, bit by bit. Season with salt and pepper. Nap the asparagus and endives with the sauce. Serve.

Artichoke Hearts with Morels

SERVES 4

It's good luck that artichokes are available during the short morel season, which lasts about a month in late spring. The earthy flavor of the wild morel—it's the most aromatic of the wild mushrooms with the exception of the truffle—goes very well with this simple vegetable salad in a lemon-and-olive-oil mayonnaise. It makes a good first course for a party, since the entire dish can be prepared well in advance, leaving the chef free to mingle.

4 large artichokes

3 lemons

Salt

12 to 16 fresh morels

1 carrot

1 rib celery

1 bulb fennel

16 haricots verts (French green beans)

1/4 cup extra-virgin olive oil

Freshly ground white pepper

1 bunch chives

SAUCE

1 egg yolk

1 teaspoon Dijon mustard

Salt and freshly ground white pepper

Squeeze of lemon juice

1/4 cup extra-virgin olive oil

1/4 cup peanut oil

MISE EN PLACE

1. "Turn" and cook the artichokes (see box, page 60).

2. If the morels are dirty, gently rinse them under cold running water. Cut the morels lengthwise into quarters or sixths, depending on their size.

3. Peel and cut the carrot into matchstick julienne. Cut the celery and the fennel into the same-size julienne. You will need a good 1/2 cup of each. String the green beans.

COOKING AND SERVING

4. Heat 1/4 cup olive oil in a large sauté pan, add the vegetables and morels, and season with salt and pepper. Gently stir-fry over moderate heat for 3 or 4 minutes or until the vegetables are tender but still firm. Add a squeeze of lemon. Be sure the morels are cooked; they should *not* be eaten raw. Allow to cool to room temperature. Reserve.

5. *To make the sauce:* Place the egg yolk and Dijon mustard in a small mixing bowl. Add a little salt and pepper and a squeeze of lemon juice. Whisk well.

6. While whisking vigorously, add the olive and peanut oils in a thread. The sauce should be thick and creamy but pourable; thin with water if necessary. Verify the seasoning and reserve.

7. Mirror 4 salad plates with two-thirds of the sauce.

8. Remove the hair from the center of the artichoke hearts and place one heart in the center of each mirrored plate.

9. Top the artichoke hearts with the salad. Pour a little of the remaining sauce over the top. Cut the chives into ½-inch-long pieces and sprinkle a few around each heart. Serve.

Morels

Five or six years ago, morels were a rare commodity—expensive, imported, and only available dried. But as fine food and cooking came into popular focus, a network of pickers, suppliers, and chefs has grown up for disseminating fresh morels, which, wonderful to say, grow abundantly throughout the entire Midwest and West Coast, particularly in recently burned areas.

Grilled Scallop Brochettes with Rainier Cherries

S E R V E S   4

This is a dish of serendipitous origin. A few years back when I had four Rainier cherries left over, it occurred to me to cook them with scallops, and I was amazed by how the flavor of the cherries so perfectly complemented the sweetness of the scallops. Unfortunately, the Rainier season was just over, and it would be another year before I served it to anybody. It was worth the wait. The cherry sauce turned out to be a hit not just with scallops but with other sweet, delicate fish, such as John Dory or pike, as well.

---

12 Rainier cherries

1 heaping tablespoon finely minced shallot

½ cup dry white wine

¼ cup heavy cream

10 tablespoons unsalted butter

Salt and freshly ground white pepper

12 large sea scallops

Special Equipment 8 bamboo skewers

1. *To make the sauce:* Cut the cherries in half with a paring knife and remove the pits. Finely mince the shallot. Place the white wine, shallot, cherries, and cream in a saucepan and reduce over moderate heat until only a few tablespoons of liquid remain. Remove from the heat and swirl in 6 tablespoons of the unsalted butter, bit by bit. Season with salt and a little white pepper. Reserve in a warm place for 15 minutes to allow the flavor of the cherries to infuse the sauce fully.

2. *To prepare the brochettes:* Remove the tough tendon from the side of each scallop. Slice the scallops horizontally in half to make 24 half-inch-thick disks. Piercing them through the sides, slide 3 scallop disks onto each bamboo skewer. Reserve.

COOKING AND SERVING

3. Make a very hot fire in your grill. (You can sauté or bake the brochettes on a buttered sheet of aluminum foil, but they will look and taste better if grilled.) Melt the remaining 4 tablespoons butter.

4. Season both sides of the brochettes with salt and a little white pepper. Brush the scallops with the melted butter.

5. Clean the grill rack with a wire brush, then season it by brushing it with a little melted butter.

6. Place the brochettes on the hot grill and cook for 45 seconds, then turn them 90 degrees to make pretty grill marks and cook another 45 seconds. Brush them again with butter, turn them over, and cook another 1½ minutes.

7. In the meantime, heat the sauce if necessary—gently! Remove the cherries from the sauce and set aside.

8. Mirror 4 warm plates with the sauce, place 2 brochettes on each plate, and top each slice of scallop with a half cherry. Serve.

Rainier Cherries

The short season for Rainier cherries (also called Royal Ann, Queen Anne, or white cherries, although they are actually yellow with a rose blush)—six or seven weeks at the beginning of the summer—used to yield just one shipment per year to restaurants in my area. With the broadening food interest in this country, this uniquely flavored fruit is now much more widely available, and we get four or five full shipments each season.

Paupiettes of Halibut and Enoki Mushrooms

S E R V E S   4

Raw fish again! But again an ideal dish for breaking down people's prejudices. Halibut is a clean-flavored, delicate, unfishy fish. Eaten with the crunchy, slightly pickled enokis, the fish tastes especially fresh and pure. A beautiful little hors d'oeuvre.

1½ cups rice wine vinegar

3 tablespoons mirin (sweet rice wine)

1½ tablespoons soy sauce

1 teaspoon *momiji* (red chili paste) or a pinch of crushed red chilies

2 packages enoki mushrooms

2 green onions

8 ounces very fresh halibut fillet (preferably from a baby halibut—less than 5 pounds)

1 teaspoon sesame seeds, toasted

MISE EN PLACE

1. In a small bowl, mix the vinegar, mirin, soy sauce, and *momiji*, adding just a little of the *momiji* at a time and tasting for desired hotness. Pour this over the enokis (with the clump of stems still intact) and let marinate 4 to 6 hours. They will keep in the marinade 2 to 3 days.

2. Finely mince just the green tops—about 4 inches—of the green onions.

3. Using a very sharp slicing knife, cut the halibut fillet into 20 very thin slices, no more than ⅛ inch thick.

ASSEMBLY AND SERVING

4. Remove the enokis from the marinade, stems still intact. Break the large bunch into 20 smaller bunches, each as big around as your finger. Roll up each bunch in a slice of halibut, leaving the stems sticking out one end. Then trim away the base of the stems so that they are even with the fish, leaving only the tender tops wrapped inside.

5. Arrange 5 *paupiettes*—wrapped, stuffed bundles—on each of 4 plates as if the points of a star. Spoon a little of the marinade over each and garnish with a pinch of minced green onion. Lightly sprinkle with toasted sesame seeds and serve.

Gratin of Salmon with Chives

SERVES 4

This is a delicate and sophisticated, yet quick and inexpensive appetizer. The use of the hot electric broiler or salamander to flash-cook the thinly sliced salmon and glaze the whipped-cream–white-wine sauce makes this an up-to-date knock-off of a classic French *glaçage*, though it is lighter, faster, and healthier since it eschews flour, egg yolks, and butter. It can also be made with scallops or any seafood sliced thin enough to cook instantly. However done, it is unique, something your guests won't have had before.

8 ounces salmon fillet

Salt and freshly ground white pepper

1 cup heavy cream

2 tablespoons minced shallots

¾ cup dry white wine

1 tablespoon minced fresh chives

Special Equipment

Electric oven broiler or salamander
4 ovenproof plates

MISE EN PLACE

1. Slice the salmon fillet crosswise into very thin (⅛-inch) strips. Season lightly with salt and white pepper.
2. Whip 3 fluid ounces of the cream until firm. Reserve.

COOKING AND SERVING

3. *To make the sauce:* Place the shallots, white wine, remaining 5 ounces cream, and a pinch of salt in a small saucepan and reduce substantially until just under a third remains. It will be too thick to be a sauce. Remove from the heat and gently stir in the whipped cream and chives. Don't overstir—you'll break it. Verify the salt seasoning.
4. Mirror the sauce on 4 ovenproof plates. Arrange thin slices of salmon on top of the sauce, but do not place so much salmon on each plate as to cover all the sauce.
5. Glaze close to a very hot broiler for 1 minute or until the sauce is golden brown. Fear not: a minute is plenty to cook the fish perfectly. Serve.

Seared Foie Gras with Artichoke, Port, and Truffles

SERVES 2

This is a bit expensive to serve to a whole tableful, but for your special friend, it's food at its sensual best—the perfect pearl. The seared foie gras medallions are buttery rich by themselves, but in the port-and-truffle sauce, an orgy—best enjoyed in small quantities. Adapted from the classic *Fond d'Artichaut Lucullus.* That's Lucius Licinius Lucullus, Roman consul notorious for his extravagance.

1 artichoke

1 lemon

Salt

6 ounces fresh duck foie gras

1 teaspoon very finely minced shallot

2 teaspoons unsalted butter

¼ cup vintage port

1 teaspoon finely julienned truffle

½ cup Veal Stock (page 109)

Freshly ground white pepper

MISE EN PLACE

1. "Turn" and cook the artichoke (see box, page 60).

2. In the meantime, slice the foie gras into ⅓-inch-thick medallions.

3. In a small saucepan, sweat the shallot with about 1 teaspoon butter until softened but not colored. Deglaze the pan with the port, add the truffle, and reduce until almost dry. Add the veal stock; reduce slightly and reserve.

4. Clean the hair from the cooked artichoke heart and slice the heart into matchstick julienne.

COOKING AND SERVING

5. Heat a small sauté pan—with no oil, nothing—over moderate heat for 4 or 5 minutes.

6. In the meantime, heat the artichoke julienne in another pan with the remaining butter and a sprinkle of salt. When warm, divide the artichoke between 2 plates, placing each half in the center of the plate. Heat the port-and-truffle sauce and verify the seasoning. Pour this over the artichoke and reserve the plates in a warm place.

7. Season the foie gras medallions with salt and white pepper. Quickly sear the medallions in the by-now very hot sauté pan *no more than 20 seconds on each side.*

8. Arrange the medallions atop the artichoke julienne and serve immediately.

Tuna and Octopus Fan with Miso Dressing

SERVES 4

The possibilities for raw fish go far beyond sushi. Here, the complexly intriguing sauce takes raw tuna past the plain rice and soy sauce treatment, and the octopus, I should clarify, is cooked. It is a perfect light first course for a multicourse French menu. With your eyes closed, you who have never tasted octopus might very well mistake it for lobster or crab.

2 green onions

2 tablespoons brown miso (soybean paste)

½ teaspoon *momiji* (red chili paste)

2 tablespoons mirin (sweet rice wine)

¼ cup rice wine vinegar

1 teaspoon soy sauce

2 packages *kaiware* (daikon radish sprouts)

1 tentacle octopus, cooked

8 ounces very fresh tuna (center cut)

2 tablespoons sesame seeds, toasted

1. *To make the dressing:* Finely chop just the green tops of the green onions. In a small mixing bowl, mix together the green onions, miso, *momiji*, mirin, vinegar, and soy sauce. Depending on the strength of your specific ingredients, you may need to fine-tune the mirin, vinegar, chili, and soy seasonings to balance the pleasing sweet-sour and hot-salty flavors properly.

2. Mirror the dressing on 4 chilled plates and arrange a small bed of radish sprouts in the center of each plate.

3. Slice the octopus and the tuna into thin petal-shaped slices. Fan alternating slices of red tuna and white octopus atop the beds of radish sprouts. Sprinkle with toasted sesame seeds. Serve.

Cèpes with Bone Marrow

SERVES 4

This is a dish straight from Bordeaux, where they have two things in abundance: good red wine and cèpes growing wild in the hills. Grilled cèpe caps filled with red wine and marrow make a wonderful small but choice appetizer in a multicourse menu. It's not a dish for dieters, however: marrow, so good just by itself on toast points, is beyond rich. Try this dish poured over steak as a sauce—one of my favorite indulgences.

---

10 pieces (1-inch) cut beef marrow bones (cut by your butcher)

1 bunch chervil

4 large or 8 medium fresh cèpes

4 tablespoons (½ stick) unsalted butter

Salt and freshly ground pepper

2 tablespoons very finely minced shallots

5 fluid ounces good Cabernet Sauvignon or red Bordeaux

¾ cup Veal Stock (page 109)

CLEANING THE MARROW THE NIGHT BEFORE

1. Carefully pop the marrow out of the bones and soak the marrow overnight in a bowl of generously salted water in the refrigerator. This will leach some of the blood out of the marrow and leave you with a cleaner taste and a creamy white color.

2. Preheat the oven to 400°F. or make a nice hot fire in your grill.

3. Pluck 3 dozen chervil leaves. Reserve.

4. Thoroughly clean the cèpes with a towel or a brush. Do not rinse them unless they are so dirty that you have no choice. Break the stems from the caps and reserve. Sauté the caps in 1 tablespoon of the butter over moderate heat for about 1 minute. Turn the caps cup side up, season with salt and pepper, and either bake them in the same pan for 7 to 8 minutes or, better yet, finish cooking them cup side up on the grill. The slightly charred, smoky flavor is worth the extra effort.

5. In the meantime, cut the stems into round, ¼-inch-thick slices. Sauté in 1 tablespoon of the remaining butter until they begin to turn golden brown. Add the shallots and sauté until softened, about 30 seconds. Deglaze the pan with the red wine and reduce until almost dry.

6. While the sauce is reducing, cut the marrow into ¼-inch-thick slices. Reserve.

7. Add the veal stock to the pan and reduce slightly until the sauce begins to thicken. Remove the pan from the heat, add the marrow, and allow it to sit for a minute to soften. You may need to add a little more heat—*just don't boil the marrow.*

8. Verify the seasoning and finish the sauce by swirling in the remaining 2 tablespoons butter, bit by bit.

9. Place 1 large or 2 medium cèpes in the center of each of 4 plates. Using a slotted spoon, fill the caps with marrow and sliced cèpes. Nap with the sauce. Sprinkle with chervil leaves and serve.

Paupiettes of Gravlax and Smoked Salmon with Beluga

MAKES ABOUT 18 PIECES

A very elegant dish and easy to make. Although the gravlax has to cure for 48 hours, the dish can be finished entirely ahead of time, making it ideal as finger food or as the first course for a dinner party. Served with freshly baked brioche, it's as memorable a first course as you'll find.

GRAVLAX

1 teaspoon black peppercorns

1 bunch fresh dill

10 ounces fresh salmon fillet, scaled but unskinned

2 tablespoons salt

1 teaspoon sugar

1 tablespoon vodka

5 ounces fine smoked salmon, skinless and boneless

3 ounces cream cheese

½ cup crème fraîche (page 55)

Squeeze of lemon juice

2 ounces Beluga caviar

MAKING THE GRAVLAX

1. Crush the black peppercorns with the flat side of a cleaver or the bottom of a pan. Stem and chop the fresh dill.

2. Make a couple of shallow slits through the skin of the salmon fillet. Generously season both sides of the fillet with the salt, crushed pepper, sugar, and dill. Place in a small Pyrex, stainless steel, or ceramic dish. (Do not use aluminum—the salt will eat into it.) Sprinkle with the vodka. Cover with plastic wrap and refrigerate for 48 hours. Turn the fillet over once or twice during this period.

MAKING THE SMOKED SALMON MOUSSE

3. Remove any skin and bones from the smoked salmon—make sure you have 5 full ounces of the salmon left. Purée it in a food processor for 1 minute. Then force the purée through a sieve. (This isn't absolutely necessary but will make for a perfectly smooth mousse.)

4. Place the smoked salmon in the bowl of an electric mixer with the cream cheese, 2 tablespoons of the crème fraîche, and the lemon juice. Whip at medium speed 2 or 3 minutes, until the mixture is light and smooth.

5. In a separate bowl, whip the remaining 6 tablespoons crème fraîche until it holds a firm peak.

6. Gently fold the whipped crème fraîche and half the caviar into the smoked salmon mixture. Reserve.

ASSEMBLY AND SERVING

7. Carefully slice the gravlax into approximately 18 paper-thin slices, leaving the skin behind. Roll up each thin slice with a heaping spoonful of mousse inside. Stand on end and top with a dollop of the remaining caviar. Serve.

Fish and Shellfish

Whitefish with Leek and Truffle

SERVES 4

I've been cooking whitefish, or *fera*, since my schoolboy days on Lake Geneva, where the native fish is so highly regarded they call it "the fisherman's fish." They treat it delicately—they poach it and serve it with a number of different light cream sauces. I've adapted one of them here, a rustic-flavored sauce in which the sweet onioniness of the leek complements the earthiness of the truffle. Surprisingly, the two tastes remain distinct yet subtle as they mix. It's one of the first fish sauces I ever learned—easy, a real confidence builder—and still one of my favorites. The fresh truffle isn't absolutely necessary for this sauce, but adding it makes the whole dish twice as rewarding.

4 small or 2 large skinned whitefish fillets
(1½ pounds total)

1 leek

4 tablespoons (½ stick) unsalted butter

2 tablespoons finely minced shallots

Salt and freshly ground white pepper

¾ cup dry white wine

¾ cup heavy cream

1 small black truffle (optional)

1. *To skin the fillets* (if your fishmonger hasn't done it already): Place the fish skin side down on a cutting board, grasp the tail with one hand, and insert a long thin knife between the skin and flesh. Hold the knife flat against the cutting board and slide it away from you, separating the fish from the skin.

2. If you have 2 large fillets, cut them in half for 4 portions. If you have 4 small, thin fillets, cut these in half crosswise and stack the two pieces together to make thicker portions that will cook more delicately and fit better on the plate.

3. Put a small pot of water on to boil. Prepare an ice bath by placing ice cubes and water in a bowl.

4. Cut the roots from the bottom of the leek. Cut the stalk off about halfway up where it begins to branch out and turn green. Save the prettiest green leaf to make chevrons for garnish later. Split the white of the leek in half lengthwise and rinse thoroughly under cold running water (leeks grow in mud). Slice the leek crosswise into very thin julienne.

COOKING AND SERVING

5. Melt 2 tablespoons of the butter in a large sauté pan. Add the leeks and stir-fry over low heat for about 2 minutes until tender and just barely brown. Remove from the heat.

6. Sprinkle the shallots in the pan. Arrange the 4 portions of whitefish on top of the shallots and leek. Sprinkle with salt and a few grinds of white pepper. Add the white wine, cover tightly, and place the pan

Fish and Shellfish

∎

81

over moderate heat. Allow the wine to come to a boil. Reduce the heat and let the wine simmer for 2 minutes. Remove from the heat and let rest, still tightly covered, for another 2 minutes.

7. Carefully remove just the fish from the pan. Blot lightly on a towel. Reserve in a warm place.

8. *To finish the sauce:* Add the cream to the wine in the pan and place it over high heat for 3 to 4 minutes to reduce by about half. When the sauce begins to thicken, turn off the heat. Gently grate the entire truffle, if using, into the sauce. Swirl in the remaining 2 tablespoons butter and verify the seasoning.

9. For literally 3 seconds, no more, plunge the green leek leaf into boiling water, remove it immediately, and chill in the ice bath. You will have softened the leek and set a vivid green color. Cut the folded leaf on the bias into twelve ¼-inch-wide chevrons.

10. Arrange the fish on 4 warm plates and nap with the sauce. Garnish each plate with 3 leek chevrons. Serve.

Broiled John Dory with Zucchini

S E R V E S   4

The unloved zucchini! Here it redeems itself: sliced paper-thin and overlapped like the scales of a fish along the John Dory's back, then toasted crisp and golden brown under a red-hot broiler. The zucchini positively makes the dish—a crunchy contrast to the wonderfully moist fish flesh and the zesty herb *beurre blanc*.

B E U R R E   B L A N C

1 teaspoon chopped mixed fresh herbs (basil, thyme, tarragon, rosemary, sage)

2 medium shallots

5 fluid ounces dry white wine

2 tablespoons heavy cream

Salt

12 tablespoons (1½ sticks) unsalted butter, softened

Squeeze of lemon juice

3 small zucchinis

4 skinned John Dory fillets (2 fish, 2½ to 2¾ pounds each; see Note)

Freshly ground white pepper

4 tablespoons (½ stick) unsalted butter

Special Equipment
Electric oven broiler

MAKING THE BEURRE BLANC

1. Chop 1 teaspoon of herbs—any combination of your favorite herbs will do, so long as no one of them overpowers the flavor of the fish and all together serve as a subtle herbal foil. Finely mince the shallots.

2. Add the herbs, white wine, cream, and a good pinch of salt to a saucepan. Reduce over high heat until about 3 tablespoons of liquid remain.

3. Remove the pan from the heat and immediately start to swirl in the softened butter, bit by bit, taking care to keep the sauce warm by adding low heat from time to time—but only low heat, lest you break it.

4. Once the butter is incorporated, whisk in the lemon juice. Verify the seasoning. Reserve the sauce in the same pan in a warm place (see Note).

COOKING AND SERVING

5. Preheat the broiler.

6. Slice the zucchinis into paper-thin pennies.

7. Place the fish fillets skinned side down on a buttered baking sheet. Lightly season with salt and white pepper.

8. Starting at the tail end, arrange the zucchini circles in overlapping rows like the scales of a fish. Lightly salt and pepper the zucchini. Place 5 or 6 dabs of butter atop each zucchinied fish.

9. Cook the fish under the very hot broiler for just 2 minutes—until the zucchini is golden brown and the fish is just cooked.

10. Mirror the beurre blanc on 4 warm plates. Using a wide spatula (so the fish won't split), carefully place the fish on top of the sauce. Serve.

Note Ask your fishmonger to do the filleting and discard the bones.

If your beurre blanc at any time seems too thick, whisk in a tablespoon or two of warm water. It will loosen the sauce without changing the balance of flavors.

Lobster with Turnips and Pernod

SERVES 2 AS AN
ENTRÉE, 4 AS AN
APPETIZER

Can lobster ever taste better than with simple lemon and butter? Hard to believe, but yes. I sometimes call this a stew (in the sense of chunks in a sauce), but this preparation is in reality a light, delicately cooked, sophisticated melding of perfect strangers into a happy marriage. The almost candied, earthy turnip in a silken Pernod sauce makes an unforgettable foil to the sweet, oceany lobster.

2 small live lobsters (1¼ pounds each)

2 turnips

8 tablespoons (1 stick) unsalted butter

1 tablespoon minced shallot

12 fresh snow peas

1 shot Pernod or Ricard (1½ fluid ounces)

½ cup dry white wine

¾ cup heavy cream

MISE EN PLACE

1. Heat a large pot of salted water to a rolling boil. Add the live lobsters, allow the water to return to a boil, and cook exactly 2 more minutes. Remove the lobsters and let cool. Save the hot water for cooking the snow peas.

2. Cut off both ends of the turnips, stand them up, and cut each one into 6 or 8 long wedges. Using a paring knife, "turn" each wedge—that is, round all the edges with the paring knife, removing the peel and fashioning rounded ovals.

3. In a small saucepan, cook the turnips with 2 tablespoons of the butter over low heat (just barely sizzling), shaking and turning frequently, for a good 10 minutes, until well done and completely golden brown—so that they are, in effect, candied. Reserve.

4. Finely mince the shallot and remove the strings from the snow peas.

5. When the lobsters are cool enough to handle, carefully break off and remove all the meat from the claws, knuckles, and tail. Cut each tail in half lengthwise and remove the vein. Reserve the meat. You will have 4 tail halves, 4 claws, and 8 knuckles. For the sauce, cut the heads into 1- to 2-inch pieces.

Lobster Cracking the Easy Way

Starting with the claw, bend the thumb back until it cracks, then pull it all the way off, leaving the sliver of meat behind. Crack the main claw shell by breaking the softer underside—the lighter colored side.

Then the tail: The whole tail meat will come out in one piece if you lay the curled up shell on its side and squeeze down on it to crack the cross ribs. The underside will then break open easily.

6. Preheat the oven to 450°F. Bring the lobster water back to a boil.

7. In a saucepan, briefly sweat the shallot in 2 tablespoons of the remaining butter over low heat for about 30 seconds, not enough to allow them to color. Add all the cut pieces of lobster head and continue to cook for I more minute.

8. Deglaze the pan with the Pernod and flambé. When the flames extinguish, add the white wine and I cup water. Increase the heat and reduce the liquid by half, then strain it through a very fine strainer into a clean saucepan. Add the cream and reduce again until it just begins to thicken. Reserve in the saucepan.

9. Arrange the pieces of lobster meat on a buttered baking sheet and top each piece with a small dab of butter, using about 2 tablespoons. Heat for 2 minutes in the preheated oven.

10. Plunge the snow peas into the boiling lobster water and cook until tender, approximately 45 seconds. Remove and keep warm.

11. Add the candied turnips, and the lobster roe if available, to the sauce and give it a final boil. Verify the seasoning— you may wish to add a few more drops of Pernod. Stir in the remaining 2 tablespoons butter into the sauce.

12. Arrange the pieces of lobster on warm plates. Nap with the sauce and randomly sprinkle a few bright green snow peas on each plate. Serve.

Salmon with Cabernet

SERVES 4

According to the age-old culinary taboo, fish must be poached in and drunk with white wine only. He or she was a gastronomic misfit who cooked any fish other than eel in red wine. Baloney! This is a narrow and outmoded notion—deserving of proper burial. Here the sturdy Cabernet plays off very well against the meaty, rich, slightly oily salmon. The *beurre rouge* is as easy to make as the familiar *beurre blanc.*

2 tablespoons finely minced shallots

I teaspoon fresh tarragon leaves (I stem)

1½ to 2 pounds skinned salmon fillet

12 tablespoons (1½ sticks) unsalted butter, softened

I cup Cabernet Sauvignon

Salt and freshly ground white pepper

¼ cup Veal Stock (page 109)

1. Finely mince the shallots. Peel the tarragon leaves from the stem. Reserve.

2. Cut the salmon fillet into 4 portions—6 ounces for a moderate portion, 8 ounces for large.

3. Smear the bottom of a large sauté pan with I teaspoon of the butter. Sprinkle evenly with the shallots. Place the salmon fillets on the shallots, add the wine, and

Fish and Shellfish

■

85

season with salt and pepper. Cover the pan tightly and place over high heat until the wine begins to boil. Reduce to a simmer and poach gently for 2½ more minutes. Remove from the heat and let rest, still covered, an additional 3 to 4 minutes to finish cooking.

4. After the resting time, remove the fillets with a slotted spatula, blot on a towel, and reserve on warm plates while making the sauce.

5. *To make the* beurre rouge: Place the pan with the wine over high heat. Add the veal stock and reduce until just 3 to 4 tablespoons liquid remain. Remove from the heat. Swirl in the remaining butter, bit by bit, as if making a *beurre blanc.* Verify the seasoning.

6. Nap the fish with the sauce and sprinkle with the fresh tarragon leaves. Serve.

Saddle of Lotte Roasted with Oyster Mushrooms

S E R V E S   4

The lotte (or angler, or monkfish) is an horrendously ugly brute—with a disproportionately large, heavy head, pointed vicious teeth, and a tapering tadpole's body. This prehistoric creature from the deep ocean must be cooked very fresh—the same day you buy it—or it will start gaining on you. Prepared just right, though—roasted and served on a bed of spinach with nutty, buttery mushrooms in an herb *beurre blanc*—it is one of the best fish in the sea, slightly chewy and sweet as lobster.

2 bunches fresh spinach

1 pound oyster mushrooms

2 pounds fresh lotte (monkfish) fillets (2 or 3 pieces)

2 tablespoons finely minced shallots

¾ cup dry white wine

1 tablespoon heavy cream

14 tablespoons (1¾ sticks) unsalted butter, softened

1 tablespoon chopped mixed fresh herbs (tarragon and thyme, chervil, chive, basil)

Salt and freshly ground white pepper

Flour for dredging

2 tablespoons oil for cooking

1 clove garlic, peeled

1. Preheat the oven to 475°F.

2. Rinse and stem the spinach. Remove the stems from the oyster mushrooms and discard the stems. If unusually large, cut them in halves or quarters.

3. Using a very sharp knife, trim away the pinkish membrane covering the lotte, leaving only the white meat.

4. Finely mince the shallots and reserve half of them. Put the other half in a small saucepan with the wine and cream. Reduce to no more than 3 to 4 tablespoons.

5. Remove the pan from the heat and swirl in 10 tablespoons of the butter, bit by bit. If the butter is cold and hard, add a bit of heat but don't let it boil.

6. Finely chop the tarragon with at least 2 of the other herbs. Add to the *beurre blanc,* season with salt and pepper, and reserve, allowing the flavor of the herbs to infuse the sauce.

COOKING AND SERVING

7. Season the lotte fillets with salt and pepper. Dredge them lightly in flour and pat off all the excess.

8. In a large ovenproof sauté pan or small roasting pan, heat the oil with 1 tablespoon of the remaining butter until the butter begins to brown. Add the fillets and brown on both sides, about 1 minute total.

9. Place the pan with the fillets in the hot oven and roast 4 to 6 minutes (depending on the size of the fish), turning the fillets over halfway through. The fish is done when it feels firm to the touch or when you see the first drop of "milk" oozing from the flesh. If undercooked, the fish will be a little too chewy; if overcooked, crumbly and dry. Remove and let rest 4 to 5 minutes before slicing.

10. Sauté the oyster mushrooms in 2 tablespoons of the remaining butter for 3 or 4 minutes until all the juice they exude cooks away and the mushrooms are slightly crisp and golden brown. Remove from the heat, season with salt and pepper, toss with the remaining raw shallot, and reserve in a warm place.

11. *To flash-cook the spinach:* Rub the bottom of a large sauté pan with a tight-fitting lid with the clove of garlic. Leaving the clove in the pan, add the remaining 1 tablespoon butter and the stemmed spinach and sprinkle lightly with salt. Cover and cook over moderate heat for about 2 minutes, shaking and stirring often, until the spinach has steamed in its own juice. Drain in a colander and remove the garlic.

12. To finish, make beds of spinach on 4 warm plates. Slice the lotte into thin medallions and fan them on the spinach beds. Nap with the herb beurre blanc and heap the oyster mushrooms on top. Serve.

Salmon with Lettuce and Champagne Sauce

SERVES 4

A very elegant recipe, but fast and easy—20 minutes from start to finish. The fish we wrap with lettuce is salmon, but almost any poachable fish will do—halibut for one. The *beurre de champagne* is as simple as a *beurre blanc,* but it's a different order of taste—delicately sweet and slightly, pleasantly yeasty. For the *coup de graĉe,* add a dollop of caviar.

---

8 large, pretty lettuce leaves (red leaf, green leaf, butterhead, or Bibb—not iceberg or romaine)

Salt and freshly ground white pepper

4 pieces skinned salmon fillet (6 ounces each)

12 tablespoons (1½ sticks) unsalted butter, softened

¾ cup dry Champagne (brut)

2 tablespoons finely minced shallots

2 teaspoons heavy cream

Dollop of caviar per serving (optional)

MISE EN PLACE

1. Rinse and dry the lettuce leaves. Cut out the bottom 2 inches of the thick, crunchy stems, leaving only the tender leaves. Stack the leaves neatly atop each other.

2. Bring an inch of water to boil in a covered saucepan. Remove from the heat and place the stacked lettuce leaves in the pan. Cover the pan and allow the leaves to wilt for just 1 minute. Drain off the water and, keeping the lettuce leaves whole, carefully remove them from the pan.

3. Slightly overlap 2 lettuce leaves on your cutting board. Lightly salt and pepper both sides of a salmon fillet. Place it face down in the center of the lettuce and fold the leaves over the fillet. Turn the package over to hold the leaves in place. Season and wrap the remaining fillets.

COOKING AND SERVING

4. Smear the bottom of a large sauté pan with some of the butter. Place the wrapped fillets in the pan, lightly sprinkle with salt, and add the Champagne. Cover tightly. Simmer gently for 2 minutes, then remove from the heat and let sit, still tightly covered, for 2 more minutes to finish cooking.

5. Using a wide spatula, carefully remove the wrapped salmon and reserve in a warm oven.

6. Place the pan over high heat, add the shallots and cream to the Champagne, and reduce until almost dry—about 2 tablespoons. Remove from the heat and swirl in the remaining butter, bit by bit, as you do in a *beurre blanc.* Verify the seasoning.

7. Mirror the sauce on 4 warm plates. Carefully blot any excess liquid from the wrapped fish and place it on the sauce. Top with caviar if using and serve.

Pompano with Two Butters

Pompano is a fish-lover's fish—oily and full-flavored. Barbecuing or sautéing it, and serving it with these two savory sauces—onion butter and red-bell-pepper butter—brings out its toothsome best. The fish must be absolutely fresh, though—smell it at the market before buying.

½ sweet white onion (such as Vidalia, Maui, or Walla Walla)

12 tablespoons (1½ sticks) unsalted butter, softened

1 red bell pepper

2 tablespoons finely minced shallots

¾ cup dry white wine

1 tablespoon heavy cream

Salt and freshly ground white pepper

4 large pompano fillets (6 to 8 ounces each)

Unsalted butter, melted, if grilling

Oil, butter, and flour if sautéing

MAKING THE TWO SAUCES

1. Thinly slice the onion. Cook it slowly in 1 tablespoon of the butter over low heat until the exuded juice cooks off, allowing it to brown as little as possible. Purée in a food processor and reserve.

2. Roast the red bell pepper over an open flame until the skin is blistered and charred. Rinse away the charred skin under cold running water. Remove and discard the stem, core, and seeds. Purée the pepper meat in the food processor (no need to wash out the bowl after puréeing the onion). Reserve.

3. Finely mince the shallots and put in a saucepan with the white wine and cream. Reduce over moderate heat until only a few tablespoons of liquid remain. Turn off the heat and swirl in the remaining butter, bit by bit, to make a *beurre blanc.* Season with salt and white pepper.

4. Divide the *beurre blanc* in half. Stir the pepper purée into half of it and the onion purée into the other half. Reserve in a warm place.

COOKING AND SERVING

5. *If grilling* (which I recommend): First make a very hot fire. Season the fish with salt and pepper and brush with melted butter. Clean the hot grill rack with a wire brush and brush with melted butter to season it. Immediately grill the buttered fish fillets approximately 2 minutes on each side, turning each fillet 90 degrees after the first minute to make pretty cross hatchings.

6. *If sautéing:* Heat ⅛ inch oil with 1 tablespoon butter in a sauté pan over moderate heat until the butter begins to brown. In the meantime, season and lightly dredge the fillets in flour, patting off all excess. Sauté about 2 minutes a side.

7. Mirror each of 4 warm plates with half pepper sauce and half onion sauce. Top with the fish fillets and serve.

Salmon Trout en Papillote

Salmon trout *en papillote*, highly popular with my lunch clients as a low-calorie dish, uses the classic French technique of flash-steaming fish inside a paper pouch in a scorching hot oven. When you cut it open at the table, the aroma of fish and seasonings billows out. The classic papillote is served with rich, creamy, and, in my opinion, rather flat sauces. I feel that lighter, more aromatic sauces take fuller advantage of the papillote's virtues—orange zest sauce, for example, or a sauce made with truffles, ginger, saffron, or fresh herbs.

Zest of ½ orange

2 teaspoons finely minced shallot

4 fresh boneless salmon trout, about 10 to 12 ounces each

12 tablespoons (1½ sticks) unsalted butter, softened

Salt and freshly ground white pepper

½ cup dry white wine

1 teaspoon heavy cream

Special Equipment 4 pieces parchment paper (18 by 14 inches each)

M I S E   E N   P L A C E

1. Peel the zest from half an orange and thinly julienne. Finely mince the shallot.

2. Behead the trout and remove the gills and side fins from the body. Fillet each trout and skin the fillets. You will have 8 fillets; keep the pairs of fillets together.

3. Clean your work area (you'll have made a mess), then fold each of the pieces of parchment paper in half widthwise and cut out paper hearts as large as the paper will yield. Butter the center few inches of one side of each parchment heart.

4. *To make the papillotes:* Place one fillet on the buttered part of each heart. Season with salt and pepper and sprinkle with a few pieces of orange zest (save the rest of the zest for the sauce). Top with the other fillet from the same fish. Season with salt and pepper and dab with a little more butter. Fold the other half of each paper heart over the fillets. Starting at the round end of the heart, start enclosing the fish with a ½-inch border—folded over twice—done in segments 2 or 3 inches long, each one overlapping the one before, all along the curved edge of the heart to the point. Tuck the fold that overlaps past the end of the point underneath the package to prevent unraveling. Crimp all the folds tightly.

C O O K I N G   A N D   S E R V I N G

5. Place a large cookie sheet (or a pizza brick if you have one) on the lower rack of your oven. Preheat the oven to 450°F.

6. In a small saucepan, combine the shallot, white wine, and cream. Reduce over moderate heat until just a few tablespoons remain.

7. Remove the saucepan from the heat. Swirl in the remaining 8 tablespoons

butter, bit by bit, to make a *beurre blanc*. Add the remaining julienned orange zest (to taste). Let the flavor develop over the few minutes the sauce sits while the fish cooks.

8. When the oven is fully preheated and not before, place the packages on the hot cookie sheet and bake 1½ to 2 minutes only—until the parchment is puffed and well browned.

9. Remove the packages from the oven, place them on 4 plates, and take them to the table unopened. To open the papillotes, tear the top with your fingers, allowing the steam and aroma to escape. Slip the trout onto the plates and serve with the orange sauce on the side.

Citrus Zest

The "zest" of a citrus fruit is the flavorful, colored outside layer of skin only. The white part just underneath is bitter and should be left behind.

Sole with Curry and Shrimp

SERVES 4

My wife keeps asking for this, so it must be good. The dish came to me in the market when I was looking for something she would like instead of the oysters I was using in a new curry sauce at the restaurant. I thought of wrapping sole around shrimp to make turbans. It turned out very dramatic—turbans served on beds of dark green spinach with the bright-yellow cream-and-curry sauce. And it's a good beginning recipe, a graceful dish with room for error—sauce that won't break, flavors that almost everybody likes—guaranteed to make you look good.

---

4 large or 8 small skinned sole fillets (buy good firm ones)

8 medium shrimp

1½ tablespoons minced shallots

2 bunches fresh spinach

4 tablespoons unsalted butter

½ cup dry white wine

Salt and freshly ground white pepper

¾ cup heavy cream

2 teaspoons curry powder

MISE EN PLACE

1. If using large fillets, split them lengthwise in half, making 8 strips. Place

them "skin" side up on your work surface.

2. Peel the shrimp and place one on the large end of each piece of sole. Roll it into a turban—skin side in, so when they cook they won't unroll.

3. Mince the shallots. Rinse the spinach.

COOKING AND SERVING

4. Smear the bottom of a medium saucepan with butter and sprinkle with the shallots.

5. Stand the turbans in the saucepan. Add the white wine, season with salt and pepper, cover tightly, and bring to a boil over high heat. Reduce the heat and gently poach for 2 minutes. Remove from the heat and let sit tightly covered for 2 more minutes to finish cooking.

6. Place 1 tablespoon of the remaining butter in a large saucepan, add the rinsed spinach, sprinkle lightly with salt and pepper, and cover tightly. Cook over moderate heat, shaking often, for about 1 minute, until the spinach is slightly wilted and just cooked.

7. Make a bed of spinach in the middle of each of 4 plates. Remove the poached turbans from the pan, blot them on a towel, and place on the spinach beds. Keep warm.

8. Place the saucepan over high heat, add the cream and curry powder, and reduce until slightly thickened, 2 or 3 minutes. Remove from the heat and swirl in the remaining 3 tablespoons butter. Verify the seasoning, especially the salt and curry.

9. Nap the sauce over and around the turbans. Serve.

*Ken Frank's
La Toque
Cookbook*
■

Grilled Swordfish with Kalamata Olive Sauce

SERVES 4

Tapenade is a traditional Mediterranean condiment. Made from good Provençal olives, garlic, and anchovies and often mixed into salads or spread on croutons, it is by no means subtle—the garlic makes it almost fiery. The garlic is used with a lighter hand in this recipe, and the rich tapenade flavors are wonderful with stronger-flavored fish such as swordfish, snapper, or mullet.

TAPENADE

3 cloves garlic

10 Kalamata olives or other good Mediterranean olives in brine

3 anchovy fillets

1 red, ripe tomato

2 tablespoons very finely minced shallots

½ cup dry white wine

1 tablespoon heavy cream

Freshly ground white pepper

10 tablespoons unsalted butter, softened

3 tablespoons melted butter for grilling

4 fresh swordfish steaks, 7 to 8 ounces each

Salt

1. *To make the tapenade:* Peel the garlic, pit the olives, and with a chef's knife, chop all together with the anchovies until you have a smooth paste.

2. Liquefy the tomato in a blender and strain through a fine strainer into a small saucepan.

3. Add the shallots, white wine, and cream to the saucepan, along with a few grinds of white pepper. Reduce until just a few tablespoons of liquid remain.

4. Off the heat, swirl in the butter, bit by bit. Stir in the tapenade. Verify the seasoning; between the anchovies and the olives, there should be enough salt. Reserve in a warm place.

COOKING AND SERVING

5. Make a very hot fire in your grill. Melt a few tablespoons of butter. Once the grill is hot, clean the rack well with a wire brush.

6. Lightly season both sides of the steaks with salt and white pepper. Brush the steaks with melted butter.

7. Brush the hot grill rack with melted butter. Immediately place the buttered steaks on the grill. Cook approximately 2 minutes on each side, turning the fish halfway through to mark each side with pretty crosshatchings.

8. Heat the sauce if necessary. Place the cooked steaks on 4 warm plates. Nap with the sauce and serve.

John Dory with Sea Urchin Sauce

SERVES 4

Sea urchin, or, more precisely, the eggs, are one of my absolute favorite seafood flavors. Inside the spiny sea urchin there is no meat, just liquid, membranes, and five sacs of gelatinous orange roe. A highly prized delicacy in France and Japan for centuries, urchin roe can be scooped out of the shell and eaten raw, souféed in the shell, or mixed into Japanese salads. The sauce we make from it here is smooth and oceany fresh and goes swimmingly with the sweet, clean-flavored John Dory.

2 medium sea urchins or 8 to 10 pieces sea urchin roe (you can buy it separately)

2 tablespoons finely minced shallots

4 tablespoons (½ stick) unsalted butter, softened

¾ cup dry white wine

2 or 3 threads saffron

1 cup heavy cream

4 John Dory fillets (2 fish, 2¾ to 3 pounds each; ask your fishmonger to do the filleting)

Salt and freshly ground white pepper

MISE EN PLACE

1. *To clean the sea urchins:* With small kitchen scissors, cut a 2-inch-diameter hole around the beak; remove and discard

Fish and Shellfish
∎
93

the beak and all attached cartilage and membranes. Pour off all the dark purple juice. Using a soup spoon, carefully scoop out the 5 tongue-shaped pieces of orange roe. Carefully rinse the roe, picking away any remaining small pieces of membrane. Reserve.

2. Finely mince the shallots.

COOKING AND SERVING

3. If grilling the fillets, make a very hot fire. If baking, preheat the oven to 500°F. Melt 2 tablespoons of the butter and reserve.

4. Place the shallots, white wine, and saffron in a saucepan over moderate heat. Reduce the liquid by about two-thirds. Add the cream and reduce until the sauce is slightly thickened. Reserve in a warm place until the very last moment.

5. Season both sides of the fillets with salt and brush with melted butter. Brush the grill (or baking sheet) with melted butter as well. Grill or bake the fillets over very high heat for 2 to 3 minutes—no longer. If grilling, turn the fillets after 1 to 1½ minutes.

6. While the fish is cooking, whisk the sea urchin roe in a small bowl with a fork to liquefy it, then stir it into the sauce. Stir in the remaining 2 tablespoons butter. Strain the sauce through a fine strainer. Season with salt and pepper.

7. Place the just-cooked fillets on 4 warm plates. Nap with the sauce and serve immediately.

Ken Frank's
La Toque
Cookbook

■

94

Sea Bass with Mussels and Saffron

SERVES 4

The traditional combination of mussels and saffron is usually found in soups, so why not in a sauce? Here the mussels are in a rich, saffron-bright *beurre blanc*. Aside from sea bass, it's an excellent sauce with almost any other salt-water fish, especially the sweet, chewy lotte.

---

18 to 24 mussels

1 cup dry white wine

1 heaping tablespoon finely minced shallot

10 tablespoons unsalted butter, softened

1½ to 2 pounds striped or black spotted bass fillet

Freshly ground white pepper

5 or 6 saffron threads

2 tablespoons heavy cream

Salt

MISE EN PLACE

1. Rinse the mussels in a large bowl, bucket, or sink under cold running water, discarding any mussels that gape open. Scrape off any barnacles by rubbing the mussels together and tear away the beards.

2. Place the mussels and ¼ cup of the wine in a tightly covered pan and cook 7 to

8 minutes, allowing the mussels to steam in the wine and in their own juices. The mussels will be done when all of their shells have opened wide.

3. Remove the cover and allow the mussels to cool slightly. Pluck the meat of each mussel from its shell and reserve. Take the mussel juice from the pot and pour it through a fine strainer over the mussels, removing any sand or sediment. (The mussels will keep 2 or 3 days in their own juice in the refrigerator.)

4. Finely mince the shallot.

COOKING AND SERVING

5. Lightly smear the bottom of a large sauté pan with a little butter and sprinkle with the shallot. Cut the bass fillet into 4 portions and arrange on top of the shallots.

6. Add the remaining ¾ cup wine, ¼ cup of the mussel juice, and a few grinds of white pepper. (No need to add salt at this point; the mussel juice will provide plenty.) Cover tightly and bring to a boil over high heat, then reduce to a simmer and poach gently for 2 to 3 minutes. Remove the pan from the heat and place it, still tightly covered, in a warm place for another 3 or 4 minutes to finish cooking.

7. Using a slotted spatula, remove the fish fillets from the pan and reserve. Add the saffron threads and cream to the pan, return it to the heat, and reduce until just a few tablespoons of liquid remain. Swirl in the remaining butter, bit by bit.

8. Remove the mussels from their juice (discard the remaining juice) and add them to the sauce. Heat the sauce gently, taking care not to boil and break it. Season with salt and pepper.

9. Blot the fish fillets on a towel and place on 4 warm plates. Nap with the sauce and serve.

Mussel-Shell Potato Peeler

For the person who has always wanted a mussel-shell potato peeler, like the ones used by natives in the South Pacific, simply rub the convex surface of a mussel shell on a sharpening stone or fine file until you've worn an oblong slit through the shell. There you have your peeler, with a surprisingly sharp edge.

Salmon Trout Soufflé with Julienne of Vegetables

This handsome dish is full of delightful contrasts: a smooth white scallop mousseline puffing up prettily through the firm pink salmon trout. But while it's an elaborate-appearing dish, most of the work can be done ahead of time, leaving just the poaching and sauce-making—and the laurel-gathering—for last.

SCALLOP FILLING

3 ounces fresh scallops
1 large pinch salt
Freshly ground white pepper
1 egg
2 tablespoons heavy cream

3-inch piece of white part of leek
3-inch piece of carrot
3-inch piece of celery
2 large mushrooms, stems removed
4 tablespoons unsalted butter, softened

4 fresh boneless salmon trout (8 to 9 ounces each)
1½ tablespoons chopped shallots
5 fluid ounces dry white wine
¾ cup heavy cream

MISE EN PLACE

1. *To start the scallop filling:* Purée the scallops in a food processor with a good pinch of salt and 2 grinds of white pepper for about 30 seconds. Add the egg and process another 30 seconds. Remove the food processor bowl, keeping the blade in and top on, and refrigerate at least 25 to 30 minutes. Add the heavy cream according to the directions in step 5 when you are ready to stuff the trout.

2. Meanwhile, split the leek in half lengthwise and rinse thoroughly. Cut lengthwise into a julienne as fine as a pencil line. Julienne the length of carrot just as fine. With a potato peeler, peel the strings off the outside of the celery, then julienne the celery to the same fineness. Slice the mushroom caps into thin wafers and finely julienne.

3. Put 1 tablespoon of the butter in a small sauté pan over low heat and stir-fry the leek, celery, and carrot for about 2 minutes until they become tender but not browned. Add the mushrooms, season lightly with salt and white pepper, and stir-fry another 30 seconds.

FILLETING THE TROUT

4. Open up the boneless salmon trout and spread it out on a cutting board skin

Ken Frank's La Toque Cookbook

■

96

side down. Cut off the head and the tail, trim away the little fins on the side, and cut each fish down the middle to make two fillets. Skin the fillets, keeping the pairs together.

STUFFING THE TROUT

5. *To finish the scallop filling:* Return the refrigerated bowl to the food processor. While adding the 2 tablespoons cream, process for 30 to 45 seconds.

6. Place the bottom fillet from each fish on the cutting board. Reserve a third of the julienne for the sauce and spread the rest of it evenly over the fillets.

7. On top of the julienne in a row down the center of each fillet place 4 to 5 heaping teaspoons of filling.

8. In the center of each *top* fillet, make a slit to within an inch of either end. Place each top fillet over its matching bottom, opening the slit slightly to allow the filling to puff through while cooking.

9. Use a large sauté pan (or 2 smaller pans) with a tight-fitting lid. Smear the bottom of the pan with a little of the butter, sprinkle with chopped shallots, and place the fish over the shallots. Add the wine and sprinkle with salt.

10. Cover the pan tightly and place it over high heat. After the wine comes to a boil, reduce the heat to a gentle simmer for 2 minutes. Remove the pan from the heat and let it sit covered for 2 more minutes to finish cooking. With a long, thin spatula, remove the fillets and blot on a towel. Place them on 4 warm plates.

11. Add the remaining julienned vegetables and ¾ cup cream to the wine in the pan, place it over high heat, and reduce for 2 or 3 minutes until slightly thickened. Remove from the heat and swirl in the remaining 3 tablespoons butter. Taste the sauce for salt and adjust if necessary. Nap the trout with the sauce and serve.

Sturgeon with Three Zests

SERVES 4

Sturgeon languishes in the shadow of its own more-famous roe. Unjustly so, for sturgeon flesh is very firm, sweet, and satisfying. It goes deliciously with this three-zest *beurre blanc,* a simple sauce that mates well with virtually any fish. When blood oranges are in season, I vary this sauce by leaving out the lemon and lime and just going with the oranges. The blood oranges provide a bright red color and a gutsier, more citric flavor than the usual orange.

1½ to 2 pounds skinned sturgeon fillet

1 lemon

1 lime

1 orange

2 tablespoons finely minced shallots

5 fluid ounces dry white wine

1 tablespoon heavy cream

10 tablespoons unsalted butter, softened

Salt and freshly ground white pepper

Flour for dredging

Oil for cooking

MISE EN PLACE

1. Cut the sturgeon fillet into 4 portions. Trim away and discard the brown flesh from the skinned side of each piece. Reserve.

2. With a paring knife, peel and finely julienne 1 teaspoon each lemon, lime, and orange zest. Use just the brightly colored outer layer of skin containing the aromatic oils; the underlayer is intolerably bitter. Reserve the fruit.

3. Put the shallots, white wine, and cream in a small saucepan. Reduce over moderate heat until almost dry. Swirl in 10 tablespoons butter, bit by bit, to make a *beurre blanc.* Season the sauce with salt and add the zests and a little squeeze of juice from each of the three fruits. Reserve in a warm place to allow the flavors to develop.

COOKING AND SERVING

4. Season both sides of the sturgeon fillets with salt and white pepper. Dredge the fillets in flour and pat off all excess.

5. Just cover the bottom of a large sauté pan with cooking oil. Add butter and heat over a high flame until the butter begins to brown. Add the fish fillets, skinned side up. Reduce the heat slightly and cook about 2½ minutes or until golden brown. Turn the fillets and finish cooking another 2½ minutes.

6. Remove the fish from the pan and blot the oil on a towel. Transfer to 4 warm plates, nap with the sauce, and serve.

Turbot with Lobster and Truffle Mousseline

SERVES 4

This dish was on the menu at the first French restaurant I ever worked at in the United States, when I was in high school in Pasadena. In those culinary dark ages before "truth in menus," we used frozen North Sea turbot. Sauce Riche, a classic sauce, was made by simply taking a ladle of hollandaise out of the pot and stirring in a little chopped lobster and canned truffle. And although I've greatly improved on it in the past dozen years—using only fresh turbot and developing a far lighter and more flavorful sauce—it was a fabulous combination even then. As an interesting variation, serve this sauce over poached eggs for breakfast and put eggs Benedict to shame.

I lemon

Salt

White peppercorns for the lobster pot

I small live Maine lobster, I to 1¼ pounds

I teaspoon finely minced shallot

12 tablespoons unsalted butter, softened

¼ cup dry white wine

2 egg yolks

Freshly ground white pepper

I small fresh black truffle

4 pieces North Sea turbot fillet, 6 to 8 ounces each (see box)

Turbot

Beware of any fish labeled turbot that is low-priced, as miscellaneous white-fleshed fish are often sold as such; true turbot is an expensive, luxuriously flavored fish. Among the family of flatfish, such as sole and flounder, which are valued for making stock, turbot makes the ultimate fish stock because of the intense concentration of gelatin in its bones. If you buy a whole turbot, be sure to poach the head and eat the highly prized oyster-like morsels in the cheek.

COOKING THE LOBSTER

1. Season a large pot of boiling water with the juice of half a lemon, salt, and a few peppercorns. Plunge the lobster into the boiling water and cook for 7 to 8 minutes. Remove and let cool. When cool, remove all the meat from the shell and reserve (see box, page 84). Break the head into small pieces and save for the sauce.

MAKING THE SAUCE

2. Sweat the minced shallot in I teaspoon of the butter in a saucepan until tender. Add the wine, I cup water, and the pieces of lobster head. Simmer, covered, for 10 minutes, pour through a fine strainer, and reduce the liquid until just 6 tablespoons remain.

3. Put this concentrated lobster essence into a stainless-steel mixing bowl with the 2 egg yolks. Place the bowl over

Fish and Shellfish

■

99

a saucepan of simmering water—do not let the bowl actually touch the water—and whisk until the mixture is frothy and quite warm to the touch and begins to hold a peak. Take care not to scramble the eggs. Immediately turn off the flame and, still keeping the bowl over the pan of simmering water, continue whisking while you add the remaining butter, bit by bit. When all the butter is added, remove from heat and season with salt and white pepper and a squeeze of lemon juice.

4. Dice the lobster meat into ½-inch chunks. Finely chop the truffle. Fold these into the sauce and reserve in a warm place.

COOKING AND SERVING

5. Preheat the oven to 450°F. Lightly butter a baking sheet.

6. Season the turbot with salt and a little freshly ground white pepper and place on the baking sheet. Bake it in the oven for 5 minutes or until done. The fish is done when a congealed droplet or two of milk forms on the surface.

7. Blot the fish on a towel and place on a warm plate. Nap with the sauce and serve.

Striped Bass with Bourride Sauce

SERVES 4

Bourride is the less famous of the two Mediterranean fish stews, but both bourride and bouillabaisse are made with the same grab bag of a half dozen or so Mediterranean rockfish. While bouillabaisse is based on a clear broth with saffron and tomato, bourride is thicker, made with cream and potatoes and a touch of garlic and cayenne—a great-flavored soup. So why not a sauce? Here I serve a bourride sauce with the king of bass, the striped bass. It's a fabulous sauce, rich without being heavy or too strong.

I small clove garlic

4 silver-dollar-size fresh mushrooms

I stalk celery

I leek

½ carrot

2 teaspoons unsalted butter

ROUILLE

I egg yolk

Pinch of salt

¼ teaspoon Cayenne peppers

I teaspoon finely chopped garlic

Squeeze of lemon juice

¼ cup extra-virgin olive oil

I tablespoon finely minced shallot

4 pieces skinned striped bass fillet (6 to 8
ounces each)

Salt

¾ cup dry white wine

5 fluid ounces heavy cream

¼ cup peanut oil

M I S E E N P L A C E

1. Finely julienne the small clove of garlic. Thinly slice the mushrooms. Cut the celery, leek, and carrot into paper-thin ribbons ⅓ inch wide and 3 inches long. Reserve.

2. *To make the rouille:* Mix the egg yolk, salt, cayenne, garlic, and lemon juice in a stainless-steel mixing bowl or food processor. While whisking or processing, add the olive and peanut oils in a thread to make a creamy mayonnaise. Reserve.

C O O K I N G A N D S E R V I N G

3. Smear the bottom of a large sauté pan with a little butter and sprinkle with the shallots. Add the fish fillets, skinned side down, and sprinkle with salt and the julienned garlic. Add the wine, cover tightly, and bring to a boil over high heat. Once boiling, reduce to a simmer and poach gently for 2½ minutes. Remove from the heat and allow to rest for 2 minutes, still covered.

4. While the fish is poaching, gently stir-fry the mushrooms, celery, leek, and carrot ribbons in a little butter with a sprinkle of salt until tender—a minute or two at most. Divide equally among 4 warm plates.

5. Remove the fish from the pan and reserve on a warm plate. Add the cream to the pan and reduce over high heat until the sauce is slightly thickened. Remove it from the heat and whisk in the rouille. Verify the seasoning. If the sauce is too thick, add the juice on the plate holding the fish fillets.

6. Gently blot the fish fillets on a towel and place them on the beds of vegetables. Nap with the sauce and serve.

Lotte Scaloppini with Artichoke Hearts

SERVES 4

If swordfish is the steak of the sea, lotte is the tenderloin. When perfectly cooked, it may be sliced without crumbling—like meat, and unlike any other fish. Recently I discovered another of its useful qualities: raw, it may be sliced and pounded thin like a veal cutlet. Then, when quickly sautéed in a very hot pan, it comes out quite juicy. And since it's a little easier to sauté lotte to perfection than it is to roast it, this is a good lotte recipe to start with.

2 artichokes

1 lemon

Salt

2 tablespoons finely minced shallots

2 pounds fresh lotte (monkfish) fillet

10 tablespoons plus 3 teaspoons unsalted butter, softened

¾ cup dry white wine

1 tablespoon heavy cream

8 large sweet basil leaves

Freshly ground white pepper

Flour for dredging

Oil for cooking

MISE EN PLACE

1. "Turn" the artichokes (see box, page 60). Thoroughly rub the artichoke hearts with a half lemon and cook in boiling salted water with the same lemon half until tender, approximately 10 to 15 minutes. Chill under cold running water to stop the cooking, remove any leaves and all the hair from the hearts, and cut into matchstick julienne. Reserve.

2. Finely mince the shallots. Reserve.

3. Trim the pinkish membrane from the lotte fillets and cut into 1½-inch-thick medallions. Place a lotte medallion between 2 sheets of plastic wrap and pound into a thin scaloppine, under ¼ inch thick, with the flat side of a cleaver. Repeat with the remaining medallions and reserve.

COOKING AND SERVING

4. In a sauté pan, quickly heat the artichoke julienne with 2 teaspoons of the unsalted butter and a sprinkle of salt. Arrange in the center of 4 plates.

5. Put the shallots, white wine, and cream in a small saucepan and reduce until almost dry. Off the heat, swirl in 10 tablespoons butter, bit by bit, to make a *beurre blanc*. Julienne the basil leaves and add to the sauce. Season with a touch of lemon juice, salt, and white pepper. Reserve in a warm place.

6. Salt and pepper the scaloppini and dredge in flour, patting off all excess. Warm the plates with artichoke julienne in the oven.

7. Add enough oil to a large sauté pan to cover the bottom. Add the remaining teaspoon butter and heat over high heat until it begins to brown. Add the lotte and cook approximately 30 seconds on each side. Blot the excess oil from each medallion with a towel and place atop the artichoke julienne. Nap with the sauce and serve immediately.

Halibut with Roasted Red Bell Pepper Sauce

SERVES 4

Halibut is truly the steak of the sea. It's a big slice with no bones. You can bake it or broil it and it's good grilled. People who don't like fishy fish tend to like halibut—and they love this sauce. The roasted red bell pepper coulis is extremely versatile, good on any delicate white fish. If you can ever find it, try cooking a rare fish called louvar with this sauce.

1 large red bell pepper

2 medium shallots

6 fluid ounces dry white wine

4 tablespoons heavy cream

10 tablespoons (1¼ sticks) unsalted butter

Salt

4 halibut steaks, 6 to 8 ounces each

Freshly ground white pepper

Oil if grilling

ROASTING THE PEPPER AND MAKING THE SAUCE

1. Roast the red bell pepper over an open flame until the skin is charred and blistered. Let it sit off the heat for 5 minutes to finish cooking, then rinse away the blistered skin under cold running water. Remove and discard the stem, core, and seeds. Purée remaining meat in a food processor.

2. In the meantime, finely mince the shallots and place them in a saucepan with the wine and cream. Reduce until the sauce begins to thicken.

3. When the sauce is reduced so that just a few tablespoons remain, remove it from the heat and swirl in 10 tablespoons of butter, bit by bit. Season with salt and check the sauce's temperature: if it is only lukewarm, add a little heat before whisking in the cold pepper purée. You may now reserve the sauce in a warm place for up to a half hour.

COOKING AND SERVING

4. Make a very hot fire on the grill. Season the fish on both sides with salt and freshly ground white pepper. Brush both sides with a little oil if grilling. Clean the grill with a wire brush and "season" it by brushing it with oil to prevent sticking.

5. Grill the fish 2 to 3 minutes on each side, rotating the fish 90 degrees halfway through the cooking of each side to make pretty crosshatchings.

6. Mirror the sauce on 4 warm plates, top with the grilled fish, and serve.

Pike with Red and Black Pepper

SERVES 4

This is an unexpected use of pepper. During the pink-peppercorn rage a few years ago, I discovered that, in careful doses, fiery black peppercorns and sweet, aromatic pink peppercorns together make an intriguing sauce with lots of character and contrast. The basic white-wine-and-cream sauce here is a very versatile one, good for any number of fish, particularly salmon and sea bass.

½ teaspoon pink peppercorns

8 black peppercorns

2 tablespoons unsalted butter

1 heaping tablespoon finely minced shallot

4 pike fillets (6 to 8 ounces each)

Salt

½ cup dry white wine

¾ cup heavy cream

1. Coarsely crush the pink and black peppercorns using either the flat side of a cleaver or the bottom of a pan. Reserve.

2. Smear the bottom of a sauté pan with butter, sprinkle with the shallot, and add the 4 pike fillets, skin side down. Sprinkle lightly with salt and add the white wine. Tightly cover the pan and allow the wine to come to a boil over moderate heat. Then reduce to a simmer and poach the fish gently for 2 minutes. Remove from the heat and let rest, still covered, for 2 more minutes to finish the cooking.

3. Using a slotted spatula, remove the pike fillets from the pan. Blot them on a towel and reserve in a warm place.

4. Add the cream and coarsely crushed peppercorns to the wine in the pan and reduce over moderate heat until the sauce just begins to thicken. Swirl in the remaining butter. Verify the salt seasoning.

5. While the sauce is reducing, remove the pin bones from each pike fillet using tweezers (or long fingernails if you have them). To make sure you get them all, lightly run your fingertip along the pin bone line from the head toward the tail.

6. Blot the fillets with a towel and place them on 4 warm plates. Nap with the warm sauce and serve.

Pink Peppercorn False Alarm

The pink peppercorn alarm was sounded a few years ago by the Wall Street Journal: *poison—arsenic—beware. Be assured that the quantities called for in any of my recipes are miles below the lethal or even discomfort-causing dosage. Lots of foods contain arsenic—almonds, for example—but in minute and harmless amounts.*

Whitefish with Tomato and Green Peppercorns

SERVES 4

Green peppercorns are traditionally associated with steak or duck, but the same smooth pepperiness is good with a full-flavored, meaty fish like whitefish. Not to be confused with the spice-it-to-death approach of blackened redfish, this is a subtle recipe—your brow won't sweat and your nose won't run. It uses only enough peppercorns to complement but not dominate the flavor.

---

1 red, ripe tomato

12 tablespoons (1½ sticks) unsalted butter

2 tablespoons finely minced shallots

1¾ to 2 pounds skinned whitefish fillet

½ cup dry white wine

Salt

1 tablespoon heavy cream

1 teaspoon green peppercorns

---

1. Peel the tomato by quickly charring it over an open flame. Rinse away the charred skin under cold, running water; cut the tomato in half and squeeze out all the juice and seeds. Finely dice the tomato meat. Reserve.

2. Smear the bottom of a large sauté pan with butter, then sprinkle with the shallots. Cut the whitefish into 4 portions. Put the fish in the pan on top of the shallots, add the white wine, and season with salt. Tightly cover the pan and allow the wine to come to a boil over moderate heat. Then reduce to a simmer and poach gently for 2 minutes. Remove from the heat and let rest, still covered, for 2 more minutes to finish cooking.

MAKING THE SAUCE AND SERVING

3. Remove the fish fillets to a warm place. Return the pan with the wine to a moderate flame. Add the cream, chopped tomato, and green peppercorns, crushing them slightly with your fingers to release their flavor. Reduce until just a few tablespoons of liquid remain. Remove from the heat and swirl in the remaining butter, bit by bit. Verify the seasoning—the salt and especially the green peppercorns.

4. Blot the fish fillets on a towel and place them on 4 warm plates. Nap with the sauce and serve.

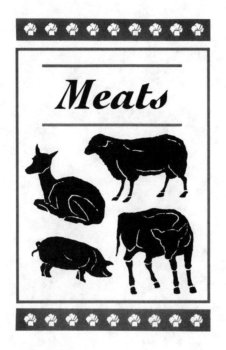

Meats

State-of-the-Art Veal Stock

MAKES 2 GALLONS

Don't skip these two pages. They contain the most important information in the book—the key to the greatness of many of the recipes that follow.

I do not subscribe to the garbage-can school of stock making, where everyone in the kitchen adds just about any kind of scrap to an endlessly boiling stockpot. That's a good way to ensure that your sauces taste like the kitchen sink. Whenever I do a demonstration or celebrity dinner and have to use another restaurant's stock, I'm always disappointed.

I make a very pure, clean-flavored stock, not vegetabley (which limits what you can do) and never thickened with any kind of binder. It is the key to my sauces—easily the most raved-about aspect of my cooking—and is probably the primary difference between my professional kitchen and your home kitchen. Having the stock on hand will make many of the recipes in this book quick, easy, and unbelievably rewarding.

Stock is a very simple but serious business: we make a new one every night. Everyone in my kitchen knows how to pamper it to the point of perfection. In your kitchen, a stock properly made—religiously made—can make the critical difference that will elevate your cooking to the highest level.

Stock is best made in large amounts. The best approach is to then freeze it so it is always available. It keeps indefinitely and will greatly expand your options for spontaneous cooking.

Without stock you are basically roasting and grilling. With stock you have dozens of simple classy options open to you. There is certainly a time and place for simple grilled foods, but in cooking, sauce separates the men from the boys.

I make this stock from both duck and veal bones, a combination I find best for brown sauces. A stock made from veal bones (expensive to be sure) has great body. Adding duck carcasses gives a fuller flavor, making an ideal stock—a great vehicle for your sauces. (Beef bones, by contrast, make a fine consommé but not a stock.)

---

8 pounds cut veal bones (joints are best)

I duck carcass, quartered and trimmed of all large pieces of fat

6 ounces tomato paste

3 gallons water

I bay leaf

Pinch of dried thyme or I stem fresh thyme

½ teaspoon white or black peppercorns

Special Equipment Large stockpot, 4-gallon size minimum

1. Preheat the oven to 450°F.
2. Roast the veal bones and the trimmed duck carcass in a roasting pan for approximately 30 minutes until golden brown, turning once halfway through to promote even browning.
3. Remove the bones from the pan and put them in the stockpot. Pour off the

grease from the still-hot roasting pan, then deglaze it with a few cups of water. Scrape the bottom of the pan with a wooden spoon to loosen and dissolve the browned, crusted drippings.

4. Add this water and the drippings to the stockpot along with the tomato paste. Fill the pot with about 3 gallons water, to within 2 inches of the top. Cover, place over high heat, and bring to a boil.

5. As soon as the stock comes to a boil, remove the cover and reduce the heat to a steady simmer. Immediately skim all fat and impurities from the surface before the fat and foam have a chance to boil back into the liquid. A large ladle is the ideal tool for skimming.

6. Simmer 10 to 15 minutes, then thoroughly skim off the newly accumulated fat. It's inevitable that you'll lose some stock in the process of a thorough skimming, but it's better to sacrifice a bit of stock than to leave any fat behind. Fat ruins a stock, it's as simple as that. It makes it taste fatty, it won't reduce and thicken properly, and it will look cloudy.

7. After this second thorough skimming, add the bay leaf, thyme, and pepper-corns. Continue to simmer the stock for 6 to 8 hours, skimming every 30 minutes or so. Six hours of simmering is the minimum required to extract enough flavor; 8 hours is plenty to extract the maximum.

8. After simmering and reducing the stock for 6 to 8 hours, give it a final skimming and strain it through a fine strainer.

9. A properly reduced stock should amount to no more than 20 percent of the original quantity of water. It should not be thick like a sauce but should gel when a spoonful is chilled for 20 minutes or so on a plate in the refrigerator. If the stock requires further reduction at this point, gently reduce the strained liquid over low heat.

10. To save the stock for just 4 or 5 days, pour the just-boiled strained liquid into a clean container and let cool to room temperature before refrigerating. To freeze the stock and save it indefinitely, pour the just-boiled stock into clean ice cube trays, let cool, then freeze. Once the stock is frozen, unmold the cubes and freeze them in a tightly sealed plastic bag for use as needed. The frozen cubes, which average about an ounce apiece, may be added to a sauce straight from the freezer.

Venison with Cracked Black Peppercorns

SERVES 4

Pepper sauce in the traditional French manner, with Cognac, cream, and cracked peppercorns, is always good with a nice piece of red meat. Good venison is just that. Don't be misled by the strong, gamy stuff you may have inherited from your neighbor's annual hunting trip. The venison I'm talking about is farm-raised meat flown in fresh from New Zealand. It's lean and healthy and really incredibly tender and sweet. A properly balanced pepper sauce—with black, white, green, pink, or all four peppercorns—is venison's perfect foil.

---

1 tablespoon black peppercorns

4 venison steaks (7 to 8 ounces each)

Salt

Oil for cooking

¼ cup Cognac

1 cup Veal Stock (page 109)

2 tablespoons heavy cream

1 tablespoon unsalted butter

---

1. Crack the black peppercorns (don't grind them finely) by mashing them against your cutting board with the bottom of your sauté pan. Do not substitute ground or other pepper: it must be freshly cracked.

2. Season the steaks with salt and dredge them in the black peppercorns. Do not shake off the excess.

3. Heat a few tablespoons of oil in a sauté pan over high heat until very hot but not yet smoking. Add the steaks to the pan and brown well for a minute or so on each side, sealing in all the juices. Reduce the heat slightly to prevent burning and cook the steaks approximately 3 more minutes on each side, or until medium-rare. Cooked past medium-rare, venison gets very dry and tough because it is so lean. Remove the steaks from the pan and allow them to rest in a warm place.

4. Pour off all the grease in the pan, being careful to retain any pepper and crusted brown drippings. Deglaze the pan with the Cognac and flambé. Add the stock and cream and reduce the sauce until slightly thickened. Swirl in the butter. Verify the seasoning.

5. Cut the venison steaks across the grain into ¼-inch slices. Arrange on 4 warm plates, nap with the sauce, and serve.

The Pepper Steak Test

The pepper steak is a curious animal, with its sauce that is easy to do but not at all easy to do perfectly — because the flavor balances are so critical. For that reason, and because it is such a standard in France, chefs will order a pepper steak when they dine out — as a test of the palates and skills of their peers.

Rack of Lamb with Pommery Mustard

This is a dish I've been making since I started cooking—and a shining example, I think, of why things are often best left simple. The crunchy mustard crust encasing the juicy pink lamb chop needs no improvement. It's a basic recipe that illustrates the importance of letting red meat rest after cooking to become tender and evenly pink throughout. The rule is: Let a piece of red meat rest at least half as long as it takes to cook it. Here we cook the lamb 15 minutes; let it rest a good 10.

¼ cup breadcrumbs

1 heaping tablespoon finely minced chives

6 tablespoons Pommery mustard

2 racks of lamb with 8 or 9 ribs each (ask for a "Frenched" lamb rack)

Oil for cooking

Salt and freshly ground white pepper

1 heaping teaspoon finely minced shallot

3 fluid ounces dry white wine

1 cup Veal Stock (page 109)

1. Preheat the oven to 475°F. for at least 15 minutes.

2. Mix the breadcrumbs, the chives, 5 tablespoons of the mustard, and enough water in a small dish to make a sticky paste. Reserve.

3. Trim the excess fat from the racks so that no more than ¼ inch remains to insulate the meat.

4. Heat 2 tablespoons oil in a large ovenproof sauté pan or roasting pan until hot. Season the lamb with salt and pepper. Brown the racks on both sides in the hot pan—a good 2 minutes a side.

5. Turn the racks meat side down and roast 5 to 6 minutes. Turn the racks over and spread the meat side with the mustard paste. Roast 8 to 9 more minutes.

6. Remove the racks from the oven and place them on a plate to rest in a warm place.

7. Pour off all the grease in the pan, leaving the crusted drippings. Add the shallot to the still-hot pan and allow it to soften. Deglaze with the white wine and reduce until almost dry. Add the veal stock and the remaining tablespoon of mustard and reduce again until the sauce is slightly thickened. Verify the seasoning and reserve.

8. Slice each rack into individual chops, and arrange on 4 plates. Nap with the sauce and serve.

Saddle of Lamb with Cabernet and Shallots

SERVES 4

If I were offered a choice for my final meal, it might well be this fatted lamb. There is no better cut of lamb than the saddle, and bundled and cooked in its own fat, it is truly the tenderest, juiciest piece of meat you'll ever eat.

1 saddle of lamb

Salt and freshly ground white pepper

Garlic or Pommery mustard (whole-grain) (optional)

2 plump shallots

Oil for cooking

1 cup Cabernet Sauvignon

1 cup Veal Stock (page 109)

4 tablespoons (½ stick) unsalted butter, softened

BUTCHERING THE LAMB SADDLE (MAY BE DONE WELL IN ADVANCE)

1. Carve first one side of the saddle, then the other, away from the backbone, ending up with two rolled pieces, each to serve 2. Proceed as follows with each side.
  a. Keeping the fat casing and long flaps attached, remove the fillet and loin by carefully carving around the protuberances of the backbone.
  b. Leaving the fat casing intact on the backs of the fillet and loin, trim away all other fat from the meat. Trim away also the tough outside skin of the fat casing. Trim down the inside of the flaps leaving a thin—about ¼ inch—but wide belt of fat in which to roll the meat.
  c. Before rolling, lightly season the meat with salt and pepper (or with a couple of crushed cloves of garlic or a smidgen of Pommery mustard). Roll the meat in its belt of fat, but only once around; cut off any excess length. Tie the rolled meat snugly with 4 or 5 pieces of kitchen twine.

COOKING THE LAMB

2. Preheat the oven to 450° to 500°F. Mince the shallots.
3. Heat 1 tablespoon cooking oil in a large ovenproof sauté pan until hot. Season the lamb generously with salt and pepper. Sauté both rolls of lamb until golden brown on all sides.
4. In the same sauté pan, roast the lamb in the hot oven for 13 to 15 minutes for pink lamb—the tip of a knife or brochette inserted into the center should feel warm on your lower lip. For well-done lamb, roast another 4 minutes.
5. Remove the lamb from the pan and let them sit in a warm but not hot place for 7 to 8 minutes. This "resting" allows the juices, which have been driven into the center, to redistribute, leaving the meat pink and juicy throughout.

6. Pour off the grease in the still-hot pan and immediately add the shallots. Sweat for 30 seconds while stirring with a wooden spoon to loosen the drippings.

7. Deglaze the pan with the wine. Reduce over high heat for 2 or 3 minutes until the mixture becomes a glaze—a syrupy coating on the bottom of the pan. Add the veal stock and reduce by half. Remove from the heat. Swirl in the butter. Verify the seasoning and reserve in a warm place.

SLICING AND SERVING

8. Snip the strings from the lamb rolls. Remove the fat casings and either discard them or cut into small pieces to serve separately—the golden-brown crusts make irresistible nibbling. Slice the meat ¼ inch thick and fan the slices on 4 warm plates. Nap with the sauce. Serve.

Veal Sweetbreads with Port and Green Peppercorns

S E R V E S   4

Sautéed sweetbreads, golden brown and crisp on the outside, buttery smooth on the inside, are sweetbreads at their best. People who may have been grossed out by the tough, rubbery, chewy, slimy texture of sweetbreads improperly stewed or otherwise bungled will flip for the crunchy, contrasting textures of these, here perfectly mated with a piquant sweet and hot sauce.

2 pounds sweetbreads (these will require 10 minutes of preparation 24 hours in advance)

Juice of 1 lemon

Salt

2 medium shallots

2 silver-dollar-size fresh mushrooms

2 bunches fresh spinach

5½ tablespoons unsalted butter, softened

Flour for dredging

Oil for cooking

1 teaspoon green peppercorns

¼ cup vintage port wine

6 to 7 fluid ounces Veal Stock (page 109)

Freshly ground white peppers (optional)

1. One day in advance, rinse the sweetbreads thoroughly. Let them soak in cold water in the refrigerator, changing the water 3 or 4 times throughout the 24-hour period.

2. The next day, add the lemon juice to a large pot of salted water and bring it to a boil. Add the sweetbreads and cook at a gentle boil for 5 minutes until they are firm and springy to the touch but not hard.

3. Remove the sweetbreads from the water and press them between 2 nesting cake pans in the refrigerator, using something like a half-gallon container of milk for a weight. Cool for 2 hours.

4. Peel the sweetbreads thoroughly, removing all membranes, connective tissue, and fat and keeping them in as large pieces as possible.

5. Slice the larger pieces horizontally into ½-inch-thick medallions. Butterfly the smaller pieces to the same thickness.

6. Chop the shallots. Julienne the mushrooms.

7. Rinse and stem the spinach. Place 1 tablespoon of the butter in a saucepan, add the spinach leaves, sprinkle with salt, and cover tightly. Cook over moderate heat, shaking the pan often, for about 2 minutes, until the spinach has flash-cooked in its own steam. Keep warm.

COOKING AND SERVING

8. Salt and flour the sweetbreads, patting off all excess flour. Heat ⅛ inch of cooking oil in a sauté pan with ½ tablespoon of the remaining butter until the butter just begins to brown. Add the sliced sweetbreads and sauté over moderate heat for about 2 minutes on each side until golden brown. Transfer to a paper towel to absorb the oil. Reserve.

9. Pour off the grease in the pan, add the mushrooms, and return the pan to moderate heat. Gently stir-fry the mushrooms to a light golden brown, taking care not to scorch the drippings. Add the shallots and stir-fry 15 seconds more.

10. Crush the green peppercorns between your fingers as you add them to the pan. Deglaze with the port. Add the veal stock and reduce slightly—about 20 percent—until the sauce just begins to thicken.

11. Remove the pan from the heat, swirl in the remaining 4 tablespoons butter, and verify the seasoning, adding a smidgen of port or pepper to perfect the balance.

12. Place a bed of spinach on each of 4 warm plates. Top with the sweetbread medallions and nap with the sauce. Serve.

Veal Sweetbreads with Shallots and Sherry Wine Vinegar

SERVES 4

The lively sauce, with sherry wine vinegar and lots of shallots, makes this a great dish for people still acquiring a taste for sweetbreads. Cooked to a crisp golden brown on the outside, still meltingly tender on the inside, and infused with the rich, piquant sauce, these sweetbreads are hard to resist. The sauce is terrific on calves' liver and just plain great on foie gras as well.

2 pounds veal sweetbreads

Juice of 1 lemon for the sweetbreads

Salt

4 plump shallots

3½ tablespoons unsalted butter

2 tablespoons sherry wine vinegar

1 cup Veal Stock (page 109)

Freshly ground white pepper

Flour for dredging

Oil for cooking

1. Prepare the sweetbreads as directed on page 115 (don't forget to start a day ahead.)

2. Thinly slice the shallots and place them in a small saucepan with 1 tablespoon of the butter. Cook, stirring frequently, over moderate heat until the shallots are light golden brown. Deglaze with the vinegar and add the veal stock. Reduce the sauce until it just begins to thicken, then finish by swirling in 2 tablespoons of the remaining butter. Season with salt and white pepper. Verify the seasoning: The vinegar must complement but not overpower the sauce. In any sharp, vinegary sauce, it is critical to salt adequately in order to mute and balance the acidity. Keep the sauce warm but not hot.

3. Salt and flour the sweetbreads, patting off all excess flour. Heat ⅛ inch of cooking oil in a sauté pan with the remaining ½ tablespoon butter until the butter just begins to brown. Then and only then add the sliced sweetbreads and sauté over moderate heat for about 2 minutes on each side until golden brown. Transfer to a paper towel to absorb the oil.

4. Divide the sautéed sweetbreads among 4 warm plates. Nap with the sauce and serve.

Veal Chops with Artichoke Mousseline

Veal with lemon is an old and good standard, here made superb with a savory artichoke-and-lemon mousseline and a light lemon sauce. It's basically a peasant dish made elegant, still simple and satisfying.

2 artichokes

2 lemons

Salt

4 tablespoons (½ stick) unsalted butter

4 veal chops

Freshly ground white pepper

Flour for dredging

Oil for cooking

¼ cup dry white wine

I cup Veal Stock (page 109)

Special Equipment Pastry bag with large star tip

MAKING THE ARTICHOKE MOUSSELINE (MAY BE DONE HOURS AHEAD OF TIME IF YOU LIKE)

1. "Turn" and cook the artichokes (see box, page 60), cooking the artichokes until very tender, 15 to 20 minutes, in order to make a smooth mousse.

2. Purée the still-warm hearts until smooth with 2 tablespoons of the butter, a small squeeze of lemon juice, and salt. Verify the seasoning and reserve in a warm place. (If making well in advance, allow to cool and reheat later.)

COOKING AND SERVING

3. Preheat the oven to 450°F.

4. Season the veal chops with salt and white pepper. Dredge in flour and pat off all excess.

5. Heat 2 tablespoons oil in an oven-proof sauté pan over medium heat until very hot but not smoking. Add the chops and brown about 1 minute per side to seal in the juices. Transfer to the oven and roast for 7 or 8 minutes or until done. ("Done" for veal means medium—neither well-done nor pink in the middle but still juicy.)

6. Remove the chops from the pan and pour off the grease. Deglaze the pan with the white wine and the rest of the juice from the ½ lemon. Add the veal stock and reduce by about half until the sauce just begins to thicken. Verify the seasoning; the lemon flavor should not dominate but complement the artichoke flavor. Swirl in the remaining 2 tablespoons butter.

7. Fit the small pastry bag with the star tip and fill it with the artichoke mousseline. Pipe a dab of mousseline on each of 4 plates to anchor the veal chops and pipe the remaining mousseline in pretty rosettes atop the meat. Nap with the sauce. Serve.

Fillet of Veal with Paprika

SERVES 4

Make a bed of spinach and roasted red bell peppers, top with tiny veal fillets, nap the whole thing with a richly flavored onion, butter, and paprika cream sauce, and what you have is an international *ménage-à-quatre* of tastes that is fairly quick and simple to achieve but wholly unforgettable. It's one of my favorite sports—melding ideas from different classic cuisines—here, basically a French *sauce soubise* lit up with Hungarian paprika.

You can use other cuts of veal, but remember that cutlets or medallions from the loin or leg are always cut thin, so you would need to reduce the cooking time accordingly.

1 onion

4 tablespoons unsalted butter

1 tablespoon good Hungarian paprika

1 red bell pepper

2 bunches fresh spinach

1 pound veal tenderloins (fillets)

Salt and freshly ground white pepper

Flour for dredging

Oil for cooking

3 fluid ounces dry white wine

½ cup Veal Stock (page 109)

6 tablespoons heavy cream

MISE EN PLACE

1. Thinly slice the onion. Simmer the slices in 2 cups water in a saucepan for 10 minutes. Drain and rinse the onion in a strainer. Purée the cooled, rinsed onion with 4 tablespoons butter and the paprika in a food processor. Force the purée through a fine sieve and reserve.

2. Roast the red bell pepper over an open flame until the skin is blistered and charred. Rinse away the charred skin under cold running water. Remove and discard the core and seeds. Finely dice half the meat of the roasted pepper and reserve.

3. Rinse and stem the spinach. Reserve.

4. Slice the veal tenderloins into 1- to 1½-inch-thick fillets and flatten them slightly with the heel of your hand. Reserve.

COOKING AND SERVING

5. Preheat the oven to 450°F.

6. Salt and pepper the veal on both sides and lightly dredge in flour, patting off all excess. Heat cooking oil in an ovenproof sauté pan with a tab of butter until the butter just begins to brown. Add the veal and brown approximately 1 minute each side. Place the pan with the veal in the oven and bake another 4 to 5 minutes or until done.

7. In the meantime, flash-cook the spinach in a tightly covered pan with 1 tab butter, the diced red pepper, and a pinch of salt—2 minutes should do it. Reserve in a warm place.

8. When the veal is cooked, remove it from the oven and reserve on a plate. Pour off all the grease in the pan, place the pan over moderate heat, and deglaze with the white wine. Add the veal stock and cream and reduce until the sauce begins to thicken.

9. While the sauce is reducing, arrange the spinach with peppers in the center of each of 4 plates and top with the veal.

10. Whisk the paprika-onion butter into the sauce. Verify the seasoning. Pour the sauce around the veal and serve.

◀

Leg of Lamb with Roasted Garlic Sauce

S E R V E S   8   T O   1 0

Greeks, Italians, French, Chinese, Persians—everybody loves lamb with garlic. This is my favorite way to serve lamb and has become something of a signature dish at La Toque. Inserting cloves of garlic into the meat is a very traditional French technique. But as I wanted to make a garlic sauce as well, I threw in a handful of unpeeled garlic to roast with the lamb and made a sauce with white wine, shallots, stock, and a bit of cream. I knew right away—it was on my opening menu at La Toque.

2 large heads garlic

1 leg of lamb, bone in (about 8 pounds), trimmed of any large chunks of fat

Salt and freshly ground white pepper

Oil for cooking

¼ cup finely minced shallots

1 cup dry white wine

2 cups Veal Stock (page 109)

¼ cup heavy cream

1. Preheat the oven to 450°F.
2. Break apart the 2 heads of garlic. Peel 4 of the cloves and reserve the others unpeeled. With a paring knife, stab 4 deep

holes in the thickest parts of the leg of lamb and push 1 peeled garlic clove into each. If time permits, let the leg sit out a couple of hours before cooking. Allowing the roast to warm up to room temperature shortens the cooking time and results in a juicier roast.

3. Generously season the leg with salt and white pepper. Heat a few tablespoons of cooking oil in a roasting pan over high heat and sear the meat on all sides to a nice golden brown.

4. Place the roasting pan in the oven to roast. (An average leg of lamb should take between 35 and 45 minutes to be cooked "pink"—somewhere between medium-rare and medium; the texture and flavor of lamb are not at their best cooked either rare or well-done.) Turn the roast every 10 minutes or so to ensure even cooking. Fifteen minutes before the meat will be done, add the remaining unpeeled garlic to the pan.

5. When the roast is done, remove the pan from the oven, place the roast on a large platter, cover it loosely with aluminum foil, and allow to rest for at least 20 minutes. It is during this resting that the meat will become a tender, juicy pink throughout.

6. Meanwhile, pour off all the fat in the roasting pan, leaving the roasted garlic in the pan. Add the shallots to the still-hot pan and stir for 30 seconds, allowing them to soften. Deglaze with the white wine and stir to loosen the crusted drippings.

7. Pour the wine, shallots, and garlic into a saucepan, add the veal stock and cream, and reduce over moderate heat by about half, until the sauce begins to thicken. Season with salt and white pepper. Strain

through a fine strainer into a sauceboat and reserve the sauce and garlic cloves separately.

8. Slice the leg of lamb, arrange the slices on 8 to 10 warm plates, and garnish each serving with a couple of roasted garlic cloves. (The now mild, tender cloves can be squeezed directly out of their skins into your mouth.) Serve.

Testing Meat for Doneness

Although attention to time and oven temperature is important, the only way to tell for sure when meat is perfectly done is to check the internal temperature. The best way to do this—after about 30 minutes of cooking—is to stick a skewer or long, thin knife into the heart of the roast, wait 5 seconds, retract it, and immediately touch the tip to your lower lip. Keep checking every 5 minutes or so until the skewer feels warm but not uncomfortably hot to your lip. Experienced chefs often simply insert their index finger along the thigh bone to check the temperature inside the roast.

Calves' Liver Sautéed with Zante Currants

SERVES 4

It is unfortunate that Zante currants have such a short season, because they are the ideal grape with which to cook— colorful, tiny as pearls, tender-skinned, seedless, and very flavorful. There are so many nice ways to use them—with fish, meat, or as a garnish. This particular dish is fast, simple, and unique: The just barely cooked, slightly tart grapes burst in your mouth like caviar, giving the needed touch of acidity for the liver. For the truly decadent, try this with a piece of seared foie gras as an appetizer.

12 ounces fresh Zante currants
(champagne grapes)

Oil for cooking

6 tablespoons unsalted butter

4 portions calves' liver

Salt and freshly ground white pepper

Flour for dredging

2 tablespoons minced shallots

1. Rinse and pluck the currants from the stems. Reserve.

2. Heat a sauté pan with $\frac{1}{8}$ inch cooking oil and a tab of the butter until the butter begins to brown. Meanwhile, season the liver with salt and white pepper and dredge lightly in flour. Quickly sauté the liver for no more than 45 seconds on each side if you like it rare, or 1½ minutes if you prefer it well done. Remove the liver from the pan and blot it on a towel.

3. Pour off the grease and return the pan to moderate heat. Add the remaining butter and cook until the butter just begins to brown. Remove from the heat and add the shallots and currants, tossing them in the brown butter to soften them slightly.

4. Place the liver on 4 warm plates, smother with the currants and butter, and serve.

Calves' Liver with Shallots and Gherkins

SERVES 4

I agree with the French that *"Tout est bon quand c'est bien fait"*—any food is good if made right. Liver is one of those foods that has to be made right. Bacon or onions is fine, but there's so much more you can do. This sauce of pickles, shallots, and vinegar provides a really satisfying tang and crunch—great with a perfectly cooked piece of liver.

4 plump shallots

12 cornichons (French gherkins)

6 fresh mushrooms

4 tablespoons (½ stick) unsalted butter

2 tablespoons sherry wine vinegar

¾ cup Veal Stock (page 109)

Salt and freshly ground white pepper

Oil for cooking

4 portions calves' liver

Flour for dredging

MAKING THE SAUCE

1. Peel and thinly slice the shallots. Cut the gherkins and the mushrooms into matchstick julienne.

2. Melt 1 tablespoon of the butter in a small saucepan. Add the shallots, gherkins, and mushrooms and cook over moderate heat, stirring from time to time, until they just begin to brown. Deglaze with the vinegar, add the veal stock, and reduce by about one-quarter until the sauce just begins to thicken. Season with salt and pepper. Swirl in 2 tablespoons of the remaining butter. Reserve the sauce in a warm place.

COOKING AND SERVING

3. Heat a sauté pan with ⅛ inch cooking oil and a tab of butter until the butter begins to brown. Meanwhile, season the liver with salt and white pepper and dredge lightly in flour. Quickly sauté the liver for no more than 45 seconds on each side if you like it rare or 1½ minutes if you prefer it well done. Remove the liver from the pan and blot it on a towel.

4. Place the liver on 4 warm plates, nap with the sauce, and serve.

Note Whether you like liver rare or well done, it should be cooked quickly and only at the last second.

Grilled Lamb Loin with Herbs

SERVES 4 TO 6

This uses the same cut as the Saddle of Lamb with Cabernet and Shallots (page 113), but the meat is trimmed differently and it is grilled instead of roasted. You can use either cooking method with either recipe, however. Make sure to tell your butcher you want the loin (saddle) in one piece, not cut into chops. (You don't want the rack; you want the loin which is found just behind the rack.) The white-wine-and-herb sauce for this recipe is lighter than the other recipe's red wine sauce, and, hence, is more appropriate in hot weather. This is a very traditional way of cooking lamb—the kind of sauce a French housewife would make, though she wouldn't be using the stock we use. (She would deglaze with white wine, a little bit of water, a little broth maybe, and she might add a few herbs and shallots.) It's a 30-minute, marketbag-to-table recipe.

1 lamb loin (both sides)

2 plump shallots

1 handful fresh herbs (basil, thyme, chervil, chives, the smallest amount of rosemary and sage—any 3 or 4)

½ cup dry white wine

¾ cup Veal Stock (page 109)

1 tablespoon unsalted butter

Salt and freshly ground pepper

Oil for cooking

1. Make a hot fire in your grill.

2. Carefully carve both loins and both small tenderloins from the lamb saddle. Trim away all fat and silver skin, leaving perfectly lean meat.

3. Finely mince the shallots. Finely chop the fresh herbs.

4. Put the herbs, shallots, and white wine in a small saucepan and reduce until almost dry. Add the veal stock and reduce slightly until the sauce begins to thicken. Swirl in the butter. Season and reserve.

5. When the grill is hot, clean the rack with a wire brush. Season the grill rack by brushing it with cooking oil. Season the meat with salt and pepper, then brush with oil. Grill the meat approximately 2½ minutes on each side for the loins and about 1 minute on each side for the tenderloins for medium-rare. Remove the meat from the grill and allow it to rest for at least 3 to 4 minutes before slicing.

6. Reheat the sauce if necessary. Cut each tenderloin into six 1-inch slices and each loin into ten to twelve ½-inch slices. Place the small slices of tenderloin in the center of each of 4 to 6 plates and fan the loin slices in front of them. Nap with the sauce and serve.

Venison with Pears and Red Wine

SERVES 4

One night when I was working at Club Elysée, the owner called to say that a car had killed a deer in front of his house. His wife wanted to bury it in the back yard and plant flowers on the grave. But no, good Frenchman that he was, he had visions of fresh venison. We hung it from the pot rack in the restaurant kitchen, bled it, and butchered it. How to make the best of this opportunity? My mind kept going back to pears poached in red wine that a visiting French chef had made for dessert at L'Ermitage. The pear-infused wine became the heart of a wonderful sauce for a *gueuleton*—a feast—for the staff and owner's friends. (Of course this feast was strictly a private affair; it is illegal to sell wild game in restaurants.) Since good fresh venison was otherwise unavailable in those days, I soon learned how good this sauce could be with duck as well.

1 ripe pear

1½ cups Cabernet Sauvignon

8 black peppercorns

Oil for cooking

1½ pounds venison tenderloin (fillet) or loin

Salt and freshly ground pepper

2 tablespoons finely minced shallots

12 fresh tarragon leaves

1¼ cups Veal Stock (page 109)

2 tablespoons unsalted butter

MISE EN PLACE

1. Peel, quarter, and core the pear, then poach it in the red wine with the peppercorns for 5 minutes. Remove from the heat and let cool to room temperature. Refrigerate the pear in the wine at least 3 or 4 hours, or overnight if possible.

COOKING AND SERVING

2. Preheat the oven to 450°F.

3. Heat enough oil to cover the bottom of an ovenproof sauté pan until very hot but not yet smoking. Season the meat with salt and pepper.

4. Sear the meat on all sides, then place it in the oven to roast. A small tenderloin will cook in as little as 4 to 5 minutes; a larger piece from the loin will take closer to 10 minutes. In either case, turn the meat over halfway through the cooking. Venison is best cooked rare or medium-rare, as it tends to get tough and dry. While the meat is cooking, bring the pear in the red wine just to a boil. Reserve.

5. Place the cooked meat in a warm place to rest and pour off all grease in the pan. Add the shallots to the still-hot pan and sweat until tender. Remove the pear quarters from the red wine, strain, and reserve, then deglaze the pan with the wine. Add the tarragon and reduce over high heat until almost dry. Add the veal stock and reduce again until the sauce begins to thicken. Swirl in the butter and season with salt and pepper. Keep warm.

6. Cut each pear quarter into 3 or 4 long slices and arrange in a fan at the top of each of 4 warm plates. Cut the meat into ¼-inch slices and fan them on the plates just below the pears. Nap with the sauce and serve.

Grilled Pork Tenderloin with Honey and Mustard

SERVES 4

This is one of the most popular dishes on our lunch menu. I can trace my craving for it back to breakfast as a child, to pancakes and the pork sausage that I stirred around in honey or maple syrup—the pork and sweet were so good together. My favorite part of this dish is the charred honey-mustard crust on the meat. The end cuts are the best—not pretty enough to serve customers but eagerly devoured in the kitchen.

2 pounds pork tenderloin (fillet)—2 or 3 pieces

1/3 cup honey

3 tablespoons Pommery mustard (whole-grain)

2 tablespoons sherry wine vinegar

2 tablespoons finely minced shallots

2 tablespoons unsalted butter

1/4 cup dry white wine

3/4 cup Veal Stock (page 109)

Salt and freshly ground white pepper

Oil for cooking

MARINATING THE PORK (BEST DONE A DAY AHEAD)

1. Trim away all the fat and silver skin from the tenderloin.

2. Mix the honey, mustard, and vinegar in a Pyrex baking dish. Thoroughly roll the tenderloins in the marinade, cover the dish, and refrigerate overnight.

COOKING AND SERVING

3. Make a hot fire in your grill.

4. Sweat the shallots in a saucepan with 1 teaspoon of the butter until they begin to brown. Deglaze with the white wine, 1/4 cup of the marinade, and the veal stock. Reduce over high heat until the sauce begins to thicken. Swirl in the remaining butter and season with salt and pepper—you may want to add a touch more of the honey-vinegar marinade to adjust the balance.

5. When the grill is nice and hot, clean the rack well with a wire brush. Season the grill rack by brushing it with cooking oil, then immediately grill the tenderloins for about 5 minutes, turning them from time to time to sear the outside and seal in all the juices.

6. Let the meat rest for a good 3 or 4 minutes, then carve the tenderloins on the bias into oval, petal-shaped slices. Arrange the slices on warm plates, nap with the sauce, and serve.

Poultry
and Game

Chicken with Oyster Mushrooms and Garlic

S E R V E S   4

This classic provincial French recipe is a simple but tasty combination—chicken in a cream and oyster mushroom sauce. And it is a practical and very satisfying dish for beginning cooks who haven't made a lot of sauces. You can also use regular button mushrooms or more exotic varieties like chanterelles or morels.

2 small frying chickens (2½ pounds each) or 2 whole breasts and 4 legs, boned

8 ounces fresh oyster mushrooms

1 plump shallot

2 bunches fresh spinach

1 clove garlic

Salt and freshly ground white pepper

Flour for dredging

Oil and butter for cooking

1½ tablespoons unsalted butter

¼ cup dry vermouth

½ cup Veal Stock (page 109)

½ cup heavy cream

M I S E   E N   P L A C E

1. Preheat the oven to 450°F.

2. If using chicken parts, skip to the next step, otherwise cut the breasts off the chickens and bone the legs, keeping the thigh and drumstick meats in one piece.

3. Trim the tough stems from the oyster mushrooms. Finely mince the shallot. Rinse and stem the spinach. Slightly crush the garlic clove and peel.

4. Season the chicken with salt and white pepper. Dredge lightly in flour, patting off all excess.

C O O K I N G   A N D   S E R V I N G

5. Heat a little oil with a tab of butter in an ovenproof sauté pan until the butter begins to brown. Add the pieces of chicken and brown about 1 minute on each side. Remove the chicken from the pan and put aside.

6. Pour off all the grease in the pan and add the mushrooms. Sprinkle with the shallot, season with salt, and put the browned chicken pieces on top. Place the pan in the oven and bake for 7 or 8 minutes.

7. In the meantime, rub the bottom of a medium saucepan with the slightly crushed clove of garlic. Add the remaining 1 tablespoon butter and the spinach; sprinkle lightly with salt. Cover tightly and cook over moderate heat for about 2 minutes, shaking occasionally, until the spinach is wilted and steamed in its own juices. Reserve.

8. Remove the cooked chicken from the pan and reserve in a warm place. Add the vermouth, veal stock, and cream to the mushrooms and reduce until the sauce begins to thicken. Verify the seasoning.

9. Make a bed of spinach on each of 4 warm plates. Place a breast and a leg on each plate. Nap with the sauce and serve.

Breast of Duck with Apples and Calvados

SERVES 4

This dish, which was an immediate success when I introduced it at La Guillotine in 1976, was a personal landmark. I was twenty-one and it was the first dish of my own I put on a menu.

In those days the hoary old standard in Los Angeles French restaurants was "duck a l'orange" (or duck with some other sweetly caramelized fruit), served in the form of a reheated, dried-up half duck carcass spilling off the plate. When Jean Bertranou broke that mold with his sliced duck breast at L'Ermitage, it gave me the freedom and inspiration to do duck my way: sliced pink *aiguillettes* of duck alternating with toasted apple slices and a smooth Calvados sauce.

---

2 large fresh ducks (at least 5½ pounds each)

2 Red Delicious apples

5 tablespoons unsalted butter

Oil for cooking

Salt and freshly ground white pepper

¼ cup Calvados

¾ cup Veal Stock (page 109)

2 tablespoons heavy cream

MISE EN PLACE

1. Cutting along each side of the breastbone with a sharp boning knife, carve the duck breasts away from the body (see Note), keeping intact about as much skin and fat as there is meat.

2. Preheat the broiler.

3. Peel, halve, and core the apples. Cut them crosswise into ⅛-inch slices. Tilt the slices of each half and spread them slightly like overlapping fallen dominoes on a buttered baking sheet. Top each apple half with a couple dabs of the butter cut in bits. Cook them under the broiler for a few minutes until the slices are tender and the edges are golden brown. Reserve.

COOKING AND SERVING

4. Heat a tablespoon of oil in a sauté pan until hot but not smoking. Season the duck breasts with salt and white pepper. Prick the skin with a fork.

5. Place the breasts skin side down in the hot pan. Cook 4 to 5 minutes—90 percent of the time on the skin side—until the skin is dark golden brown and has rendered most of its fat. The breast meat should be medium-rare, slightly springy to the touch. Remove the breasts from the pan and allow them to rest in a warm place.

6. Pour off all the grease in the pan, leaving the crusted drippings, then deglaze with the Calvados, stirring with a wooden spoon to loosen the drippings.

7. Add the veal stock and the cream to the pan. Reduce over high heat until the sauce begins to thicken. Remove the pan from the heat and swirl in the remaining

tablespoon of butter. Verify the seasoning and reserve.

8. Cut the skin from the duck breasts and discard. Slice the duck breasts, skin side up, into *aiguillettes*—thin, angled slices—cutting crosswise and on the bias.

9. Alternating slices of apple and slices of duck, reassemble the duck breasts in a fan on each of 4 warm plates. Nap with the sauce and serve.

Note Save up your duck legs—freeze them—for one of the duck leg recipes (see Index). Use the wings and carcass for Veal Stock (page 109).

Breast of Duck with Pink Peppercorns and Honey

SERVES 4

Sweet-and-sour duck is an old Chinese-French chestnut to be sure, but in this new version, pink peppercorns add a spicy, aromatic edge to the honey. The result is an especially complex palate experience, as rich and stimulating as any dark, winy sauce, yet with a surprising lightness and tanginess.

1 tablespoon pink peppercorns

2 tablespoons Cognac

1 shallot

2 large ducks (5½ pounds each)

Oil for cooking

1 teaspoon honey

1 tablespoon sherry wine vinegar

¾ cup Veal Stock (page 109)

4 tablespoons (½ stick) unsalted butter

Salt

MISE EN PLACE

1. The day before if possible, crush and soak the pink peppercorns in the Cognac to bring out the flavor.

2. Mince the shallot.

3. Cutting down along each side of the breastbone, remove the breasts from the duck (see Note).

4. Sauté (or grill) the duck breasts in a little oil over moderate heat for 5 minutes. Whether grilling or sautéing, do 90 percent of the cooking with the skin side down. Cook only until the meat is medium-rare—it will go from being flaccid to slightly springy to the touch. Let the breasts rest—and this is most important—for 3 or 4 minutes in a warm place, during which they will achieve a uniform tender pinkness throughout.

5. Pour off the grease in the pan, leaving the crusted drippings (unless you've burned them, in which case start with a clean pan). Add the shallot and let sweat for 15 seconds until softened but not browned.

6. Deglaze the pan with the Cognac and peppercorn mixture, stirring with a wooden spoon to loosen the drippings. Add the honey, vinegar, and veal stock and reduce over high heat by about a third or until slightly thickened.

7. Remove from the heat and swirl in the butter, giving the sauce a nice smooth sheen.

8. Season with salt, and verify the seasoning, especially the honey/vinegar balance. The two flavors should complement without overpowering each other. Perfect the balance by adding just a drop or two of either—it can make all the difference.

9. Cut the skin from the duck breasts and discard. Slice the duck breasts into *aiguillettes*—thin, angled slices. Fan the slices on warm plates and nap with the sauce. Serve.

Note Freeze the duck legs for use in Duck Chili or Duck Salad. Use the wings and carcass for Veal Stock (page 109).

Fillet of Rabbit with Ginger

SERVES 4

The nutritious, economical rabbit is perennially popular in Europe, yet a gastronomic dud in the United States. Why should that be? The Easter Bunny? Bugs Bunny? With apologies to the bunnies, this is an ideal introduction to the fine texture and subtle flavor of rabbit—tender, boneless, bite-sized slices of loin arranged like flower petals around a tasty timbale, all in a tangy ginger sauce.

4 large frying rabbits (3½ pounds each) with livers and kidneys

1 egg

¼ cup heavy cream

Salt and freshly ground white pepper

1 medium shallot

1 small piece ginger

Flour for dredging

Oil for cooking

3 tablespoons unsalted butter

½ cup dry white wine

¾ cup Veal Stock (page 109)

Special Equipment 4 ovenproof espresso cups or small timbale molds

MISE EN PLACE

1. Pull the hind legs away from the rabbit carcass and cut off at the hip joint. Do the same with the front legs and cut off behind the shoulder blades. Save these legs for other rabbit recipes.

2. Remove the liver and kidneys from each rabbit. (Save the kidneys for other recipes.) Cut away and discard any large veins or connective tissue from the livers. Reserve two-thirds of the livers for this recipe; save the remaining third for other recipes.

3. With a boning knife, cut down along the backbone, carefully removing each fillet. Reserve.

4. Transfer the livers to a food processor and purée with the egg, cream, salt, and white pepper until smooth. Thoroughly butter the insides of the espresso cups and fill to within ¼ inch of the tops with the liver purée.

5. Finely mince the shallot. Reserve. Peel and finely julienne 1 tablespoon ginger. Reserve.

COOKING AND SERVING

6. Preheat the oven to 400°F.

7. Put 1 inch of water in a baking pan large enough for the 4 espresso cups and bring the water to a boil on top of the stove. Place the 4 timbales in the boiling water, transfer the pan to the oven, and bake for 8 to 10 minutes, until the mousse is set and has risen slightly in the center. Remove from the water.

8. Season the rabbit fillets with salt and pepper and dredge lightly in flour, patting off all excess.

9. Heat 2 tablespoons oil with a dab of the butter until the butter begins to brown. Add the rabbit fillets and sauté 3 to 4 minutes until golden brown and slightly firm to the touch. Reserve the fillets on a warm plate and allow to rest for another 3 to 4 minutes before slicing.

10. Pour off the grease in the pan. Add the shallot and allow to soften for 30 seconds. Deglaze the pan with the white wine, add the veal stock, and reduce by about half until the sauce begins to thicken. Remove from the heat.

11. Add the ginger and swirl in a tablespoon of butter, bit by bit. Verify the seasoning and reserve in a warm place.

12. Unmold the liver timbales by running the point of a paring knife around the edge and upending the timbales in the center of 4 warm plates.

13. Thinly slice the rabbit fillets on the bias into petal-shaped slices. Arrange the slices around the timbales like a flower. Nap with the sauce and serve.

Chicken with Fresh Tomato Coulis

SERVES 4

This is a wonderfully simple and satisfying dish. The sauce, which has no stock, no cream, and very little butter, depends for its unusually fresh flavor on good, ripe tomatoes accented with hints of onion, garlic, and tarragon. In addition to chicken, try the coulis with fish, scallops, rabbit, ravioli, and other pasta.

---

3 or more red, ripe tomatoes, chosen for flavor not beauty (plum or pear tomatoes are ideal, but small, so use twice as many)

¼ medium onion

1 clove garlic, peeled

1 small shallot, minced

2 small frying chickens (2½ pounds each) or 2 whole breasts and 4 legs, boned

Salt and freshly ground white pepper

Flour for dredging

Oil for cooking

6 tablespoons unsalted butter, softened

¼ cup dry white wine or vermouth

1 tablespoon fresh tarragon leaves

1. *To make the coulis:* Place the to-matoes, onion, and garlic in a food proces-sor and process for about 1 minute. Strain the mixture through a fine strainer, push-ing through as much as you can. Reserve.

2. Mince the shallot and reserve.

3. If using chicken parts, skip to the next step, otherwise cut the breasts off the chickens and bone the legs, keeping the thigh and drumstick meats in one piece.

COOKING AND SERVING
(SEE NOTE)

4. Preheat the oven to 450°F.

5. Salt and pepper the chicken, dredge in flour, and pat off all excess flour between your hands.

6. Heat 2 tablespoons oil with a dab of the butter in an ovenproof sauté pan until the butter turns golden brown. Brown the chicken on both sides about 1 minute each. Transfer the pan to the oven and bake the legs and breasts another 4 or 5 minutes until they are slightly firm to the touch. Remove the chicken from the pan and reserve in a warm place.

7. Pour off all the grease in the pan, leaving the browned drippings. Place the pan over moderate heat, add the shallots, and stir with a wooden spoon to loosen the drippings.

8. Deglaze immediately with the white wine. Add the tomato coulis and re-duce the sauce a bit more than half until it begins to thicken. Off the heat, swirl in the remaining butter, bit by bit. Verify the sea-soning.

9. Mirror the plates with the sauce and sprinkle with the fresh tarragon leaves. Place a breast and a leg on each plate. Serve.

Note You can either sauté or grill the chicken. I love it grilled myself. It's healthier—you cook the fat out when grill-ing. Make the sauce the same way but in a fresh pan.

Pigeon with Honey and Peppermint

SERVES 4

This dish has a slightly Oriental character, thanks to the rice wine vinegar, peppermint, and honey. It makes vivid use of contrasts—strong, sweet, and hot, with the rice vinegar playing off the pungent peppermint. Still, it remains distinctly French, and heartily so—pigeons have more meat on their bones than you might expect.

4 pigeons

½ cup rice wine vinegar

2 teaspoons soy sauce

2 teaspoons honey

1 tablespoon oil for cooking

¾ cup Veal Stock (page 109)

2 tablespoons unsalted butter

Salt

12 fresh peppermint leaves (do *not* chop ahead of time)

MISE EN PLACE

1. Cut off each pigeon's wing tips at the elbows and discard. Cut off the excess flaps of skin around the neck and the dorsal vent. To prevent overcooking the drumsticks, tuck them tightly against the body by inserting the ankles into small knife slits in the skin of each side.

2. Mix the vinegar, soy sauce, and honey in a large mixing bowl. Bathe the pigeons in the mixture for 2 to 3 minutes. Remove and let them dry at room temperature, ideally for an hour but at least a few minutes. Save the marinade.

COOKING AND SERVING

3. Preheat the oven to 450°F.

4. Heat a tablespoon of oil in a large ovenproof sauté pan until hot. Brown the pigeons breast side down until they turn a deep golden brown. Turn them over, transfer the pan to the oven, and roast for 8 to 9 minutes, until the breasts begin to feel firm. Remove the pigeons from the pan and let rest in a warm place for 5 minutes.

5. Pour off the grease in the pan and deglaze with the marinade. Reduce over medium heat until almost dry. Add the veal stock and reduce again until slightly thickened, with the sheen of a sauce.

6. Off the heat, swirl in the butter. Verify the seasoning—the soy sauce should supply enough salt. Keep warm

7. Exactly as if boning a chicken, cut off the pigeon legs and, with a small paring knife, carefully remove an discard just the thigh bones, leaving the drumsticks intact and keeping all the leg meat in one piece. Cut the breasts from the carcasses and cut each one into 7 or 8 thin slices.

8. Cross the legs at the top of each of 4 plates and fan the breast slices in front of them.

9. Warm the sauce if necessary and, only now, chop and add the fresh peppermint. Nap the pigeons with the sauce and serve.

Chicken with Cucumber and Ginger

SERVES 4

This is intensely flavorful yet extraordinarily light summer fare. The sauce, with its bit of sharp ginger and the soft crunch of cucumber, is wonderfully refreshing without a hint of richness or heaviness. And despite the Japanese-sounding ingredients, it's a distinctly French dish.

2 small frying chickens (2¼ to 2½ pounds each) or 2 whole breasts and 4 legs, boned

1 hothouse cucumber

1 small piece (1-inch) fresh ginger

Salt and freshly ground white pepper

Flour for dredging

Oil for cooking

2 tablespoons unsalted butter

¼ cup dry white wine

¾ cup Veal Stock (page 109)

1. Preheat the oven to 450°F.

2. If you are using chicken parts, skip to the next step, otherwise cut the breasts off the chickens and bone the legs, keeping the thigh and drumstick meats in one piece.

3. Cut the cucumber into 2-inch lengths, then cut each section lengthwise into 6 wedges. "Turn" the wedges—that is, round them with a paring knife into nice ovals. Peel and finely julienne the ginger.

4. Season the chicken with salt and pepper. Dredge lightly in flour and pat off all excess.

5. Heat ⅛ inch oil with a tab of the butter in an ovenproof sauté pan until the butter begins to brown. Add the pieces of chicken and brown about 1 minute on each side. Place the pan in the oven and bake 5 to 6 minutes more. Transfer the cooked chicken to a warm place.

6. Pour off all the grease in the pan and place over high heat. Add the white wine, veal stock, and cucumbers and reduce by about half or until the sauce just begins to thicken. Verify the salt seasoning. Add a little of the julienned ginger, stir, and taste—then add more if you like. Remove from the heat and swirl in the remaining butter. Reserve.

7. Arrange the chicken on 4 warm plates. Nap with the sauce and garnish with the cucumbers, which will be cooked just al dente by the reduction of the sauce. Serve.

Chicken with Tarragon

I had a chicken dish I've never forgotten at La Mère Blanc in Vonnas in the Bresse region. It was the famous *poulet de Bresse* with blue feet —a tender, large, juicy bird with a meatier flavor than any other chicken. This dish, inspired by that *poulet de Bresse* with its delicately sweet tarragon and tomato sauce, is a good approximation of the original, no matter where your chicken grows up.

---

1 plum tomato

1 branch fresh tarragon

2 small frying chickens (2½ pounds each) or 2 whole breasts and 4 legs, boned

Salt and freshly ground white pepper

Flour for dredging

Oil for cooking

Unsalted butter

2 tablespoons minced shallots

¾ cup dry white wine

1 teaspoon sherry wine vinegar

¾ cup Veal Stock (page 109)

3 tablespoons crème fraîche (page 55) or heavy cream

MISE EN PLACE

1. On a barbecue fork or skewer, roast the tomato over an open flame to blister and loosen the skin, about 30 seconds. Remove the skin under cold running water. Cut the tomato in half and squeeze out the seeds and juice. Finely mince the remaining meat. Reserve.

2. Pluck the tarragon leaves off the stem and coarsely chop.

3. If using chicken parts, skip to the next step, otherwise, cut the breasts off the chickens and bone the legs, keeping the thigh and drumstick meats in one piece.

COOKING AND SERVING

4. Preheat the oven to 450°F.

5. Salt and pepper the chicken breasts and legs and dredge in flour. Pat off all excess flour between your hands.

6. Heat 2 tablespoons oil with a dab of butter in an ovenproof sauté pan until the butter turns golden brown. Sauté the chicken pieces about 1 minute on each side. Transfer the pan to the oven and bake for another 4 or 5 minutes or until slightly firm to the touch. Remove the chicken from the pan and keep warm.

7. *To make the sauce:* Pour off all the grease in the pan, leaving the browned drippings. Add the shallots and sweat briefly. Deglaze with the white wine, stirring with a wooden spoon to loosen the drippings.

8. Add the chopped tomato, tarragon, vinegar, and veal stock. Reduce by about half until the sauce just begins to thicken. Whisk in the crème fraîche and reduce a bit more. Verify the seasoning. If the sauce is a little thick, stir in any juice collected on the chicken plate.

9. Arrange a breast and a leg on each of 4 warm plates. Nap with the sauce and serve.

Chicken Sausage

SERVES 4

This is a unique way of doing chicken and perfect for feeding lots of people. Whether cooking for four or forty, you can prepare and cook this ahead of time and keep it warm for a good half hour—it will stay nice and juicy inside its skin while waiting. Offered with a colorful stir-fry of fresh vegetables, it doesn't need much of a sauce, just a simple *jus,* as here, or any sauce you like—mustard, tomato, or tarragon, for instance. The stir-fry, with its variety of fresh flavors and textures, is also versatile.

---

2 small frying chickens (2¼ to 2½ pounds each), with giblets

Salt and freshly ground white pepper

1 egg

¼ cup heavy cream

1 carrot

1 rib celery

2 small turnips

4 green onions

8 pencil-thin asparagus

16 snow peas

4 large mushrooms

1 tablespoon finely minced shallot

Flour for dredging

Oil for cooking

4 tablespoons unsalted butter

¼ cup dry white vermouth

½ cup Veal Stock (page 109)

---

1. If you are buying chicken parts, skip to the next step, otherwise remove the leg and the breast from each side of each chicken in one piece, keeping the skin intact: Do this by cutting along the breastbone to loosen the breast meat, then pulling the leg away from the body and cutting at the hip joint. Chop the knuckle off the bottom of the drumstick. Pull the leg—bone and meat together—out of its skin, leaving behind a breast with a large flap of skin attached.

2. Cut the meat from the thighs and drumsticks, cutting away and discarding the tendons from the lower end of the drumstick. Dice the leg meat into small pieces.

3. Transfer the diced meat to a food processor. Add the livers and season with salt and pepper. Process for 1 minute. Add the egg and cream and process 30 seconds more.

4. Place the breasts skin side down on a work surface. Spoon one-quarter of the mousse onto each breast. Wrap the skin around the breast, enclosing the mousse. Tie each "sausage" securely at the ends and middle with 4 pieces of string.

COOKING AND SERVING

5. Preheat the oven to 400°F.

6. *To prepare the vegetables:* Peel the carrot and thinly slice on the bias. Peel the strings from the celery with a vegetable peeler and thinly slice on the bias. Peel the turnips and slice into thin circles. Trim the roots from the bottoms of the green onions and the greens from the tops. Cut the woody ends off the bottoms of the asparagus. Snap off the ends and pull any

strings off the snow peas. Slice the mushrooms. Mince the shallot.

7. Salt and pepper the chicken sausages and dredge in flour, patting off all excess between your hands. Heat 2 tablespoons oil in an ovenproof sauté pan with a dab of the butter until the butter begins to brown. Brown the chicken on all sides, then bake in the oven 8 to 9 minutes. Remove and let rest in a warm place at least 5 minutes before slicing.

8. Pour off the grease in the pan, leaving the crusted drippings. Add the shallot, sweat for 30 seconds, then deglaze the pan with the vermouth, stirring with a wooden spoon to loosen the drippings. Add the veal stock and reduce slightly over moderate heat. (No need to reduce this to a sauce thickness, since we are after a light *jus* accompaniment rather than an intense flavor focus.) Verify the seasoning. Reserve in a warm place.

9. *To stir-fry:* Heat the remaining 4 tablespoons butter in a sauté pan until hot but not brown. Add the carrots and stir-fry over moderate heat for 30 seconds, taking care not to brown the butter. Add the celery, green onions, turnips, and asparagus; sauté 2 more minutes, still being careful not to burn the butter. Add the mushrooms and snow peas; finish cooking for 30 more seconds. Season and divide equally onto 4 plates.

10. With the point of a sharp scissors, snip the strings from the rested chicken sausages and cut into ½-inch slices. Arrange the slices atop the beds of vegetables. Nap with the sauce and serve.

Ken Frank's
La Toque
Cookbook
■
140

Chicken with Crayfish and Morels

S E R V E S   4

If you were surprised to see me pair fish with a red wine sauce, then you'll find this combination unusual too—chicken in a seafood sauce. Though it sounds *nouvelle,* it's my contemporary version of the classic *"Poulet* George Sand"—chicken sautéed in crayfish sauce. Here the sauce is a rich mélange of sweetness from the crayfish and earthiness from the morels, a sensual, stick-to-your-ribs sauce. It's also good on other white meats—such as rabbit and sweetbreads, and wonderful on fettuccine and other pastas. Add truffles to make it unforgettable.

24 live crayfish or 24 crayfish tails and I cup Lobster Fumet (page 29)

4 tablespoons (½ stick) unsalted butter

⅓ cup diced peeled carrot

⅓ cup diced onion

⅓ cup diced celery

2 shots brandy

½ cup dry white wine

2 red, ripe tomatoes

I stem fresh tarragon

2 frying chickens (2½ to 3 pounds each) or 2 whole breasts and 4 legs, boned

12 large fresh morels or 2 ounces dried morels

(ingredients continued)

Salt and freshly ground white pepper

Flour for dredging

Oil for cooking

¼ cup Veal Stock (page 109)

¾ cup heavy cream

MISE EN PLACE

1. *To cook the crayfish:* Put an inch of water in a large pot and bring to a boil. Add the crayfish, cover tightly, and steam for 5 to 6 minutes. Drain in a colander and allow to cool enough to handle.

2. To peel the crayfish, tear the tail away from the head, pinch the tail slightly to crack its shell, and pry it open with your fingers, removing the meat. Reserve the meat and save the shells and heads to make the crayfish stock. Put aside 4 good heads for garnish.

3. *To make the crayfish stock:* Peel the carrot. Dice the carrot, onion, and celery and chop the tomatoes. Melt 1 tablespoon of the butter in a large saucepan and sweat the carrot, onion, and celery until they are tender and just begin to turn golden brown. Add the crayfish heads and shells and sauté for another minute. Deglaze with the brandy and flambé. When the flames die down, add the wine, tomatoes, tarragon, and a cup or so of water. Simmer gently for 30 minutes. Strain through a fine strainer and reserve. You should have approximately 1 cup of stock. (You may substitute 1 cup Lobster Fumet for the crayfish stock.)

4. If using chicken parts, skip to the next step, otherwise cut the breasts off the chickens and bone the legs, keeping the thigh and drumstick meats in one piece.

5. Rinse the morels if they are dirty. If using dried morels, soak them in warm water to soften for a few minutes. Cut the morels into quarters or sixths, depending on their size. Reserve.

COOKING AND SERVING

6. Preheat the oven to 450°F.

7. Season the chicken with salt and freshly ground white pepper. Dredge in flour and pat off all excess.

8. Cover the bottom of a large oven-proof sauté pan with oil and add a tab of the remaining butter. Heat over high heat until the butter begins to brown. Add the chicken and brown approximately 1 minute on each side. Then transfer to the oven and bake for 5 minutes. Remove the pan from the oven, pour off all the grease, add the morels, and return it to the oven to bake for another 3 to 4 minutes.

9. Transfer the chicken to a platter and reserve in a warm place. Leaving the morels in the pan, deglaze with the crayfish stock, then add the veal stock and cream and reduce until the sauce begins to thicken.

10. Add the crayfish tails and any juice from the chickens resting on the platter. Verify the seasoning.

11. Place a chicken breast and a leg on each of 4 warm plates. Using a slotted spoon, divide the crayfish and morels among the portions. Nap with the sauce, garnish each plate with a crayfish head, and serve.

Quail with Roasted Shallots

SERVES 4

This is quail stuffed with whole candied shallots, roasted to a rich golden brown, and napped with a lively sweet-and-sour sauce. The preparation of the shallots is unorthodox: They are wrapped in a many-layered pouch of aluminum foil and cooked in a blasting hot oven. It's a surprisingly gentle technique that slowly candies the shallots and leaves them meltingly tender. The simple honey-vinegar sauce is irresistible with almost any fowl—squab, duck, chicken.

16 plump shallots, whole and unpeeled

2 tablespoons oil for cooking

Salt and freshly ground white pepper

4 bunches fresh spinach

8 fresh quails

2½ tablespoons unsalted butter

2 teaspoons sherry wine vinegar

½ teaspoon honey

1 cup Veal Stock (page 109)

MISE EN PLACE

1. Preheat the oven to 450°F.
2. Snip off the excess skin from the tops and roots of the shallots but leave them unpeeled and still sealed at both ends.
3. Line the bottom and sides of an ovenproof medium saucepan with 7 or 8 layers of aluminum foil, using pieces large enough to stick out at least an inch beyond the edges of the pan.
4. Place the shallots with 1 tablespoon of the oil in the foil-lined pan. Sprinkle with salt and white pepper and stir well to coat the shallots evenly.
5. Cover with an additional 5 or 6 layers of aluminum foil and crimp tightly around the edges. Bake for 45 minutes, making sure to shake the pan every 10 minutes or so to prevent burning. You will know the shallots are done when they feel soft and unresisting through their skins. Keep the oven on.
6. Snip off one end of each roasted shallot and squeeze out the soft pulp. Finely chop a third of the pulp and keep the rest whole.
7. Rinse and stem the spinach.

COOKING AND SERVING

8. Lightly season the cavity of each quail with salt and pepper.
9. Stuff the quails with the whole shallot pulp, reserving the chopped pulp for the sauce.
10. Heat the remaining tablespoon oil in a large ovenproof sauté pan until hot. Brown the quails breast side down. Turn them over and roast them in the same pan in the oven for 6 to 7 minutes.
11. In the meantime, flash-cook the spinach by placing it with ½ tablespoon of the butter and a sprinkle of salt in a large, tightly covered saucepan. Cook over moderate heat for no more than 2 minutes, shaking firmly from time to time to ensure even cooking. The spinach will wilt and

steam in its own juice. Reserve in the same covered pan.

12. Remove the roasted quails from the pan and reserve in a warm place. Pour off all the grease in the pan, leaving the browned drippings. Add the finely chopped shallots and deglaze with the vinegar, stirring with a wooden spoon to loosen the drippings. Add the honey and veal stock and reduce over high heat by about half.

13. While the stock is reducing, drain any liquid from the spinach, then make a bed of it on each of 4 warm plates and top with 2 quails.

14. Remove the sauce from the heat and swirl in the remaining 2 tablespoons butter. Verify the honey/vinegar seasoning. Nap the quails with the sauce and serve.

Quail Stuffed with Fennel and Mushrooms

SERVES 4

Quail really is more for the palate than the stomach. They are different and tasty, but with only 2 ounces of meat per bird, I could eat four at a sitting. If you serve just one bird per person, however, it's an ideal small course in a "menu dégustation"—a tasting menu comprising many dishes in small portions. Here the fennel, mushroom, and spinach stuffing and the smooth Cognac-and-garlic sauce gives a peasant heartiness to an elegant dish.

8 cloves garlic, unpeeled

2 bunches fresh spinach

4½ tablespoons unsalted butter

1 bulb fresh fennel

8 ounces fresh mushrooms

1 tablespoon finely minced shallot

Salt and freshly ground white pepper

8 fresh quails (boneless if available)

Oil for cooking

1 shot Cognac

¾ cup Veal Stock (page 109)

MISE EN PLACE

1. Preheat the oven to 475°F.
2. Roast the unpeeled garlic cloves for ½ hour or until the garlic skins begin to

turn golden brown. Reserve. Keep the oven on for step 6.

3. Rinse, stem, and flash-cook the spinach by placing it with ½ tablespoon of the butter in a large saucepan with a tight-fitting lid and cooking it over high heat for about 2 minutes, shaking the pan from time to time. The spinach will wilt and steam in its own juices in this short time. Drain the spinach and finely chop it with a chef's knife. Reserve.

4. Cut the fennel into fine (⅛-inch) dice. Chop the mushrooms just as fine. Very finely mince the shallot and reserve.

5. Melt 2 tablespoons of the remaining butter in a large sauté pan over moderate heat. Add the fennel and stir-fry for 2 or 3 minutes, just until it begins to soften. Add the mushrooms and continue to sauté until all the rendered juices are cooked off. Mix in the chopped spinach, season with salt and pepper, and reserve.

COOKING AND SERVING

6. Lightly season each bird inside and out with salt and pepper. Fill with the spinach-fennel-mushroom stuffing and tie the legs together with a bit of string.

7. Heat 3 tablespoons oil in a large ovenproof sauté pan until oil is hot but not yet smoking. Brown the quails breast side down for about 1 minute. Turn the quails over, transfer the pan to the oven, and roast for 4 to 5 minutes, basting the birds once halfway through the cooking. Remove the quails from the pan and reserve in a warm place.

8. Pour off all the grease in the pan, leaving the browned drippings. Add the shallot and cook over low heat, stirring with a wooden spoon to loosen the drip-

pings, until the shallot is soft and translucent. Deglaze with the Cognac and flambé.

9. When the flames have died down, add the veal stock and the roasted garlic cloves and simmer gently until reduced by about a third and beginning to thicken. Remove from the heat and swirl in the remaining 2 tablespoons butter. Verify the seasoning—the sauce usually requires a little salt.

10. Place 2 birds on each of 4 plates and garnish with a pair of roasted garlic cloves—to be squeezed out of their skins into your mouth! Nap with the sauce and serve.

Peeling Garlic

The best way to loosen garlic cloves from an intact bulb? With the palm of your hand, simply crush the bulb against your work board. Sufficient force will snap all the cloves neatly from the root.

The best way to peel a garlic clove—always a painstaking and annoying task—is to crush the individual unpeeled cloves against your work board with the flat of a chef's knife or cleaver. Broken, the skins pull away with almost magical ease.

Duck Chili

Even for the most refined palates there is a time and a place for a big bite of Texas—*real* chili, hot and spicy with meat in big chunks and no beans. Early westerners used pork, chicken, beef, buffalo, venison, squirrel—whatever came to hand. To my taste, fresh, red, juicy duck meat steeped in this rich beer-and-garlic sauce makes the best, heartiest bowl of chili you'll ever have. It's a constant request from my lunchtime customers.

24 duck legs

2 onions

16 cloves garlic

1 jalapeño pepper (or more to taste)

Salt

⅔ cup chili powder

2 teaspoons ground cumin

¼ cup tomato paste

2 heaping tablespoons masa harina (corn flour)

1 bottle (12 ounces) beer

Sour cream, chopped onions, and/or grated cheddar cheese for garnish

1. Cut the meat off the duck legs, discarding the bones, tendons, and all the skin except 3 or 4 pieces. Dice the meat into ½-inch chunks.

2. Dice the onions. Chop the garlic and jalapeño. (If you don't like your chili really hot, remove the seeds from the jalapeño.)

3. In a cast-iron pot or Dutch oven, fry the duck skin over low to moderate heat to render the fat. Once you have 4 to 5 tablespoons fat, discard the skins.

4. Turn the heat all the way up and add the diced duck meat. Sauté for 4 or 5 minutes until the copiously exuded liquid has boiled off and the meat sizzles and browns well. Season with salt. (You won't need pepper!)

5. Add the onions and sauté another minute. Add the garlic, jalapeño, chili powder, cumin, tomato paste, and masa. Cook while mixing and stirring for another minute. Deglaze with the beer, making sure to scrape loose all the crusted drippings on the bottom of the pan.

6. Add enough water to cover the meat by an inch or so, cover, and bring to a boil. Verify the salt seasoning but remember that the salt will intensify as the chili reduces. Reduce the heat to a simmer. Cook partially covered for a good 2 hours.

7. Serve with a garnish of sour cream, chopped onions, and/or grated cheddar cheese.

Variation Beef, pork, or rabbit make perfectly fine supplements or substitutes here if you don't have enough duck legs saved. Figure ½ pound of meat per person.

Note Do *not* use MSG in this or any other recipe. Many prize chili recipes call for MSG, which is incomprehensible to me. It's a crutch, quite simply unnecessary if you're a decent cook, especially when, as here, there is an abundance of strong, natural flavors available to you.

Duck Confit

MAKES 8 LEGS

If meat could ever be candy, it would be duck confit. (The word confit literally translated means candied.) A relic from the past, a confit is pork, goose, or duck meat cooked slowly in its own fat and juices and redolent of garlic and herbs. This duck confit is tender and incredibly flavorful—sheer duckness.

Mother Nature has gifted us with the duck, and I haven't found a part of the duck that I don't like and use: crisp skin for snacking, carcasses to enrich my veal stock, sliced pink duck breast (about as good as red meat gets) and of course foie gras. Duck is great meat for chili, too.

Duck confit enriches my cooking in a multitude of ways. I use it in pastas, salads, and soups, as well as the more traditional uses such as cassoulet and rillettes.

To make confit, you'll need a large cast-iron pot with a tight-fitting lid. Accumulate duck legs in the freezer until you have enough. The first time you make confit, you'll need duck fat too, so save and freeze a few of the big flaps of fatty skin—about 2 pounds.

2 cups duck fat (see box at right)

8 duck legs

1 whole head garlic

1 small sprig fresh thyme (2 inches)

Pinch of crushed red chilies

1 bay leaf

Salt

1. Preheat the oven to 300°F.

2. Melt the duck fat over low heat in your cast-iron pot. Add the duck legs to the pot—skin, bones, and all. Cut the unpeeled head of garlic horizontally in half. Add both halves to the pot, skins and all. Add the thyme, chilies, and bay leaf and a generous sprinkle of salt.

How to Render Duck Fat

Place 2 pounds of fatty duck skin in a medium saucepan with 2 cups of water and bring it to a low simmer. As you allow it to simmer for an hour or so, the water will melt the fat from the skin and will itself slowly evaporate, and the liquid will change from milky white to clear pure duck fat. When the skins turn crisp light brown, strain off your rendered duck fat. Pure duck fat can be refrigerated indefinitely.

---

3. Cover the pot, place it in the oven, and leave it to cook a good part of the day. After the first half hour, check from time to time to see that it has reached a simmer; continue to cook thereafter for a good 3 hours. (As with anytime you are cooking with fat, do not leave it unattended.)

4. Remove the pot from the oven, carefully lift out the duck legs, and place them in a storage container. Carefully strain enough of the fat onto the duck legs to cover them and seal out the air. Let cool and refrigerate. (For long-term storage, place each leg in a Zip-closing freezer bag

with some of the fat. Seal and freeze indefinitely.) The juice left in the bottom of the pan underneath the fat is unbelievably flavorful—essence of duck—and should be saved to enhance a soup or cassoulet or other future dish.

5. When ready to use the confit, remove it from the refrigerator and let soften to room temperature. Using your fingers, peel the skin from the legs and discard. Pull the meat from the bones and carefully shred it, discarding any tendons and cartilage. Once shredded, the confit must be used within 48 hours.

6. Be sure to save the fat for your next batch: Heat and re-strain the fat into a clean container. Allow to cool and refrigerate until next time.

Braised Duck Legs with Cabbage

SERVES 4

This is one of my fondest memories from Yvoire—a country duck stew whose simplicity goes to the heart of my cooking identity. What appeals to me is the good rich taste of the duck meat slowly braised and infused with the sweetness of the vegetables. Duck hunting was an everyday thing in Yvoire—the family of fishermen I lived with took their guns along and shot duck on the way back from pulling in their nets at dawn. Though only 15 minutes from Geneva, it was real countryside—a village with a population of only 307. You could hunt outside your door.

8 duck legs

Salt and freshly ground white pepper

½ head cabbage

½ carrot

½ onion

½ stalk celery

1 tablespoon unsalted butter

⅔ cup dry white wine

2 cups Veal Stock (page 109)

1. Preheat the oven to 400°F. Trim all the excess fat from the duck legs and chop the knuckle off the end of each drumstick. Season with salt and pepper. Brown

both sides over moderate heat in an oven-proof sauté pan, then transfer to the oven and bake for 15 to 20 minutes. Remove and reserve.

2. In the meantime, cut the cabbage half into 4 wedges and blanch for 2 minutes in boiling salted water.

3. Peel the carrot and cut into pretty ¼-inch dice. Dice the onion and celery similarly. Sweat the diced vegetables with the butter in a heavy pan with a tight-fitting lid until they just begin to brown.

4. Add the blanched cabbage wedges and browned duck legs to the pan. Deglaze with the wine, add the stock, and season with salt and pepper. Bring the liquid to a boil, then allow to simmer covered for 1½ hours. Skim the fat from the surface from time to time.

5. When ready to serve, use a slotted spoon to remove the duck legs and cabbage wedges carefully from the sauce. Place a cabbage wedge on each plate and top with a pair of duck legs.

6. Skim any remaining fat from the sauce and return to a boil, reducing further if necessary. Verify the seasoning and pour the sauce over the duck legs. Serve.

Braised Duck Legs with Green Peppercorns

S E R V E S   4

This is a straight-ahead, traditional French recipe (with green peppercorns giving it a slightly modern touch) and great winter food with its hearty satisfying sauce. Here is another good way to use the duck legs you've collected in your freezer. The difference between fresh and frozen legs disappears after braising them slowly for a long period of time. In fact, if you make this a day ahead of time, you will find the flavor fully developed and the dish improved.

8 duck legs

Salt

½ onion

1 tablespoon green peppercorns

¼ cup Cognac

2 cups Veal Stock (page 109)

2 tablespoons heavy cream

1. Preheat the oven to 400°F.

2. Carefully remove just the thigh bone from the duck legs by cutting along the inside of the thigh. Remove all chunks of excess fat and skin, leaving only enough skin to cover the meat. Using a cleaver, chop the knuckle off the bottom of each drumstick. Season with salt.

3. Heat a heavy ovenproof pot with a tight-fitting lid over moderate heat until hot. Fit the duck legs skin side down into the pot and cook until the skin is golden brown and has begun to render its fat. Turn the legs over and cook the other side briefly to seal in the juices. Turn the legs back onto the skin side and place the uncovered pot in the oven to roast for about 20 minutes.

4. Meanwhile finely dice the onion and crush the peppercorns slightly

5. Remove the duck legs from the pot and pour off all the grease. Add the onion to the still-hot pot and place the duck legs, skin side up, on top. Cover tightly and roast another 10 minutes.

6. Add the peppercorns and Cognac to the pot and flambé the Cognac. Add the stock and cream. Barely simmer, partially covered, on top of the stove for another 45 minutes until the duck legs are meltingly tender.

7. Carefully remove the duck from the pot and arrange on 4 plates. Reduce the sauce further if necessary—until it just begins to thicken. Verify the seasoning and spoon the sauce over the duck legs. Serve.

Roasted Rabbit Saddle with Morels

SERVES 4

The boning required here is somewhat complicated, but it's worth the trouble and can be done a day ahead of time. The boneless rabbit stays juicy and tender. If you'd prefer to avoid boning, however, just carve off the fillets, grill them separately, and serve them with this wonderful, easy sauce. If fresh morels are not in season (spring is their time), it is perfectly acceptable to use dried morels; oddly, good dried morels are better than mediocre fresh ones.

4 rabbit saddles (save the legs for a stew or pâté)

Salt and freshly ground white pepper

2 bunches fresh spinach

1 clove garlic, crushed but unpeeled

2 dozen fresh morels

1 plump shallot

Oil for cooking

1½ tablespoons unsalted butter

1½ fluid ounces Armagnac

1 cup Veal Stock (page 109)

¼ cup heavy cream

1. *To bone and stuff the saddles:* Carefully cut the backbone out of the 4 rabbit saddles, keeping the flanks and the fillets all in one big piece. Save the liver and kidneys. Lay out each boneless saddle, skin side down, and season lightly with salt and white pepper.

2. Cut the kidneys in half and cut each liver into 3 or 4 pieces. Place the liver and kidney pieces on the center of each saddle and roll them up inside the meat. (You've simply removed the bones and put the saddle back together again.) Tie each stuffed saddle with string and wrap tightly with aluminum foil.

3. Rinse and stem the spinach. Crush, but do not peel, the garlic. Reserve. Clean and quarter the morels. Finely mince the shallot. Reserve.

COOKING AND SERVING

4. Preheat the oven to 450°F.

5. Heat ⅛ inch oil in an ovenproof sauté pan over high heat until hot. Add the foil-wrapped saddles to the pan and cook for 1 minute on each side. Transfer to the oven and cook 8 more minutes.

6. In the meantime, smear the bottom of a saucepan with ½ tablespoon of the butter. Add the spinach and the garlic clove, season lightly with salt, and cover tightly. Cook over moderate heat, shaking the pan from time to time, for about 2 minutes, until the spinach is wilted. Reserve.

7. In another saucepan, sauté the morels in the remaining 1 tablespoon butter until tender, about 1 minute only. Add the shallot to the pan and sweat for 30 seconds. Deglaze with the Armagnac. Add the veal stock and cream and allow the sauce to reduce until it just begins to thicken. Remove from the heat, verify the seasoning, and reserve.

8. When the rabbit saddles are done, remove them from the oven and allow to rest for 5 minutes before unwrapping. Add any juice trapped in the foil to the sauce.

9. Arrange the spinach in the center of 4 warm plates. (Discard the garlic clove.) Cut the saddles into ¼-inch slices and place the slices atop the beds of spinach. Nap with the sauce and serve.

Duck with Port and Cassis

SERVES 4

Though not a red wine sauce, the combination of port and cassis complements a nice bottle of red wine as well as any sauce can. (You'll have to buy the black currants in a full basket, but they freeze wonderfully—indefinitely. Use them later for sauces, jelly, or sorbet.) The port-and-cassis sauce goes equally well with venison and other meats like pigeon or chicken.

2 large ducks (5½ pounds each)

2 plump shallots

½ basket (about ⅔ cup) fresh black currants

Salt and freshly ground pepper

3 fluid ounces vintage port (see Note)

1 cup Veal Stock (page 109)

1 tablespoon unsalted butter

1. Cutting down along each side of the breastbone, remove the breasts from each duck, and trim away all excess skin and fat. Freeze the legs for one of the duck leg recipes (see Index). Use the wings and carcass for Veal Stock (page 109).

2. Finely mince the shallots. Pick the black currants from their stems. Reserve.

3. Season the duck breasts with salt and pepper. Heat a sauté pan and add the breasts skin side down to the pan. Cook over moderate heat 4 or 5 minutes in their own fat until the skin is deep golden brown, then turn the breasts over and finish cooking for 1 more minute. Remove the meat from the pan and allow to rest.

4. Pour off all the grease in the pan, add the shallots off the heat, and stir with a wooden spoon to soften them slightly.

5. Return the pan to the heat, deglaze with the port, and add the black currants. Reduce until almost dry. Add the stock and reduce again until the sauce just begins to thicken. Remove from the heat and swirl in the butter to finish the sauce.

6. Thinly slice the duck breasts. They should be pink but not really rare. Fan the slices on 4 warm plates, nap with the sauce, and serve.

Note If using a "wood" port instead of a vintage port, you'll have to use a little more. Vintage ports are much richer and inkier.

Pigeon and Lobster with Cabernet Sauce

SERVES 2

This dish is a bit expensive and complicated, so it is not for the beginner, but it is lushly rewarding, something to cook for a special friend on a special occasion. I learned it from a cook who had learned it in France and felt it should be kept the ultimate secret—*dommage*. Since it is sublime stuff arranged in an arc, and since the French chef's name was Raimbeau (sounds like rainbow), we call it *Arc en Ciel*.

Salt and freshly ground white pepper

2 tablespoons red wine vinegar

1 small live lobster (1 pound)

1 fresh pigeon (15 to 16 ounces)

½ carrot

¼ onion

½ stalk celery

2 fresh mushrooms

Oil for cooking

2 tablespoons unsalted butter

½ cup Cabernet Sauvignon

¾ cup Veal Stock (page 109)

1 tablespoon finely minced shallot

8 fresh tarragon leaves

MISE EN PLACE

All the Mise en Place steps can be done as much as 24 hours ahead of time.

1. *To cook the lobster:* Bring 2 quarts water to a boil with a pinch of salt, a few grinds of pepper, and the vinegar. Plunge the lobster into the boiling liquid and cook for 9 minutes. Remove the lobster and allow to cool. Discard the cooking liquid.

2. *To bone the pigeon:* Cut off both legs from the pigeon and, keeping the drumstick and thigh in one piece, carefully remove just the thighbone. Cutting along the breastbone, remove both breasts and keep the wing bones attached. Cut off the wing at the elbow and discard. Be sure to save the carcass for the stock.

PREPARING THE PIGEON/LOBSTER STOCK

This is a double stock, specifically perfumed with pigeon and lobster, yet based on the standard veal stock.

3. Cut the pigeon carcass into small pieces using a large chef's knife or cleaver. Pull the head off the lobster; save the claws and tail for later. Rinse the head under cold running water to clean out the tomalley—the green liver (a delicacy to some, but unfortunately it will discolor your stock). Cut the lobster head into small pieces.

4. Peel the carrot and dice it—along with the onion, celery, and mushrooms—into a *mirepoix*—a finely chopped medley of vegetables used to flavor stocks and sauces.

5. Put 1 tablespoon cooking oil and ½ tablespoon of the butter in a large sauce-

pan and heat until the butter begins to brown. Add the chopped pigeon bones and sauté over moderate heat until golden brown. Add the *mirepoix* and continue to sauté until the vegetables are tender. Add the chopped lobster head and sauté for 1 minute more.

6. Deglaze with the red wine, then add 1 cup water and the veal stock. Bring to a boil, reduce the heat, and simmer slowly for 1 hour. Strain the stock and reserve.

COOKING AND SERVING

7. Preheat the oven to 450°F.

8. Mince the shallot. Put ½ tablespoon of the remaining butter in a small saucepan. Add the shallot and sweat until tender. Add the pigeon-lobster stock and the tarragon leaves and reduce over moderate heat until the sauce just begins to thicken. Verify the seasoning—the lobster head will probably have supplied enough salt. Swirl in the remaining tablespoon of butter. Reserve and keep warm.

9. Crack the lobster claws and knuckles and remove the meat, keeping each piece intact, if possible. Using a large chef's knife, cut the tail in half lengthwise. Arrange the lobster meat on a small buttered baking sheet or aluminum foil pan.

10. Heat ⅛ inch oil in a small ovenproof sauté pan. Season the pigeon legs and breasts with salt and pepper. When the oil is hot, brown the meat on both sides. Place the pan in the oven to roast. The legs should be done in about 2 minutes, the breasts in about 4.

11. Allow the pigeon meat to rest for a few minutes and heat the lobster in the oven for 2 or 3 minutes.

12. Slice the lobster tail and the pigeon into 5 slices each. Place 2 lobster knuckles in the center of each of 2 warm plates. Arrange a lobster claw grasping a pigeon leg at the top of each plate and fan alternating slices of pigeon and lobster in an arc at the bottom of the plate. Nap with the sauce and serve.

Pasta

Pasta

Pasta as part of every good cook's repertoire is a recent culinary phenomenon and is now a major part of the culinary revolution—which I heartily endorse. I could eat pasta every day; it's hard to imagine life before pasta.

Among the endless combination of choices—fresh or dried, rolled or extruded, store-bought or homemade, and a million shapes to boot—my preference is most definitely fresh rolled egg noodles.

The traditional Italian wisdom has it that the best pasta is made with all durum semolina flour. I find that a blend of just one-third semolina and two-thirds all-purpose flour makes pasta with great texture—that firm bite—without making it heavy. Remember, though, that great texture requires some elbow grease as well—it's the vigorous kneading that develops the gluten in the dough.

2 cups all-purpose flour

I cup semolina flour

3 eggs

I tablespoon olive oil

I teaspoon salt

MAKING THE DOUGH (BEST TO DO 2 TO 24 HOURS BEFORE ROLLING AND CUTTING)

1. Combine both flours, the eggs, oil, and salt in a food processor. Mix thoroughly until crumbly. (It will be too dry to make a ball.) Empty onto a floured work surface and sprinkle with 2 tablespoons water. Knead the dough with the heel of your hand for a couple of minutes to develop the gluten and make a smooth but very tough ball of dough. Add another teaspoon of water, if needed to bring the dough together.

2. Wrap the ball tightly in plastic wrap and refrigerate until ready to use, but for no more than 2 days.

ROLLING AND CUTTING THE PASTA

3. Dust your work surface with flour and set up your pasta machine.

4. Form the dough into a long sausage shape about 2 inches in diameter. Flatten it with the heel of your hand and roll it through the machine at the thickest setting.

5. Fold the ragged edges in toward the center and roll through the machine again at the same setting. Repeat 2 or 3 times until you have a thick ribbon with fairly smooth edges.

6. Now start to decrease the setting on the machine each time the pasta goes through until you've reached the desired thinness. Don't forget to dust the ribbon with a little flour each time too.

7. Feed the dough through the desired cutting roller and cut the pasta every 18 inches or so. As you cut each batch, dust it with flour again and heap loosely to make 8 portions. This is best used just after rolling and cutting. You can keep it fresh for a day in the refrigerator on a tray covered with a barely moist towel.

Fettuccini with Diced Tuna, Capers, and Cracked Pepper

SERVES 4

This recipe is a shining example of how far we've come since plain spaghetti and red sauce. Today pasta without the traditional sauce doesn't raise an eyebrow. What I love about this dish is the great flavor you get from the garlic, pepper, and tuna with good olive oil. Almost as quick to turn out as a can of Spaghetti-O's, it is the closest thing in this book to fast food. And it is deliciously versatile: Use diced mushrooms, shrimp, or scallops if you can't get great tuna—it's hard to go wrong.

1 pound very fresh tuna

4 large tomatoes (a heaping cupful when diced)

8 cloves garlic

12 large Kalamata olives

12 fresh basil leaves, chopped

1 tablespoon cracked black pepper

4 tablespoons capers

Salt

⅔ cup extra-virgin olive oil

½ recipe Pasta, cut into fettuccine (page 157), or 8 ounces dried

MISE EN PLACE

1. Cut off the skin and any dark meat from the tuna, then cut into ½-inch dice.
2. Peel, seed, and dice the tomatoes. Chop the garlic. Pit the olives and cut into slivers. Chop the basil. Crush the black peppercorns.
3. Combine the tuna, tomatoes, garlic, olives, basil, pepper, and capers in a mixing bowl. Season with salt. Reserve.

COOKING AND SERVING

4. Put a large pot of generously salted water on to boil.
5. When the water is boiling, heat the olive oil in a large sauté pan.
6. Start cooking the pasta, and at the same time, start sautéing the tuna mixture in the hot olive oil. Both will need to cook for about 1½ minutes. If using dried pasta—which takes longer to cook—wait and sauté the tuna mixture when the pasta is almost done.
7. Drain the pasta and immediately toss everything together in the sauté pan. Divide among 4 warm pasta bowls and serve.

Dividing and Serving Pasta

Chefs use tongs to first lift out each portion of pasta, holding it, letting loose ingredients fall back into the pan, and then place it in the bowl. After all portions of pasta are divided, go back and top each one equally with the remaining sauce and ingredients.

Angel Hair Fisherman's Style

SERVES 4

This is my version of a traditional seafood pasta I eat regularly and never get tired of. It's extremely versatile. Because a fisherman's catch is always a little different, I don't ever make it exactly the same way twice. If they are in season, top this with freshly sautéed soft-shell crab. It's also delicious made with lobster. And as some of my customers request, you can always leave the mussels out. But never never put Parmesan or Romano cheese on top of a seafood pasta. It covers up the nice oceany flavors.

2 tomatoes

1 medium onion

6 mushrooms

1 clove garlic

2 dozen mussels

Salt

¼ cup extra-virgin olive oil

8 shrimp, peeled and deveined

½ pound sea scallops

2 cups Lobster Fumet (page 29)

½ cup heavy cream

Freshly ground white pepper

½ recipe Pasta, cut to the finest width (page 157), or 8 ounches dried capellini

12 leaves fresh sweet basil

MISE EN PLACE

1. Put a large pot of generously salted water on to boil.

2. Peel the tomatoes, discard the juice and seeds, and dice the remaining meat. Peel and dice the onion. Clean and slice the mushrooms. Finely chop the garlic.

3. Wash and remove the beards from the mussels, discarding any that are already open. Place the mussels with ½ cup water in a small saucepan with a tight-fitting lid and steam them open. This should only take about 5 minutes. Do not overcook them. Turn off the heat and let them get cool enough to handle, and then pull the meat out of the shells. Save the broth.

PREPARE THE DISH

4. Heat the olive oil in a saucepan over moderate heat, add the diced onion, and stir-fry until tender but not yet colored. Add the shrimp, scallops, and sliced mushrooms and cook with the onion until it just begins to turn golden brown. Add the diced tomato, lobster fumet, and cream. Season with a few turns of fresh ground white pepper and cook 5 or 6 minutes, until reduced by about a third. Add the mussels and a few tablespoons of the mussel broth to taste. Verify the seasoning (the broth should supply enough salt) and reserve.

5. Cook the pasta in the boiling salted water for about 1½ minutes, or until tender. Reheat the sauce if necessary. Then and only then, julienne the fresh basil. Drain the cooked pasta, toss with the seafood sauce, and divide evenly among 4 warm pasta plates. Sprinkle with basil and serve.

Pasta
■
159

Angel Hair Pasta with Roasted Peppers and Porcinis

SERVES 4
AS A FIRST COURSE

The porcini (little pig) is the great mushroom of Italy. Fortunately, it is native to the United States also. Young, small specimens are what the French know as cèpes, but it's the larger, fully opened, mature mushrooms that the Italians love, and justly so. Though they have a slippery cap with a thick black spore mass underneath when mature, they more than make up in rich flavor what they lose in appearance. (The French and Italians can't believe these are the same mushrooms—both are *boletus edulis.*)

This is a great combo—crème fraîche and red bell pepper purée—and there is no better way to top it than with porcinis. But if porcini or another great mushroom isn't available, it's still hard to go wrong. Another favorite combination is crumbled goat cheese and broccoli florets added to the red bell pepper cream.

2 large red bell peppers

2 large red, ripe tomatoes

2 large porcinis (2 cups when diced)

3 cloves garlic

1 bunch fresh sweet basil

Salt

¼ cup extra-virgin olive oil

Freshly ground white pepper

⅔ cup crème fraîche (page 55)

½ recipe Pasta, cut to the finest width (page 157), or 8 ounces dried capellini

MISE EN PLACE

1. Roast the red bell peppers over an open flame until charred. Rinse away the skin, then remove the stems, cores, and seeds. Purée in a blender and reserve.

2. Peel and seed the tomatoes and cut them into ½-inch dice. Rinse and cut the porcinis into ½-inch dice. Finely chop the garlic and julienne the basil leaves.

COOKING AND SERVING

3. Put a large pot of generously salted water on to boil.

4. Heat the olive oil in a sauté pan, add the porcinis, and cook until light golden brown. Add the tomatoes and garlic, season with salt and white pepper, and toss over moderate heat for 30 seconds. Keep warm.

5. In a large stainless-steel mixing bowl, combine the crème fraîche and red pepper purée; thin with ¼ cup water (see Note). Season with salt and pepper and heat over the boiling pasta water. Keep warm.

6. Cook the pasta until done. Drain and toss immediately in the bowl with the red pepper cream. Divide among 4 warm pasta bowls and top each with a large spoonful of the porcini mixture. Garnish with the basil and serve.

Note With practice you will learn to make pasta sauces seemingly too thin, because when added to freshly cooked pasta, the pasta itself will absorb water from the sauce and tend to thicken it.

Fettuccine with Fresh Tomato and Two Cheeses

SERVES 4

This no-cream-or-butter recipe grew out of a tomato sauce I serve to my staff. It's a simple sauce made right, the real key being good, fresh vine-ripened tomatoes and good olive oil. Try it anywhere you need tomato sauce, or spread it on a Boboli, sprinkle with garlic salt, cheese, and basil, and pop it in the oven for 5 minutes for a great snack.

10 red, ripe tomatoes

¼ onion

½ red bell pepper

8 good black olives, pitted

5 cloves garlic

6 tablespoons olive oil

Salt and freshly ground pepper

¾ cup diced fresh mozzarella (about 4 ounces)

½ cup freshly grated Italian Parmesan cheese (about 1 ounce)

12 fresh basil leaves

½ recipe Pasta, cut into fettuccine (page 157), or 8 ounces dried

MAKING THE SAUCE

The sauce can be made ahead of time, even a day or two before.

1. Purée and strain 8 of the tomatoes. Peel, seed, and dice the remaining 2.

2. Finely dice the onion and red bell pepper. Finely chop the olives and garlic.

3. Cook the onion and bell pepper in a saucepan over moderate heat in the olive oil. Just as they begin to brown, add the tomato purée, garlic, and olives. Simmer for 10 minutes or so, stirring from time to time, until the sauce has thickened. Add the diced tomatoes, season with salt and pepper, and simmer briefly. Verify the seasoning and reserve.

COOKING AND SERVING

4. Put a large pot of generously salted water on to boil. Dice the mozzarella into ¼-inch cubes. Grate the Parmesan.

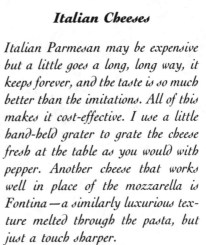

Italian Cheeses

Italian Parmesan may be expensive but a little goes a long, long way, it keeps forever, and the taste is so much better than the imitations. All of this makes it cost-effective. I use a little hand-held grater to grate the cheese fresh at the table as you would with pepper. Another cheese that works well in place of the mozzarella is Fontina—a similarly luxurious texture melted through the pasta, but just a touch sharper.

5. Add the fettuccine to the boiling water and while it is cooking, julienne the basil. Heat the sauce.

6. When the pasta is al dente, add it

to the sauce, sprinkle with about a third of the mozzarella, and toss together, gradually adding the rest of the mozzarella. Immediately divide it among 4 warm pasta bowls. Sprinkle with the basil and Parmesan and serve.

Note It is best not to store tomatoes in the refrigerator, for once chilled they forever lose some of their flavor.

Seafood Ravioli

S E R V E S 8

This is a good example of how French cuisine can borrow an idea from another culture and make it its own. We all know ravioli are Italian, but with the very light, thin pasta, the scallop, sole, and lobster filling, and a velvety lobster cream sauce, this dish is unmistakably French at heart. Be warned, however: Each ravioli contains substantially more filling than a standard ravioli. It's such a rich dish that I recommend serving only 2 plump ravioli as an appetizer, 3 or 4 as a main dish. And while it's a 2-hour recipe from start to finish, don't be daunted by the complexity—it's one of the most rewarding in the book.

FILLING

All the lobster meat from the tail, claws, and knuckles of 1 large lobster (2 to 2½ pounds) or from 2 smaller ones

Salt

2 ounces fresh sole fillet

6 ounces fresh scallops

Freshly ground white pepper

1 egg

1 cup heavy cream

¼ medium onion

½ stalk celery

½ carrot, peeled

2 tablespoons cooking oil

Head, legs, and all shell from 1 large
lobster (2 to 2½ pounds) or from 2
smaller ones

¼ cup Cognac

⅔ cup dry white wine

1 tablespoon tomato paste

1⅔ cups heavy cream

2 tablespoons unsalted butter

1 recipe Pasta dough (page 157),
formed into a ball and wrapped tightly
in plastic

1 egg for egg wash

MAKING THE FILLING

1. *To cook the lobster* (this will take 30 minutes all together, and the lobster can then be refrigerated overnight): Plunge the live lobster into a large pot of boiling salted water. Cook for 16 minutes, or less if using 2 small lobsters. Remove and let cool.

2. While the lobster is cooling, cut the sole into ½-inch cubes and mix in a food processor with the scallops, 2 good pinches of salt, and a few grinds of white pepper to taste for about 1 minute. Add the egg and process 30 seconds more. Refrigerate, leaving the mixture in the bowl with the blade and top intact, for 20 to 30 minutes.

3. While this is chilling, remove the lobster meat from the tail, claws, and knuckles, saving the head and legs for the sauce. Cut 8 thin, pretty round slices crosswise from the tail and save for garnish. Dice the remainder of the lobster meat. Reserve.

4. Put the chilled processor bowl back on the machine, add 1 cup cream to the seafood mixture, and process about 30 seconds. Fold in the diced lobster meat. Reserve.

MAKING THE SAUCE

5. Dice the onion, celery, and carrot. Sweat in a cast-iron pot with 2 tablespoons oil over moderate heat until the vegetables just begin to color.

6. Add the shells of the lobster heads and stir-fry for approximately 1½ minutes. Add the Cognac and flambé—the flame will go out by itself once the alcohol is consumed.

7. Deglaze with the white wine. Add the tomato paste and 4 cups water. Bring to a boil, then simmer for 30 minutes or until the liquid is reduced by half.

8. Strain this broth through a fine strainer and discard all the pieces of shell. Add the 1⅔ cups cream and reduce again by half until slightly thickened, about 10 minutes. Swirl in the butter and check the salt seasoning. Reserve in a warm place until ready to serve.

ASSEMBLY AND SERVING (START WHILE THE SAUCE IS REDUCING)

9. Put a large pot of generously salted water on to boil—use a good tablespoon of salt.

10. Shape your pasta dough into 2 long thin sausages, flatten them, and roll each one through the pasta machine into very thin strips (the next-to-last setting on most machines), 4 to 5 inches wide and 3 to 4 feet long.

11. Brush one of the strips with egg wash. On this strip, place heaping tablespoons of the seafood filling at even intervals down the center of the strip, leaving 1½ inches between mounds. Cover with the other strip of pasta. Press the strips together around the filling to seal thoroughly on all sides. Using a round cookie cutter (or a sharp-edged glass or espresso cup), cut the ravioli free. You should end up with about 24 pieces.

12. Make sure the sauce is ready (reheat gently if necessary). Plunge the ravioli—in a wire basket—into the boiling water; cook for 4 minutes. Carefully remove the ravioli and blot on a paper towel. Divide the ravioli among 8 warm pasta bowls. Nap with the sauce and garnish each plate with a lobster slice. Serve. Die.

Variations Pacific lobster, blue or Dungeness crab, shrimp, or live crayfish may be substituted for the lobster. Handle the meat and shells just as described here.

If you have some on hand, you may substitute 2 cups Lobster Fumet (page 29) for the sauce—just reduce with 1⅔ cups heavy cream until it's a nice creamy consistency.

Making ravioli.

Tortellini with Foie Gras and Truffles

MAKES 2 DOZEN;
SERVES 6 AS AN
APPETIZER

In jest I refer to this as my simple little peasant pasta from Bel Air. It is hard to go wrong when you stuff a tortellini with foie gras and truffles—a wonderfully unique filing, richer than sin, and another great example of French cuisine cannibalizing other cuisines for its greater glory. This dish involves a bit of work, but it's very impressive. You can do everything ahead of time, leaving only the pasta to be cooked at the last minute.

FILLING

1 onion

1 tablespoon unsalted butter

Salt

1/3 pound fresh duck foie gras

Freshly ground white pepper

1 fresh black truffle (about 1 ounce)

SAUCE

1 leek

1 shallot

1 tablespoon unsalted butter

1/4 cup vintage port

1 1/2 cups Veal Stock (page 109)

1/2 cup heavy cream

1 tablespoon finely julienned black truffle (left over from filling)

1 recipe Pasta dough (page 157), formed into a ball and wrapped tightly in plastic

1 egg for egg wash

PREPARING THE FILLING

1. Cut the onion into pretty 1/4-inch dice. Cook with the butter in a sauté pan over moderate heat, stirring from time to time, until it turns a rich golden brown—almost candied. Season with salt and reserve.

2. Cut the foie gras into 24 small pieces. Season lightly with salt and white pepper. Finely julienne the truffle. Reserve.

MAKING THE SAUCE

3. Cut the white of the leek into 1/4-inch-wide ribbons. Finely mince the shallot. Sweat the leek and shallot in a saucepan with the butter until soft and barely brown. Deglaze with the port, add the veal stock and cream, and simmer until reduced and slightly thickened. Season with salt and white pepper.

4. Add 1 tablespoon truffle julienne to the sauce. Save the rest for the filling. Reserve the sauce to allow the flavor to develop.

ASSEMBLY AND SERVING

5. Put a large pot of generously salted water on to boil.

6. Using a pasta machine, roll the dough as thin as possible into 2 long strips, each at least 42 inches long. Dust with flour and cut into 2 dozen 3½-inch squares.

7. In the center of each square, place a dab of candied onion, a piece of foie gras, and a little sprinkle of truffle julienne. Brush the edges of each square with egg wash and fold diagonally into a triangular pouch. Crimp and seal the edges tightly, squeezing out excess air. (A standard tortellini would be folded again, but it isn't practical with a good chunk of foie gras inside.)

8. Using a wire basket (for this is a fragile pasta), cook the tortellini for 4 minutes in the boiling salted water.

9. In the meantime, reheat the sauce and verify the seasoning. You should be able to taste the truffle in the sauce by now.

10. Divide the tortellini evenly among warm pasta bowls. Nap with the sauce and serve.

Angel Hair with Soft-Shell Crabs and Pesto

S E R V E S   4

As traditionally served, pesto is too dry for my taste. But the following technique, using lots of water and butter, produces a wonderfully strong sauce with a smooth, fluid consistency.

Good as pesto may be on its own, there is no better way to eat a plate of pesto than topped with a freshly sautéed soft-shell crab. The crunchy, briny crab brings out all the glory of pesto. It's a rare perfect combination, just one of those marriages that work.

The two most eagerly awaited short seasons of magical ingredients—in my universe anyway—are the truffle season and the soft-shell crab season. With soft-shell crabs, available in the spring and early summer, you eat the legs, shell, and everything. This dish is such a favorite among my clientele that we have a list of people we are instructed to call when it appears on the menu.

One of the world's rare delicacies, soft-shell crab is one hundred percent American—invented in the Chesapeake Bay. Apologies to the Academie Française, I even coined a French name for the soft-shell crab: "crabe mange-tout."

3 cups sweet basil leaves, loosely packed (about 3 bunches)

10 cloves garlic, peeled

12 walnut halves

⅓ cup extra-virgin olive oil

6 tablespoons grated Parmesan cheese

Salt

4 live soft-shell crabs

6 tablespoons unsalted butter

½ recipe Pasta, cut to the finest width (page 157), or 8 ounces dried capillini

---

1. Using a food processor, process the basil leaves, the peeled garlic, and the walnuts until very finely chopped. With the blade turning, add the oil in a thread and then the Parmesan. Season with salt and reserve.

2. Put a large pot of salted water on to boil to cook the pasta.

3. *To clean the crabs:* (do this at the last minute just before cooking.) Turn the crabs upside down. Using scissors, snip away the mouth and the tail flap. Turn the crabs back over, lift each edge of the shell to expose the gills, and cut them away.

4. Heat 4 tablespoons of butter in a large sauté pan. When the butter begins to brown, cook the cleaned crabs over high heat for 2 or 3 minutes on each side.

5. Put the pesto in a large stainless steel mixing bowl with the remaining 2 tablespoons of butter and ½ cup water. Warm the pesto over the pot of boiling water. Verify the seasoning.

6. Cook the pasta in the boiling salted water for about 1½ minutes or until tender. Drain and toss immediately in the bowl with the warm pesto. Divide the pasta evenly among 4 warm pasta bowls. Top each portion with a freshly sautéed crab and serve.

Pesto Tips

Use pesto on pasta hot or cold. Stir little bits into salads. Spread it on toast. Make a great sandwich with pesto, prosciutto, and sun-dried tomatoes.

If you have to keep your basil for a while before making pesto, you'll be amazed how much longer it stays fresh and sharp when refrigerated in a tightly sealed zip-seal bag.

If you have forever to make pesto, by all means use a mortar and pestle—the so-called "purist's" way. I don't recommend it. There's nothing to be gained for the extra time it takes. A food processor is my tool of choice.

Fettuccine with Egg and Fresh Truffle

SERVES 4

It's rare that I have a plate sent back to my kitchen, but one of the first times this went on my menu back in the early eighties was a moment I still cherish. A woman ordered the pasta special, with egg and fresh truffle. No sooner had we sent it out than the waiter brought it back: "She wants the pasta without the noodles." Hmmm . . . really? What to do? I ended up making her a truffle omelet. To the rest of my clientele, however, this recipe is a perennial favorite. The egg and the truffle have a special relationship that never ceases to amaze me. Every year when truffles come into season, I marvel at the way the egg absorbs their flavor. The best way to experience this miracle of nature is to store whole eggs in a jar with truffles overnight, then cook a few for breakfast—without adding the truffles. It's a revelation—the inspiration for this recipe.

4 eggs

1 fresh black truffle (¾ to 1 ounce)—look for a firm, fragrant tuber

Salt

12 tablespoons (1½ sticks) unsalted butter

½ recipe Pasta, cut into fettuccine (page 157), or 8 ounces dried

MISE EN PLACE

1. Carefully pack the eggs and the truffle into a jar, seal tightly, and refrigerate 24 hours or more.

COOKING AND SERVING

2. Put a large pot of generously salted water on to boil. Put the butter in a large mixing bowl and let it melt over the pot of boiling water.

3. Off the heat, whisk the eggs into the melted butter and add 4 pinches of salt. Gently grate about ¾ of the truffle into the eggs, saving the rest to garnish the top.

4. Cook the fettuccine in the boiling salted water until done. Drain and toss with the egg mixture. Divide among 4 warm pasta bowls and grate the remaining truffle on top. Serve.

Desserts

Brillat-Savarin with Truffles

SERVES 8 TO 12

This is one of the reasons I look forward to fresh truffles every winter. It puts the truffle at center stage, allowing it to exercise its sensuous, earthy pull to the absolute fullest. I first made this for Baron Philippe de Rothschild's Best-of-Ten-Decades Dinner in 1981. It was a $650-per-person meal celebrating a century of Mouton Rothschild, considered by oenophiles to be the best of the five "first growths" in Bordeaux. The baron chose the best vintage from each decade and sent four bottles of each from his personal cellar at Mouton—and of course sent along a special, temperature-controlled wine safe in which to rest the wines until serving. The fifth and final flight of wines, an 1888 and an 1899 Mouton Rothschild, accompanied the truffled cheese.

Though I've experimented with a number of cheeses, none works so well with truffles as a very fresh Brillat-Savarin. Its combination of rich texture and mildness enhances the truffle flavor. Don't use an overripe Brillat-Savarin or any stronger cheese, because the acidity will tend to bury the truffle flavor.

---

1 fresh truffle (canned truffle will not
work)

1 Brillat-Savarin

---

1. Chop the truffle exceedingly fine—it should be almost powdery.

2. Unwrap the Brillat-Savarin. Save the wrapping. Using a cheese wire, cut the cheese into three ½-inch-thick layers. Cover the bottom layer with half the chopped truffle. Top with the middle layer and cover it with the rest of the chopped truffle. Place the top layer back on the cheese, press together gently, and rewrap tightly in the original plastic film.

3. Refrigerate 2 to 3 days before serving. Allow to warm almost to room temperature and serve.

Note There is no finer companion for this ultimate cheese than the ultimate pear, the Royal Riviera, which fortunately shares the same season as the fresh truffle.

Gratin of Apricots with Amaretto

SERVES 4

Almonds and apricots are one of the best flavor combinations around. I first tasted the two together in one of Madame Vaulot's incredible crêpes in Yvoire. Last summer when we had some good fresh apricots in season, it occurred to me that amaretto, made from almonds, would be a natural liqueur to use with them. On the first day we made an amaretto sabayon and popped it under the broiler, and it was good. On the second day we added a sprinkling of brown sugar for a crème brûlée effect, and it was lordly.

16 fresh ripe apricots

2 tablespoons unsalted butter

2 tablespoons granulated sugar

SABAYON

4 egg yolks

1 tablespoon honey

Juice of 1 orange, strained

3 tablespoons amaretto

⅓ cup crème fraîche (page 55) or sour cream

2 tablespoons brown sugar

Special Equipment 4 individual gratin dishes

SAUTÉING THE APRICOTS

1. Break the apricots in half and discard the pits.

2. Melt the butter in a sauté pan over moderate heat. Add the apricots and gently sauté 2 or 3 minutes until they have softened and exuded their juice. Add the granulated sugar and continue to cook until dissolved.

3. Pour off the juice and save for the sabayon. Arrange 8 apricot halves in each of 4 gratin dishes or ovenproof soup plates. Reserve.

MAKING THE SABAYON

4. Preheat the broiler.

5. In a large stainless-steel mixing bowl, place the egg yolks, honey, orange juice, amaretto, and apricot juice. Bring an inch or two of water to a simmer in a small saucepan and nest the stainless-steel bowl atop it, making a bain-marie. Vigorously whisk the mixture until you have a fluffy egg sauce, very hot to the touch and holding a peak like whipped cream or meringue. Watch it closely and whisk constantly: If you cook it too fast or too long you will scramble the eggs and have to start over.

6. Remove the sabayon from the heat and stir in the crème fraîche. The sauce will fall somewhat, but don't worry, it's supposed to.

7. Pour the sauce around the apricots, sprinkle with brown sugar, and cook under the broiler until golden brown. Be attentive—it should take only about a minute. Serve.

Gratin of Raspberries with Grand Marnier

SERVES 4

This is an irresistible sauce—a sabayon made with fresh orange juice, honey, and Grand Marnier and served hot over fresh raspberries or strawberries. It's the simplest of desserts in the making but results in a delightful complexity of textures and temperatures. Whip up the frothy sabayon before dinner and glaze it under the broiler at the last minute.

2 half-pint baskets raspberries

2 egg yolks

1 tablespoon honey

Juice of 1 orange, strained

2 tablespoons Grand Marnier

¼ cup crème fraîche (page 55) or sour cream

Special Equipment 4 ovenproof dessert plates or individual gratin dishes

1. Preheat the broiler (see box at right).

2. Arrange the raspberries in the center of the ovenproof dessert plates.

3. Place the egg yolks, honey, orange juice, and Grand Marnier in a large stainless-steel mixing bowl.

4. Bring an inch or two of water to a simmer in a small saucepan and rest the stainless-steel bowl atop it. Whisk the mixture continuously until you have a fluffy egg sauce, very hot to the touch, that holds a peak like whipped cream or meringue—a sabayon. But be careful—if you cook it too fast or too long you will scramble the eggs.

5. Remove the sabayon from the heat and stir in the crème fraîche. The sauce will fall somewhat, but don't worry, it's supposed to.

6. Spoon the sabayon over the raspberries and cook under the broiler until golden brown. Again, pay attention: It will take only about a minute. Serve.

On Broilers

An electric oven is preferable to gas in this one rare instance because an electric broiler radiates much more intense downward heat than gas flames. Unless, that is, you have a gas salamander—a professional gas broiler fitted with special heat-retaining and -radiating bricks above the gas element.

Pistachio Custard with Vanilla and Strawberry Sauce

SERVES 4

This is a stylish improvement on the classic crème caramel—a rich, smooth pistachio custard with chopped green pistachios mounded on top and pretty vanilla and strawberry sauces underneath. It's sophisticated-looking but in fact a simple dessert: The custard is straightforward and both sauces are easy. So is the professional-looking marbled pattern in the sauces—done with the point of a knife.

CUSTARD

¼ cup peeled pistachios (unsalted)

2 cups half-and-half

4 eggs

¾ cup sugar

STRAWBERRY SAUCE

½ pint strawberries

6 tablespoons sugar

Juice of ¼ lemon

VANILLA SAUCE (CRÈME ANGLAISE)

1 cup milk

1 vanilla bean or 2 drops good vanilla extract

4 egg yolks

⅓ cup sugar

Special Equipment 4 individual ramekins (5 fluid ounces each)

Plastic squeeze bottle or narrow-lipped pitcher

MAKING THE CUSTARD

1. Preheat the oven to 350°F. Put 2 quarts water on to boil for a bain-marie. Chill 4 dessert plates.

2. Chop the pistachios as fine as possible—use the food processor. Add the nuts to the half-and-half in a small saucepan and bring to a boil.

3. In the meantime, beat the eggs and sugar together in a mixing bowl. When the half-and-half comes to a boil, stir it into the egg mixture.

4. Pour the custard mixture through a fine strainer, separating out the nuts. Rinse the nuts under lots of cold water and save for garnish. Pour the custard into the ramekins.

BAKING THE CUSTARD

5. Place the ramekins in a baking pan and make a bain-marie by pouring the boiling water in the pan around them 1 inch deep (see box on facing page). Slide the

pan into the oven, taking care not to splash water into the custard. Bake 20 to 25 minutes or just until a knife inserted shows clean. Don't overcook this and don't let the water in the bain-marie boil, just simmer. Remove the ramekins from the water and chill for 4 hours.

MAKING THE STRAWBERRY SAUCE

6. Rinse and hull the strawberries. Purée them in a blender with the sugar and lemon juice. Strain and reserve in a plastic squeeze bottle, if available, or in a narrow-lipped sauceboat or pitcher.

MAKING THE CRÈME ANGLAISE

7. Prepare an ice bath.
8. Bring the milk to a boil with the vanilla bean, if using. In a mixing bowl, whisk together the egg yolks and sugar. Add the boiled milk, mix thoroughly, and pour back into the same saucepan if it's not scorched.
9. Cook over medium heat, stirring constantly with a wooden spoon, until the sauce begins to thicken slightly, coating the back of the spoon. Do not let it boil. Add the vanilla extract, if using. Strain the crème anglaise and chill it immediately over the ice bath to stop the cooking. (Rinse and save the vanilla bean for another time.)

SERVING

10. Mirror the chilled dessert plates with crème anglaise. Using the squeeze bottle or pitcher, decorate the surface with the strawberry sauce in a pattern of your choice and marble it by running the point of a knife through the pattern in a symmetrical fashion.

11. Unmold each custard in the center of a plate. Garnish each with a spoonful of chopped pistachios and serve.

The Bain-Marie

A bain-marie can be either a double boiler or a water bath. When you're melting chocolate over a pot of boiling water, your bain-marie is really a double boiler. However, in this recipe the bain-marie is a water bath to ensure even and gentle cooking of the custard.

The easiest way of handling this very spillable sort of bain-marie is to: (1) Preheat the oven. (2) Place the ramekins in an empty baking pan. (3) Pull the middle oven rack partway out. (4) Place the baking pan on the rack. (5) Pour the boiling water into the pan around the ramekins, removing one dish if necessary to facilitate pouring. (6) Slide the rack gently back into the oven.

Persimmon Pudding

This is an old family recipe from southern California, dating from my mother's childhood in the San Gabriel Valley in the 1930s. The dish was a specialty at a roadside restaurant on the way to a family cabin on Mt. Baldy. My grandmother's sister-in-law asked for the recipe, her husband planted a persimmon tree in their back yard, and today I use persimmons from that very tree in my persimmon pudding at La Toque. I'd gladly credit that restaurant but nobody alive remembers the name.

1 cup persimmon pulp (about 2 or 3 persimmons)

1 cup granulated sugar

1 cup flour

2 teaspoons baking soda

½ teaspoon cinnamon

Pinch of salt

1 cup raisins

½ cup chopped pecans

½ cup chopped walnuts

1 teaspoon vanilla extract

1 teaspoon fresh lemon juice

½ cup milk

¼ cup melted unsalted butter

Ken Frank's
La Toque
Cookbook

■

176

HARD SAUCE

1 pound unsalted butter, softened

1 pound powdered sugar

Juice and finely chopped zest of 2 lemons

Shot of Cognac (optional)

MAKING THE PUDDING

1. Purée the persimmons in a blender. Strain the purée to remove any pieces of skin and measure 1 cup strained pulp.

2. In a large mixing bowl, mix together all ingredients except the persimmon pulp, milk, and butter. Then stir in the persimmon pulp and the milk, and finally the melted butter.

3. Preheat the oven to 350°F. Boil water to use in your bain-marie.

4. Line the bottoms of two 2-quart loaf pans with waxed paper or parchment paper. Brush the pans and paper generously with melted butter. Fill each pan half full with batter. Cover the top of each pan with aluminum foil and crimp tightly. Place the pans in a large baking pan, add 1 inch boiling water, and bake for 2 hours. Remove the pans from the water and allow to cool to room temperature. When cool, wrap tightly with plastic wrap and store in the refrigerator until ready to serve.

MAKING THE HARD SAUCE

5. Cream together the butter, powdered sugar, lemon juice, and zest until

smooth. Although my grandparents were teetotalers, I think a touch of Cognac greatly improves the flavor, especially when the pudding is served warm.

6. The pudding is best sliced, then slightly warmed in the oven and served with hard sauce or freshly turned ice cream. However, it keeps virtually forever and makes a terrific snack straight out of the refrigerator with hard sauce.

Chocolate Pots au Crème

S E R V E S   6

The *pot au crème* has enjoyed renewed popularity in the last decade, part of a trend, I think, toward simple, fine desserts. It's basically a mousse in a cup, rich and chocolaty. It's not fancy—no sauces or chocolate fans or exotic hoopla—and it's easy to make. Prepare it way ahead of time and pop it into the refrigerator.

2 cups heavy cream

7 ounces bittersweet chocolate

4 egg yolks

¼ cup honey

¼ cup strong freshly brewed espresso

⅓ cup crème fraîche (page 55)

Sprinkle of unsweetened cocoa powder

1. Whip the cream until it holds a soft peak. Reserve in the refrigerator.
2. Melt the chocolate in the top of a double boiler. Reserve in a warm place.
3. Put the egg yolks, honey, and espresso in a stainless-steel mixing bowl. While whisking vigorously, cook over simmering water until the eggs hold a firm peak and are very warm but not hot to the touch.
4. Fold the melted chocolate into the egg mixture and allow to cool to room

temperature. Then fold in the chilled whipped cream.

5. Pour the mousse into 6 parfait glasses or ceramic chocolate pots. Chill in the refrigerator at least 2 hours or until ready to serve.

6. When ready to serve, whip the crème fraîche until it holds a soft peak. Spoon atop the mousse and sprinkle with a little cocoa. Serve.

Three Fruit Sorbets Strawberry, Lime Mint, Pear

Although all sorbets are easy to make and are all made from just fruit and sugar, fruits with a lot of pulp—berries, pears, pineapple—call for a very different technique from that used for fruits with little pulp but very concentrated juices, like lemons, limes, passion fruit, and black currants. Here are three basic kinds of fruit sorbet: one using raw fruit, one using cooked fruit, and one using fruit juice and syrup. These three flavors—inspired by the very pure, intense fruit sorbets I remember buying as a kid along the lake in Geneva—happen to play off each other very well, making an excellent three-in-one dessert. (Any more than three or four on the same plate, however, results in the loss of distinct flavors—ending up with "mud sorbet.")

Strawberry Sorbet

S E R V E S   8

This is the most common sorbet technique. It can be used with almost any raw, fresh fruit. Depending on the natural flavor and sweetness of the fruit, you'll vary the amount of sugar.

4 baskets (pints) strawberries

2 cups sugar

Juice of 1 lemon (or slightly more to taste)

Special Equipment Ice cream machine

1. Rinse, hull, and quarter the strawberries, then purée them with the sugar in a food processor. Strain through a fine strainer. Season with the lemon juice: The lemon should point up the strawberry flavor and balance the sweetness of the sugar.

2. Freeze in an ice cream machine until set. Reserve in the freezer or serve immediately.

Lime Mint Sorbet

SERVES 8

This is a syrup-based sorbet flavored with lime juice and mint—both strong flavors, but no body. The syrup will provide the body of the sorbet.

1¼ cups sugar

1 bunch fresh mint

8 limes

¼ cup light corn syrup

Special Equipment Ice cream machine

1. Dissolve the sugar in 4 cups water in a saucepan. Bring to a boil over high heat.

2. In the meantime, pluck the mint leaves from their stems and coarsely chop. Once the syrup has come to a boil, remove it from the heat, add the mint leaves, and allow to steep 15 to 20 minutes as the syrup cools. Strain the leaves out through a fine strainer.

3. While the mint is steeping, squeeze the juice from the limes.

4. Add the lime juice and corn syrup to the strained mint syrup. Chill in the refrigerator until cold, then freeze in an ice cream machine until set. Reserve in the freezer or serve immediately.

Pear Sorbet

SERVES 8

You can make pear sorbet with raw fruit, but perfect pear sorbet demands cooked fruit for two reasons: If the pears are not absolutely ripe, they must be cooked first to make a smooth sorbet; if they are ripe, they must be cooked to prevent their turning brown. The degree of ripeness determines the cooking time.

1¼ cups sugar

Juice of 1 lemon

6 ripe pears

Special Equipment Ice cream machine

1. In a saucepan, dissolve the sugar in 4 cups water and the lemon juice. Peel, core, and thinly slice the pears; immediately—to prevent browning—add the pears to the sugar syrup. If your pears are good and ripe, simmer for 3 to 4 minutes. Unripe pears, however, may need more than 10 minutes to become tender.

2. Strain the sliced pears from the syrup and reserve the syrup. Purée the pears in a blender. Using about half the sugar syrup, thin the pear purée to achieve both a smooth, runny consistency and the desired sweetness. Add more syrup if necessary.

3. Chill the mixture until cold, then freeze in an ice cream machine until set. Reserve in the freezer or serve immediately.

Tea Sorbet with Calvados

SERVES 8

While the Japanese have been making tea ice cream for a long time, I found this refreshing, sensual *entremets* at L'Oasis, the three-star restaurant in La Napoule near Cannes. Serve it between a fish and meat course or after a garlic dish—whenever you want a spirited change.

4 tea bags—Darjeeling or other fine tea

⅓ cup sugar

8 teaspoons Calvados

Special Equipment Ice cream machine

1. Bring 2 cups water to a boil in a saucepan. Remove from the heat, add the tea bags, and steep until strong but not harsh.

2. Pour the tea into a mixing bowl, add the sugar, and stir to dissolve. Let cool.

3. Freeze in an ice cream machine until set. Reserve in the freezer or serve immediately.

4. Serve in martini glasses frosted in the freezer. Sprinkle each serving with a dash of Calvados—about a teaspoon per glass. Serve.

Zinfandel Sorbet

Granité, a coarse-grained sorbet often made from fine wines and liquors, is a traditional *entremets* of classic French cuisine. I've modernized it to my taste using an idea from a French pizza parlor. A favorite hangout when I was working at the restaurant in Yvoire was a joint down the road in nearby Evian, next door to the famous springs, where along with your pizza they'd put a big bowl of sangría in the middle of the table. I can still taste it—good wine and fruit juices and pepper and spices. Frozen, it makes a zingy refresher or even a light dessert. You can substitute a blend of port and Cabernet for the Zinfandel or any other wine with a big spicy flavor.

---

1 orange

1½ cups full-bodied, spicy Zinfandel

⅔ cup sugar

Freshly ground pepper

MAKING THE GRANITÉ

1. Peel the zest from the orange and chop finely, then squeeze the juice from the zested orange.

2. Combine the orange zest and juice with the wine, the sugar, and 8 to 10 good grinds of black pepper in a mixing bowl.

3. Freeze the mixture, using one of the two following techniques:

a. For a *granité* consistency, pour the mixture into a Pyrex dish large enough so that the wine isn't more than an inch or so deep. Place in the freezer. When the top begins to freeze, stir it—a couple of turns with a fork will be enough to break it up. Continue to stir it every 20 minutes or so until the mixture has thickened and crystallization is complete. Allow a good 3 hours.

b. If you prefer a smoother consistency, freeze it in an ice cream machine until set. Transfer it to a chilled Pyrex or stainless-steel container and reserve in the freezer.

4. Serve one small scoop in a small frosted wineglass.

Note Plan to serve the *granité* within 8 to 12 hours of making; it won't keep its consistency any longer than that. You can, however, thaw and refreeze leftover *granité* if you wish to serve it again at a later date.

Fresh Peach Ice Cream

Peach ice cream is one of the hardest ice creams to get just right, but when you do, it's as subtle and delicate a flavor as you'll ever taste. I was finally satisfied with this particular approach after trying numerous versions. It's important to start with great peaches. Then I candy them to concentrate the flavor as much as possible and keep the pieces of fruit soft, even when frozen. It will be one of your all-time favorites.

2 cups sugar

5 ripe peaches, diced

3 cups milk

9 large egg yolks

3 cups heavy cream, chilled

Special Equipment Ice cream machine

CANDYING THE FRUIT (CAN BE DONE AHEAD OF TIME)

1. In a large saucepan, dissolve the sugar in 1 cup water. Using a pastry brush dipped in fresh water, rinse down any sugar crystals stuck to the sides of the pan in order to prevent crystallization while cooking. Place over moderate heat and cook, rinsing down the sides from time to time, until cooked to hard crack (300° to 310° F.)—the last stage before turning to caramel. At hard crack, the syrup becomes very thick and the bubbles grow large and lethargic.

2. In the meantime, peel and dice the fresh peaches into ½-inch cubes.

3. When the sugar gets to the hard-crack stage, remove it from the heat and add the peaches, stirring just enough to coat them with the syrup. Cover the saucepan and let sit over the pilot flame for a half hour.

4. After the peaches have candied for a half hour, place the pan over moderate heat, bring to a boil, and let boil for a minute or two, uncovered, to cook out extra moisture and concentrate the flavor. It should now be a thick syrup. Put aside to cool.

MAKING THE ICE CREAM

5. Bring the milk just to a boil in a large saucepan.

6. Whisk the 9 egg yolks together in a large mixing bowl. Gently mix in the cooled peaches and syrup, but carefully: don't mangle the soft peaches.

7. When the milk has just come to a boil, stir it into the peach mixture. Then pour everything back into the saucepan (unless it is scorched) and cook over moderate heat, stirring constantly with a wooden spoon, until the mixture has slightly thickened and coats the back of the spoon. Do not allow to boil! You'll curdle the yolks and have to start completely over.

8. Immediately remove it from the heat and stir in the cold cream to stop the cooking and prevent curdling. Let the custard cool to room temperature and the peach flavor ripen for a good 2 hours. This curing time also allows the tiny air bubbles to work their way out, making for a denser ice cream.

9. When cooled, freeze the mixture in an ice cream machine until it thickens and begins to set. Then transfer to a chilled Pyrex or stainless-steel container and place it in the freezer to firm up for 3 to 4 hours. Serve.

Fresh Truffle Ice Cream

MAKES 1 1/2 QUARTS

This recipe is dedicated to my son, Daniel, who said at the age of three, as I was showing him what goes into fruit sorbet (mainly, lots of sugar), "That's gross. I'd rather wait for twuffle ice cream." He does have a point, truffle ice cream belongs in a special niche. I wouldn't think of making ice cream with any other mushroom, but the almost sweet, earthy truffle lends fresh home-made ice cream an entrancing flavor—hard to describe, but its aromatic qualities are similar to those of the vanilla bean. I sometimes serve this on my all-truffle menu: truffles in every course from appetizer to dessert.

1 fresh black truffle (¾ to 1 ounce)

3 cups milk

10 egg yolks

⅔ cup sugar

1½ cups heavy cream, chilled

Special Equipment Ice cream machine

1. Chop the truffle exceedingly fine—almost powdered.

2. Add the milk and the chopped truffle to a large saucepan and bring just to a boil.

3. In the meantime, in a large mixing bowl, whisk the egg yolks and sugar together until smooth.

4. When the milk has just come to a boil, whisk it into the egg mixture. Then pour the mixture back into the saucepan (if not scorched) and cook over moderate heat, stirring constantly with a wooden spoon, until the mixture just begins to thicken and coats the back of the spoon. Do not overcook or let it boil—you'll curdle the eggs.

5. Immediately remove it from the heat and stir in the cold cream to stop the cooking. Let cool to room temperature, then refrigerate for a good 2 hours to allow the subtle truffle flavor to infuse deeply. Letting it "cure" overnight is even better.

6. When chilled, freeze the mixture in an ice cream machine. As soon as it's thick, transfer it to a chilled Pyrex or stainless-steel container and freeze until firm. To make a rich, smooth, dense ice cream, don't overprocess—you'll only stir in too much air.

Hazelnut Ice Cream Chocolate Mint Ice Cream Amaretto Praline Ice Cream

Nothing beats your own freshly turned ice cream. Here are three great flavors to start with. If you've read any amount of this book so far, you will know I am a serious hazelnut addict. Of these three ice creams, the rich, roasted hazelnut flavor is my favorite. Once you've mastered the basic technique, you'll be able to design your own killer concoction with other flavors to which you have a significant attachment.

C U S T A R D
3 cups milk

10 large egg yolks

2/3 cup sugar

1 1/2 cups heavy cream, chilled

F O R   H A Z E L N U T   I C E   C R E A M
1 cup hazelnuts

FOR CHOCOLATE MINT ICE CREAM

4 ounces bittersweet chocolate

¼ cup heavy cream

2 ounces peppermint schnapps or crème de menthe

FOR AMARETTO PRALINE ICE CREAM

⅔ cup slivered blanched almonds

¼ cup amaretto

Special Equipment Ice cream machine

MAKING THE CUSTARD

1. Bring the milk just to a boil in a large saucepan.

2. In a large mixing bowl, whisk the egg yolks and sugar together until smooth.

3. When the milk has just come to a boil, whisk it into the egg mixture in the mixing bowl.

4. Pour the mixture back into the saucepan (if not scorched) and cook over moderate heat, stirring constantly with a wooden spoon, until the mixture just begins to thicken and coats the back of the spoon. Do not turn your attention away even for a moment! Too much heat or a few seconds too much cooking will scramble the egg yolks irreversibly and you'll have to start from absolute scratch.

5. Immediately remove it from the heat and stir the cold cream into the mixture to stop the cooking and prevent curdling.

6. At this point, proceed with your chosen flavor according to the directions below.

MAKING HAZELNUT ICE CREAM

7. Roast the hazelnuts in a 350°F. oven for 10 to 12 minutes until the dark skins crack open and they turn golden brown. (Keep an eye on them—they burn easily.) Slough off the skins by rubbing the nuts between your hands or in a towel. Grind the nuts in a food processor or blender to a smooth fine paste.

8. Stir this hazelnut paste into the just-finished custard. Allow to cool to room temperature and let the nut flavor ripen for a good 2 hours.

9. When cooled, freeze in an ice cream machine. When finished, transfer to a chilled Pyrex or stainless-steel container (don't eat it all while doing this!) and allow to set in the freezer. Serve.

MAKING CHOCOLATE MINT ICE CREAM

7. Break the chocolate into small pieces and melt in the top of a double boiler with the cream.

8. Stir the melted chocolate into the just-finished custard. Allow to cool to room temperature. When cool, add the peppermint schnapps and freeze in an ice cream machine as directed for Hazelnut Ice Cream (above).

7. Toast the almonds until golden brown. Add the just-toasted almonds to the just-finished custard.

8. Allow to cool to room temperature. When cool, add the amaretto and freeze in an ice cream machine as directed for Hazelnut Ice Cream, page 185.

Crêpes with Sautéed Strawberries

S E R V E S   4

Once upon a time in the village of Yvoire on Lake Geneva, a little old lady named Madame Vaulot worked behind a tiny bar in a tiny restaurant for seven hours every night making and selling dessert crêpes and *cidre bouché*—nothing else. She made a killing. Working just four months of the year, she supported herself, her son, and her daughter-in-law on just those crêpes, they were that good. The little bar was a wonderful place for me to go and have a bottle of *cidre* and perfect my French. And devour crêpes. This candied-strawberries-in-Grand-Marnier crêpe is "in the manner of Madame Vaulot"—lots of fresh fruit and whipped cream topped with toasted almonds. A treat to make for friends at all hours.

C R Ê P E S

4 tablespoons (½ stick) unsalted butter

2 eggs

⅔ cup flour

Pinch of salt

¾ cup milk

FILLING

¼ cup sliced almonds

½ cup heavy cream

I quart strawberries

4 tablespoons (½ stick) unsalted butter

⅓ cup sugar

I shot Grand Marnier

Special Equipment 10-inch omelet pan with nonstick coating is ideal

MAKING THE CRÊPES

It's best if the batter is made 3 to 4 hours ahead to let the bubbles work their way out—makes for thinner, more delicate crêpes.

1. Melt 2 tablespoons of the butter. Mix the eggs with the flour and salt until smooth. Add the melted butter and mix immediately before it congeals. While stirring, thin the batter with the milk. It should be smooth and runny; if not, add more milk.

2. Melt the remaining 2 tablespoons butter in the omelet pan. Then pour off the butter into a small dish and reserve. The pan is now seasoned and ready for the first crêpe.

3. Place the buttered pan over low to moderate heat and heat until the butter begins to sizzle. Pour approximately 3 tablespoons batter into the pan—tilting and turning while pouring—to coat the entire bottom of the pan as thinly as possible.

4. Cook the crêpe about 45 seconds,

or until golden brown on the bottom. Flip and finish cooking on the other side. Slide the crêpe out of the pan onto a work surface and allow to cool. If the first crêpe is too thick, thin the batter with more milk.

5. Repeat the process with the remaining batter, lightly brushing the pan with melted butter before making each new crêpe. The batter should yield eight 8-inch crêpes. Once cooled, the crêpes may be stacked, wrapped in plastic, and refrigerated overnight.

FINISHING AND SERVING THE CRÊPES

6. Toast the sliced almonds (a toaster oven will do) until light golden brown

7. Whip the cream.

8. Rinse, hull, and quarter the strawberries.

9. Melt the butter in a sauté pan until it browns. Add the strawberries and sauté about 1 minute. Add the sugar and sauté 2 more minutes or until the sugar is all dissolved and the mixture thickens. Deglaze with the Grand Marnier and remove from the heat.

10. Divide the mixture among the crêpes. Roll them up or fold them over and place 2 crêpes on each of 4 dessert plates. Top with whipped cream, sprinkle with toasted almonds, and serve immediately.

Crêpes with Apples and Cinnamon Ice Cream

SERVES 8

This cold-weather, in-front-of-the-fireplace dessert is an American classic with a French twist. It is apple pie à la mode with cinnamon in a crêpe. The spicy cinnamon, the cold ice cream, and the hot apples are a good contrast. It is a thoroughly satisfying dessert and good dinner-party fare, as it can be prepped in advance and put together at the last minute.

CINNAMON ICE CREAM

3 cups milk

10 egg yolks

⅔ cup sugar

1½ cups heavy cream, chilled

2 teaspoons cinnamon

CARAMEL SAUCE

1 cup sugar

1 tablespoon unsalted butter

½ cup heavy cream

FILLING

4 Golden Delicious apples

2 tablespoons unsalted butter

¾ cup crème fraîche (page 55)

2 tablespoons heavy cream

8 crêpes (page 186)

Special Equipment Ice cream machine

MAKING THE CINNAMON ICE CREAM

1. In a large saucepan, bring the milk just to a boil.

2. In a large mixing bowl, whisk the egg yolks and sugar together until smooth.

3. When the milk just comes to a boil, whisk it into the eggs and sugar. Return the mixture to the saucepan (if not scorched) and cook over moderate heat, stirring constantly with a wooden spoon, until the mixture just begins to thicken and coats the back of the spoon. Do not overcook.

4. Immediately stir in the cream to stop the cooking. Stir in the cinnamon and let cool to room temperature. When cool, freeze in the ice cream machine until set. Transfer to a chilled Pyrex or stainless-steel container and reserve in the freezer.

MAKING THE CARAMEL SAUCE

5. Put the sugar in a dry saucepan and cook over moderate heat, stirring constantly and vigorously with a wooden spoon to work out the lumps, until you have a rich brown caramel.

6. Remove the caramel from the heat and immediately stir in the butter and

cream. Add the cream very carefully, as the hot caramel could splatter and cause a nasty burn. When cool, stir in a little water to thin the caramel to a nice sauce consistency. Reserve.

MAKING THE FILLING AND ASSEMBLING THE CRÊPES

7. Preheat the oven to 375°F.

8. Peel, core, and cut the apples into eighths. Carefully arrange in a sauté pan with the butter. Brown one side, then the other until both sides are a nice golden brown. Place the browned apples on a buttered cookie sheet (can be done hours ahead of time). Just before serving, bake the apple slices in the oven 7 or 8 minutes or until tender.

9. In the meantime, whip the crème fraîche with the heavy cream until stiff. Reserve.

10. Reheat the crêpes in a sauté pan brushed with a little melted butter, cooking for only a few seconds on each side. Spread the heated crêpes on your work surface.

11. Mirror 8 dessert plates with warm caramel sauce. Place 4 hot apple wedges on the front half of each crêpe. Top with a scoop of cinnamon ice cream and a generous dollop of whipped crème fraîche. Fold each crêpe over the filling and immediately place atop a mirrored dessert plate. Serve immediately.

Surprise Pear with Pistachio

SERVES 6

The "surprise" in the title is a scoop of fresh pistachio ice cream hidden inside a chocolate-coated poached pear. Hold off doing this recipe until you find really ripe, excellent pears—you can tell by the slight give around the stem but especially by the rich, ripe smell. The recipe is an adaptation of a favorite dessert of the fine Los Angeles chef Joseph Broulard, from whom I learned it years ago as he was driving me down the San Diego Freeway to a job interview in Torrance. I got the job and hated it; I tried the Poire en Surprise and loved it. Here is my version.

ICE CREAM

⅔ cup peeled pistachios (unsalted)

10 egg yolks

⅔ cup sugar

3 cups milk

1½ cups heavy cream, chilled

POACHED PEARS

1½ cups sugar

6 ripe pears

1 lemon, halved

8 ounces bittersweet chocolate

1 tablespoon peppermint schnapps or slightly more crème de menthe

Special Equipment Ice cream machine

MAKING THE ICE CREAM

1. Grind the pistachios very fine in a food processor, blender, or coffee grinder.

2. In a large mixing bowl, whisk the egg yolks and sugar together until smooth.

3. Bring the milk just to a boil in a large saucepan and then whisk it into the egg mixture.

4. Pour the mixture back into the saucepan (if not scorched) and cook over moderate heat, all the while stirring with a wooden spoon and watching carefully. Cook just until the mixture begins to thicken and coats the back of the spoon. Proceed cautiously, as cooking too fast or too much will scramble the egg yolks, and you'll have to start over.

5. Once the mixture is slightly thickened, immediately stir in the cream—this will stop the cooking and prevent the yolks from curdling.

6. Stir in the ground pistachios and set the custard aside to cool at room temperature for a good 2 hours, during which the subtle flavor of the pistachios will infuse thoroughly.

7. When cooled, freeze in an ice cream machine until set. Transfer the ice cream to a chilled Pyrex or stainless-steel container and reserve in the freezer.

POACHING THE PEARS

8. Dissolve the sugar in 4½ cups water in a saucepan large enough to hold the 6 pears.

9. Carefully peel each pear, leaving the stem intact. Rub the pears with the lemon to keep the flesh white and place them in the saucepan with the sugar water.

10. Cover, bring to a boil, then allow the pears to simmer gently for just 5 minutes—don't overcook. Remove the pears from the syrup and chill them. Reserve the hot syrup for the chocolate sauce.

MAKING THE CHOCOLATE SAUCE

11. Break or cut the bittersweet chocolate into small pieces. Put them in a small saucepan with the peppermint schnapps and add ½ cup of the still-hot pear syrup. Let them sit for a minute or two while the chocolate melts with the hot syrup.

12. When the chocolate is melted, stir with a wooden spoon and thin with a couple of tablespoons of the hot pear syrup, as needed, to reach a nice pourable consistency. Keep warm.

ASSEMBLY

13. Trim the bottoms of the chilled pears, if necessary, to make them stand up straight.

14. Cut the pears horizontally in half. With a soup spoon or melon baller, very gently hollow out each half of the pear, removing the core and leaving a cavern for a scoop of ice cream.

15. Place the bottom half of each pear in the middle of each of 6 dessert plates. Nestle one scoop of pistachio ice cream in the bottom and cover with the top half of the same pear, hiding the ice cream inside.

16. Generously nap the pears with warm chocolate sauce and surprise your guests immediately.

Chocolate Espresso Soufflé

SERVES 4

Popping lushly out of its cup as it comes from the oven, this is a no-lose dessert—sinfully rich and chastely petite at the same time. While the base of most soufflés is a batter of milk, flour, and sugar, this one is just chocolate, espresso, and egg—the good chocolate supplying the especially pure taste. Because of its simple base, it's extremely easy to make—a recipe designed to demystify soufflés forever.

3½ tablespoons strong freshly brewed espresso

5 ounces bittersweet chocolate

Granulated sugar for ramekins

4 egg whites

1 tablespoon powdered sugar, plus more for garnish

3 egg yolks

¾ cup heavy cream for whipping (optional)

Special Equipment 4 ramekins (5 fluid ounces each)

1. Preheat the oven to 400°F.
2. Brew the espresso—make it strong!
3. Melt the chocolate in the top of a double boiler or in a large stainless-steel

mixing bowl (or any heatproof mixing bowl) over simmering water until the temperature is that of a warm bath, but nowhere near boiling.

4. While the chocolate is melting, thoroughly butter the insides of the ramekins all the way to the top. Thoroughly coat with granulated sugar by pouring in a couple tablespoons of sugar, then pouring it out slowly while turning the ramekin in your hand. The unbroken butter-sugar coating is essential to the even, columnar rising of your soufflé, so don't touch the inside surface.

5. In a clean, dry mixing bowl, copper or otherwise (see Note), whip the egg whites until frothy. Add the powdered sugar and beat until they hold a soft peak—but not until hard. A softer consistency folds in easier and rises better, so don't overbeat.

6. As soon as you've finished the whites, whisk the egg yolks into the melted chocolate. While continuing to stir, add the hot espresso.

7. Immediately fold the whites into the chocolate—gently but thoroughly, a good dozen and a half strokes should do it.

8. Fill the ramekins with the batter just to the top and bake 8 to 9 minutes.

9. Sprinkle with powdered sugar and serve immediately, with a little side of whipped cream if you prefer.

Note A copper bowl might make a marginally better meringue, but it's by no means required. Egg whites beaten in a clean copper bowl are more stable, but they take longer to whip. The copper bowl is mostly an affectation, just another of the needlessly daunting myths about soufflés. Soufflés simply take a little practice. And sure you can peek at them, just don't slam the door.

Grand Marnier Soufflé

This is a contemporary version of another familiar classic dish. Nowadays chefs are taking great liberties with soufflés, often bypassing the heavy custards or doughs that were their backbone. Modern soufflés are not only lighter and purer-tasting but also much easier and faster to make. Once you've mastered this soufflé, with only a little imagination you'll be able to adapt it easily to other favorite fruit flavors and liqueurs.

---

7 tablespoons granulated sugar, plus more for coating ramekins

2 tablespoons Grand Marnier

Juice of ½ orange

1 teaspoon finely chopped orange zest

2 egg yolks

4 egg whites

Sprinkle of powdered sugar

Special Equipment 4 ramekins (5 fluid ounces each)

1. Preheat the oven to 400°F.
2. Thoroughly coat the insides of the ramekins with softened butter. Fill the ramekins with granulated sugar and slowly pour it out, turning the ramekins as you pour to ensure an unbroken butter-sugar coating.

3. In a small saucepan, briefly boil the Grand Marnier to cook off the alcohol, then remove it from the heat. (Don't worry if it flambés briefly.) Add the orange juice and zest. This should make ¼ cup of orange essence.

4. Add this orange essence to a clean mixing bowl containing the egg yolks and 4 tablespoons of the sugar. Mix thoroughly and reserve.

5. In a separate clean, dry mixing bowl, beat the egg whites until they just begin to have body. Add the remaining 3 tablespoons sugar and continue to beat until they hold a soft smooth peak.

6. Gently but thoroughly fold the meringue into the orange mixture. Fill the ramekins to the brim, but carefully, without disturbing the butter-sugar lining.

7. Bake the soufflés 8 to 9 minutes until they look like soufflés. Do not overcook: Your soufflé will continue to rise higher and higher but will only get drier and chewier. Remove from the oven. Sprinkle with powdered sugar and serve immediately.

Frozen Passion Fruit Soufflé

MAKES 1 LOAF (8 TO 12 SLICES) OR 4 INDIVIDUAL RAMEKINS

This is a very light, pretty, hot-weather dessert that involves no baking and can be made a day ahead of time. Passion fruit is as exotic and seductive in flavor as in name. It makes an irresistibly sweet/tart meringue that you can serve either sliced or in ramekins.

SOUFFLÉ

12 passion fruits (enough for ¾ cup juice)

1⅔ cups heavy cream

1 cup sugar

3 egg whites

APRICOT AND RASPBERRY COULIS

¼ cup dried apricots

¼ cup plus 3 tablespoons sugar

Squeeze of lemon juice

½ cup fresh or frozen-in-sugar raspberries

Special Equipment 4 ramekins (5 fluid ounces each), or a 2-quart loaf pan and a plastic squeeze bottle or narrow-lipped pitcher

MAKING THE SOUFFLÉ

1. Juice the passion fruit by cutting each one in half, scooping the pulp and seeds into a strainer, and pressing the juice through the strainer with the bottom of a ladle. (Don't use a food processor or blender—you'll chop up the seeds and release their bitterness.) Reserve.

2. Whip the cream to a firm peak and reserve.

3. Place the sugar in a saucepan and add enough water (about ¼ cup) to dissolve it. Carefully brush down any sugar crystals from the sides of the pan with a clean wet brush. Without stirring or moving the pan, cook over medium heat to soft ball—240°F.—just past thread.

4. Meanwhile, prepare the individual ramekins if using. (If making the loaf instead, omit this step.) Make paper collars for the ramekins by cutting out rectangular pieces of parchment paper 1 inch longer than the circumference of the ramekin and 1½ inches wider than the ramekin is tall. Wrap a collar around each ramekin and fasten with a small piece of tape.

5. Place the egg whites in a clean, dry mixing bowl.

6. As soon as the sugar reaches the soft-ball stage, remove it from the heat. Turn on the electric mixer and whip the egg whites for about 30 seconds or until frothy. While still whipping, carefully pour in the hot sugar syrup and continue to beat at full speed until the syrup has cooled—4

to 5 minutes. (You've made Italian meringue!) When finished it should be heavy, stiff, and shiny—not unlike a jar of marshmallow cream.

7. Fold the passion fruit juice into the Italian meringue, then fold in the whipped cream.

8. Fill each ramekin to the top of the collar, or fill the loaf pan, and freeze for at least 4 hours (see Note).

MAKING THE APRICOT AND RASPBERRY COULIS

9. Place the dried apricots in a saucepan with ⅔ cup water and 3 tablespoons sugar. Bring to a boil, then remove from the heat and allow to soak and soften for 45 minutes. Purée in a blender until smooth. Add sugar or water to perfect the sweetness or consistency. Add a squeeze of lemon juice to taste to accentuate the flavor and balance the sweetness. Strain and reserve.

10. For the raspberry coulis, if using fresh raspberries, purée in a food processor with ¼ cup sugar until smooth. Strain and reserve. If using frozen raspberries, simply don't add sugar.

SERVING

11. If using ramekins, peel away the paper collars and serve the individual soufflés with the two coulis in sauceboats on the side.

12. If using a loaf pan, remove the pan from the freezer, dip it for 15 seconds in warm water, then invert it and unmold the soufflé on a cutting board.

13. Mirror the entire bottom of each of 8 to 12 chilled plates with apricot coulis. Garnish each with a swirl or zigzag of raspberry coulis from a plastic squeeze bottle or narrow-lipped pitcher.

14. Slice the frozen loaf using a knife dipped in warm water before each cut. Place a slice atop each plate of coulis and serve.

Note It is human nature to keep peeking and poking to see if the soufflé is frozen yet. But don't—it is soufflé nature never to freeze if you keep opening the freezer door and spilling the cold air.

Tarte Tatin

S E R V E S   8   T O   1 0

Named after its originators, Les Mères Tatin, two old-maid sisters residing in Normandy at the turn of the century, this caramelized upside-down apple tart, served with a scoop of homemade ice cream, is the closest thing you'll get to heaven in an earthly dessert. I've seen many versions of the Tarte Tatin, but none so good as this—one of Jean Bertranou's signature dishes from La Chaumière. A gift to warm the soul on a cold night.

13 or 14 Red Delicious apples

16 tablespoons (2 sticks) unsalted butter

1½ cups sugar

8 ounces puff pastry (scraps will do fine—you can buy the dough ready-made from a pastry shop)

Special Equipment

Ovenproof 10-inch pan with straight 2½-inch sides

Gas stove strongly recommended

1. Peel, halve, and core the apples.
2. Break the butter into small pieces and place the pieces in the pan. Add the sugar. Stand the apple halves upside down—fat end down—and back to back, all around the edge of the pan. Fill in the center of the pan, packing in as many more standing apple halves as will fit. You will have half a dozen or so apple halves remaining—these will be inserted later.
3. Place the pan over a low flame. Cook 5 to 10 minutes until the butter is melted, the sugar is dissolved, and the apples have exuded some of their juice. Cook 1½ hours. Adjust the heat if necessary to achieve a slow but steady simmer. The secret here is a slow, even, patient cooking. Every 10 minutes or so, give the pan a sharp turn, rotating the apples slightly, to keep them from sticking and to ensure an even caramelization. After 20 minutes or so, the apples will have shrunk enough to

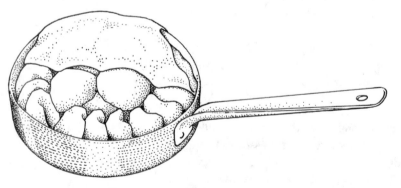

Topping tart in pan with pastry.

allow you to slip the first of the extra apple halves in between the others. After more time, you'll be able to fit all the extras in.

4. In the meantime, roll out a thin circle of puff pastry about an inch wider than the diameter of the pan. Prick the surface thoroughly with a fork. Reserve in the refrigerator.

5. Preheat the oven to 400°F.

6. If after about 1½ hours of slow cooking, all the apple halves have been fitted into the pan, and the juice has thickened considerably and caramelized to a deep golden brown, remove the pan from the heat. Otherwise, continue to cook until syrup has caramelized before proceeding. Cover the apples with the circle of puff pastry, tucking the edge slightly down inside the pan. Bake in the hot oven 20 to 25 minutes, until the pastry is browned.

7. Remove from the oven and allow to sit 3 or 4 minutes. Then carefully invert the tart onto an oversized plate. Smooth the apples with a spatula. Collect the extra caramel in the pan and pour it over the top. Serve the tart warm with homemade ice cream.

Fruit Tart

MAKES ONE 9-INCH TART, SERVING 8 TO 10

This is the one dessert I've been making my entire career, and it's the only dessert I can eat every day. In fact I often have a piece of leftover tart for breakfast. My favorite is the blueberry. This simple tart has it all over the fancy overcomplicated pastries that are the vogue today. The sugar-cookie crust, nutty brown-butter filling, and fresh fruit make it the perfect dessert. If you keep dough ready in the freezer, you can make it on a day when you just *know* you don't have the time.

PÂTE SUCRÉE
1¾ cups plus 2 tablespoons flour

10 tablespoons plus 1 teaspoon unsalted butter

3½ tablespoons granulated sugar

Pinch of salt

2 egg yolks

4 drops vanilla extract

BROWN-BUTTER FILLING
1 cup granulated sugar

4½ tablespoons flour

3 eggs

12 tablespoons (1½ sticks) unsalted butter

Variation 1: 2 to 3 heaping tablespoons
raspberry jam

2½ pints fresh raspberries or
2 pints fresh strawberries

Variation 2: 2 apples or 2 ripe pears

Variation 3: 1½ pints (3 cups) fresh
blueberries

1 shot kirsch

Sprinkle of powdered sugar

Special Equipment 9-inch tart pan with
removable bottom

MAKING THE PÂTE SUCRÉE

1. In a food processor, combine the
flour, butter, sugar, and salt and mix for 45
seconds. Add the egg yolks, vanilla, and a
tablespoon of water and mix another 30
seconds or so until the dough forms a ball.
If necessary, add more water—it should be
smooth to the touch but not sticky.

2. Wrap the dough in plastic wrap and
refrigerate at least 4 to 5 hours or preferably overnight.

ROLLING THE DOUGH

3. Remove the dough from the refrigerator (it should be hard). Cut the
dough into 4 or 5 pieces and knead to
soften without overworking the dough.

4. With your hands, shape the dough
into a disk about ½ inch thick and place on
a cool work surface sprinkled with flour.

Roll the dough out into a thin circle—⅛
inch thick—at least 2 inches larger than
your tart pan. You will need to dust the
work surface a couple of times with flour
to keep the dough from sticking, but don't
overdo it, as it will toughen the dough.

5. Roll up the dough on the rolling
pin, then carefully unroll it over the tart
pan. Press the dough carefully into the bottom and sides of the pan, crimping the
edges to remove the excess. Refrigerate
15 to 20 minutes.

MAKING THE BROWN-BUTTER FILLING

6. Whisk together the sugar, flour,
and eggs in a large mixing bowl.

7. Cook the butter in a *hot* sauté pan
over high heat without stirring until it begins to foam and turns golden brown. Don't
burn the butter, but do let it get
browned—the source of the filling's dis-
tinctive nutty flavor.

8. Whisk the brown butter into the
egg mixture, stirring until smooth.

ASSEMBLING AND BAKING THE TART

9. Preheat the oven to 350°F.

Variation 1—Strawberry or Raspberry

10. Fill the tart shell with the butter
filling. It should be about three-quarters
full. Bake for 50 to 60 minutes until it is
dark golden brown. Allow to cool thoroughly but do not refrigerate.

11. No more than an hour or two

before serving, brush the top of the tart with the jam heated with a teaspoonful or two of water. Top with fresh raspberries or hulled strawberries. Sprinkle with powdered sugar and serve.

Variation 2 —Apple or Pear

10. Peel and quarter the apples or pears. Cut the quarters crosswise into 1/8-inch slices, keeping them intact. Arrange the sliced quarters in a star pattern in the bottom of the tart shell.

11. Pour the butter filling around the fruit until the tart is about three-quarters full. You will need to use only about two-thirds of the filling (best not to overfill).

12. Bake about 60 minutes for an apple tart, or 70 minutes for a tart with juicy, ripe pears. When cool, sprinkle with powdered sugar and serve.

Variation 3 —Blueberry

10. Put 2 cups of fresh blueberries into the tart shell. Pour the butter filling over the blueberries until the tart is about three-quarters full. You will need to use only about two-thirds of the filling; do not overfill.

11. Bake for 1 hour. Remove from the oven and sprinkle with the kirsch. Top with the remaining cup blueberries and bake 10 more minutes. Remove, let cool, and sprinkle with powdered sugar before serving.

Flourless Chocolate Roulade

MAKES 1 FAT
13-INCH ROLL OR 1
SKINNY 18-INCH
ROLL

This is an extremely light, flourless cake that can be customized with any filling you like—fruits, liqueurs, chocolate chips, whipped cream, mousses, you name it. It is a quick and versatile recipe I learned from the late Jean Bertranou, the Los Angeles chef whose cooking ideas strongly influenced my style.

2/3 cup granulated sugar, plus more for the baking paper

6 large eggs

1/3 cup unsweetened cocoa, plus more for decoration

1 2/3 cups heavy cream

Additional fillings, such as fruit, liqueur, or chocolate chips, if desired

Sprinkle of powdered sugar

Special Equipment 18- by 13-inch baking sheet

1. Preheat the oven to 400°F.

2. Cover an 18- by 13-inch baking sheet with waxed paper or parchment paper. Brush the paper with melted butter and sprinkle evenly with granulated sugar. Shake off the excess sugar.

3. Separate the eggs into 2 mixing bowls. Whip the egg whites until they begin to stiffen, then add about a third of the granulated sugar. When very stiff, add the rest of the sugar.

4. Once the meringue is ready—and only then—take the bowl with the yolks and whisk in the cocoa. Immediately fold the meringue into the egg yolks gently but thoroughly.

5. Pour the batter onto the prepared pan and spread evenly to ½ inch of the edges. Bake 12 to 15 minutes until slightly firm to the touch. Remove and let cool. (When this cools, it will fall back down to the prebaked thickness; this is to be expected, don't worry.)

6. When the cake is cool, whip the cream and spread it in a thin, even layer over the whole cake. Add any additional fillings. Now the rolling: Proceeding from either one long or short edge, gently roll the cake, lifting it from the pan with the waxed paper and peeling the paper back as the cake is rolled up. With a serrated knife, cleanly trim off both ends, either squarely or on the bias.

7. Sprinkle the rolled-up cake with powdered sugar, with a stencil of your own design if desired. Add a second color of stenciling with cocoa powder.

8. To serve this very delicate cake, slice it with a serrated knife. If you wish to keep all or part of it overnight, wrap it tightly in plastic wrap to keep the whipped cream from greedily absorbing all the aromas in your refrigerator.

Strawberry Cream Cake

SERVES 8 TO 12

I can remember always requesting this cake for my birthday when I was a child—it's a great hot-weather cake because of the mounds of whipped cream and fresh strawberries. This is an excellent cake for the novice baker—a good place to learn your basic buttercream and basic sponge cake. It involves no critical chocolate, and though there is a little pastry-bag work and a crumb coat, everything here is very forgiving.

GENOISE
3 eggs

⅓ cup sugar, plus more for sprinkling

½ cup plus 2 tablespoons flour

BUTTERCREAM
⅔ cup sugar

2 eggs

3¾ sticks unsalted butter, softened

FILLING
1 shot Grand Marnier

⅓ cup sugar

2 cups heavy cream

1 pint strawberries

1 shot Grand Marnier

1 bunch fresh mint

Special Equipment Pastry bag with large star tip

MAKING THE GENOISE

1. Preheat the oven to 350°F. Liberally butter a 9-inch cake pan.

2. Whisk the eggs and sugar in the bowl of an electric mixer over moderate heat until as warm as a bath but not hot. Place the bowl on the mixer and beat for 4 minutes at full speed, then another 4 minutes at medium speed.

3. Meanwhile sift the flour. Fold the flour into the egg mixture. Pour the batter into the prepared pan and bake 18 minutes. The genoise is done when the sides pull away from the pan.

4. Invert the cake onto a baking sheet that has been sprinkled with granulated sugar and allow to cool.

MAKING THE BUTTERCREAM

5. Dissolve the sugar in ½ cup water in a small saucepan and bring to a boil over moderate heat. Cook until you have thread—the first stage after syrup, when a droplet just begins to leave a thread.

6. While the sugar is cooking, place the eggs in the bowl of an electric mixer with the whip attached. Cut the softened butter into small pieces and reserve.

7. When the sugar gets to the thread stage (230° to 234°F.), remove it from the heat. Immediately start beating the 2 eggs at full speed with the mixer. While the eggs are beating, pour in the hot sugar and

continue to beat until the mixture is light, fluffy, and only slightly warm, about body temperature.

8. Continue to beat while adding the softened butter, bit by bit. Add the Grand Marnier, then beat still more until the mixture is smooth and fluffy. Reserve in a cool place, even the refrigerator. But if it gets too cold, you will have to whip it again until it is the perfect texture for spreading on the cake.

ASSEMBLING THE CAKE

9. Dissolve ⅓ cup sugar in ⅔ cup water in a small saucepan and bring to a boil.

10. Whip the cream until stiff. Reserve.

11. Rinse, hull, and quarter all but 9 or 13 pretty strawberries (depending on the number of servings you want from the cake—8 or 12), which you will save for top decoration.

12. Cut out a 9-inch circle from corrugated cardboard. Using a serrated knife, carefully cut your genoise into 2 layers (see Note). Place a small dab of buttercream in the center of the cardboard circle and top with the first layer of genoise.

13. Sprinkle with half of the Grand Marnier—1 tablespoon—and generously soak it with sugar syrup using a pastry brush.

14. Spread a ½-inch layer of buttercream on the genoise and cover with the quartered strawberries. Top the strawberries with a ½-inch layer of whipped cream and then the remaining layer of genoise.

15. Sprinkle the top of the cake with the remaining Grand Marnier. Soak it with sugar syrup, using the pastry brush.

Desserts
■
201

16. Spread a thin coating of butter-cream all over the outside of the cake, smoothing and evening the sides. (This is the crumb coat.) Chill 15 to 20 minutes.

17. After the crumb coat has set, frost the entire cake with a ¼-inch-thick layer of whipped cream. Place the remaining whipped cream in a pastry bag fitted with the large star tip. Pipe rosettes of whipped cream around the top edge of the cake, one for every portion, then a final one in the center. Top each rosette with one of the pretty strawberries and garnish with mint leaves. Refrigerate until ready to serve.

Note To cut the sponge cake into even layers, first make a shallow cut all the way around the outside edge, then work your way gradually into the middle.

The Zigzag

SERVES 8 TO 12

A very slick, professional-looking cake that can nonetheless be made in a home kitchen. It's basically a chocolate genoise/chocolate mousse cake with some spectacular white and dark chocolate decoration. The hard part is the chocolate work, but the trick is patience—waiting for the chocolate to reach just the right consistency. A demanding dessert but one to be proud of.

CHOCOLATE GENOISE

3 eggs

⅓ cup sugar, plus more for sprinkling

½ cup flour

2 tablespoons unsweetened cocoa powder

CHOCOLATE MOUSSE

5 ounces bittersweet chocolate

¾ cup sugar

3 egg yolks

¾ cup heavy cream

2 cups heavy cream

5 ounces bittersweet chocolate

2 ounces white chocolate

1 cup fresh raspberries

Special Equipment 36-inch marble slab or other chillable work surface

MAKING THE CHOCOLATE GENOISE

1. Preheat the oven to 350°F. Liberally butter a 9-inch cake pan.

2. Whisk the eggs and sugar in the stainless-steel bowl of an electric mixer over moderate heat until the mixture is runny and as warm as a bath but not hot. Place the bowl on the mixer and beat at full speed for 4 minutes, then another 4 minutes at medium speed.

3. Sift together the flour and cocoa; fold into the egg mixture. Pour the batter into the cake pan and bake 18 minutes. You'll know it's done when the cake has shrunk 1/16 inch away from the pan all the way around.

4. Invert the cake onto a baking sheet that has been sprinkled with granulated sugar. Allow to cool.

MAKING THE MOUSSE

5. Melt the chocolate in a double boiler. Reserve.

6. Dissolve the sugar in 1 cup water in a saucepan and bring to a boil. Remove from the heat.

7. Put the egg yolks in the bowl of an electric mixer. Beat at medium speed and, while beating, add 6 tablespoons only of the hot syrup (reserve the rest). Beat at full speed for 3 to 4 minutes, until the mixture has cooled to body temperature.

8. Remove the bowl from the mixer. Pour in the still-warm melted chocolate—using a spatula to get every last drop. Stir the mixture with the spatula until it is well mixed. Cool it in the refrigerator for 10 to 15 minutes until it begins to jell and thicken, but don't let it get too hard.

9. Meanwhile, whip ¾ cup cream until it is stiff.

10. Fold the whipped cream into the cooled chocolate mixture. Return it to the refrigerator for 15 to 20 minutes, until it is set.

ASSEMBLING THE CAKE

11. Whip 2 cups cream until quite stiff. Reserve. In separate double boilers, melt the bittersweet chocolate and the white chocolate. Reserve.

12. Using a serrated knife, carefully cut the genoise into 2 thin layers.

13. Cut a 9-inch circle from corrugated cardboard. Place a dab of mousse in the middle of the cardboard circle as cement. Top with the first layer of genoise. Using a pastry brush, generously soak the genoise with some of the reserved sugar syrup.

14. Spread a ½-inch layer of mousse atop the soaked genoise, using about three-quarters of the mousse. Cover the mousse with the raspberries, then cover the raspberries with a thin layer of whipped cream. Top with the remaining layer of genoise.

15. Again with the pastry brush, generously soak the top layer of genoise with sugar syrup.

16. Using a long, thin spatula, do a "crumb coat" with the remaining mousse: Spread the top of the cake smooth and the sides of the cake straight up and down. (This is called a crumb coat because it seals in the crumbs and prevents them from surfacing when you apply the finishing layer.)

17. Measure the height and circumference of your cake, then place it in the refrigerator to chill. Cut a waxed paper strip ½ inch wider than your cake is tall and 4 inches longer than its circumference. ($C = \pi D$, so if D is 9 inches and π is 3.1416, then . . . oh, never mind. Make the strip 33 inches long.)

18. Cut a 16-inch square of waxed or parchment paper diagonally into 2 right triangles and fashion them into cornets.

19. Chill your smooth work surface for 4 or 5 minutes, using a plastic trash bag filled with ice. Wipe it dry with a towel. Smooth the waxed paper ribbon onto the chilled surface. Fill the first cornet with melted white chocolate and snip off the tip, leaving a small hole the size of a pencil lead. Moving rapidly back and forth across the width of the waxed-paper ribbon, squeeze out a tight zigzag pattern down the entire length. Immediately lift the ribbon from the surface, leaving the overlapping chocolate behind. Clean away the excess white chocolate.

20. Place the ribbon back on the chilled surface. Pour the melted dark chocolate down its center and smooth the chocolate with a long, thin spatula out past the ribbon's edges. Immediately lift the ribbon from the table, leaving the excess dark chocolate behind. Return this excess to the double boiler for later use.

21. Replace the ribbon on the chilled surface and allow the chocolate to just set—it will lose its shine and take on a matte finish. Do not let it get so hard that it will crack when flexed, however.

22. Remove the cake from the refrigerator and wrap the chocolate-coated ribbon—chocolate side in, of course—around the cake. Don't overlap the ends, but instead pinch them together. Place the cake back in the refrigerator—with the paper still on—and chill for about 10 minutes until the chocolate is hard.

23. In the meantime, remelt the leftover dark chocolate and pour it in the remaining paper cornet.

24. Remove the cake from the refrigerator. Top with all the remaining whipped cream and smooth the whipped cream even with the top of the waxed-paper ribbon, creating a level surface. Snip a pencil-lead–sized hole in the bottom of the second cornet and decorate the top of the cake with zigzags of dark chocolate. Immediately peel away the waxed paper, leaving behind the striking white-on-dark zigzag around the side, contrasting with the dark-on-white zigzagged top.

25. Refrigerate for at least 30 minutes to let set before serving.

Walnut Torte

Caveat chocoholic. For those whose weakness is anything chocolaty, nutty, and chewy, this is the apple the Serpent holds out. Disguised as a torte, it's really a 2-pound, inch-thick, chocolate-coated candy bar.

FILLING

2¼ cups sugar

⅔ cup heavy cream

14 tablespoons (1¾ sticks) unsalted butter

2¾ cups walnuts, coarsely chopped

1 recipe Pâte Sucrée (page 197), best made the day before and refrigerated

1 egg for egg wash

CHOCOLATE COATING

6 ounces bittersweet chocolate

3 fluid ounces heavy cream

Special Equipment 9-inch tart pan with removable bottom

MAKING THE FILLING

1. Combine the sugar with ⅔ cup water in a saucepan; thoroughly brush down the sides with a wet pastry brush to wash down any sugar crystals. Place over moderate heat and cook, without stirring or shaking the pan but occasionally brushing the sides down with a clean wet brush to prevent crystallization, until caramelized a deep golden brown (but not burned or smoking).

2. While the sugar is caramelizing, measure out the cream, butter, and walnuts—time will be of the essence once the sugar caramelizes.

3. When the sugar reaches the caramel stage, remove it from the heat and carefully add the butter and cream. Do it at arm's length, for the sugar may spit, and there are few things in the kitchen hotter than caramel. Then stir with a wooden spoon. Add the walnuts and continue to stir until they are thoroughly coated. Reserve and let cool.

ASSEMBLY AND BAKING

4. Preheat the oven to 350°F.

5. Remove the pastry dough from the refrigerator and knead until soft—but don't overwork it, or it will get too warm to work with.

6. Dust your work surface with flour to prevent sticking. Roll about two-thirds of the dough into a circle ⅛ inch thick and at least 2 inches larger all around than the tart pan. Save all the excess dough for the top.

7. Carefully roll the circle of dough loosely on the rolling pin and unroll it over the tart pan. Press the dough carefully into the sides of the pan and trim the top, leaving a 1/2-inch overlapping border.

8. Roll the remaining dough (including the trimmings) into a 1/8-inch-thick, 9-inch circle to serve as a top.

9. Pour the now barely warm filling into the tart shell. Paint the 1/2-inch border of dough with the egg wash. Top the tart with the second circle. Crimp the edges tightly, pinching off any large overlapping pieces. With the point of a small knife, poke 4 or 5 vents in the top.

10. Place the tart on a baking sheet to catch any overflow and bake 25 to 30 minutes until the crust is golden brown.

11. Remove from the oven and allow to cool—still in the pan—to room temperature. Then refrigerate; the tart will be too fragile to unmold unless chilled.

COATING WITH CHOCOLATE

12. Break the chocolate into small pieces and melt with the cream in the top of a double boiler until quite warm but not hot to the touch. Then stir until smooth and shiny.

13. Cut a 9-inch circle out of corrugated cardboard. Invert the chilled tart on top of the cardboard, remove the pan, and place the tart on a wire rack.

14. Pour the chocolate over the tart. Spread evenly with a long, thin spatula, making sure to cover all the sides. Chill in the refrigerator until 30 minutes before serving. Serve smallish pieces—this is almost too rich!

Note The walnut torte will keep 4 to 5 days refrigerated, though the pretty shine of the chocolate will diminish after 24 hours.

Gâteau Dacquoise

Chocolate, rum, and nuts make a rich dessert, indeed. Surprisingly, though, it's a cake that doesn't end up being very heavy—a flourless hazelnut meringue with two fillings: whipped chocolate buttercream and rum whipped cream. The flavors are vivid but the cake melts away in your mouth. I must credit my wife, Nancy, who once pitched in to serve as my pastry chef for a few months, with the *mise au point*—the perfecting of this recipe.

M E R I N G U E

1 ¼ cups hazelnuts (filberts)

¾ cup plus 2 tablespoons granulated sugar

1 heaping tablespoon cornstarch

5 egg whites

5 tablespoons powdered sugar, plus more for garnish

C H O C O L A T E   B U T T E R C R E A M

1 ½ ounces bittersweet chocolate

⅔ cup granulated sugar

2 eggs

3 ½ sticks unsalted butter, softened

R U M   W H I P P E D   C R E A M

1 ½ cups heavy cream, very cold

3 tablespoons granulated sugar

1 shot dark rum

Special Equipment
8-inch flan ring
Pastry bag with medium star tip

M A K I N G   T H E   M E R I N G U E

1. Preheat the oven to 350°F. Cover 2 baking sheets (one large enough for two 8-inch circles, the other for a single 8-inch circle) with parchment paper.

2. Roast the hazelnuts in the oven for 10 to 12 minutes or until medium golden brown, shaking the pan every couple of minutes to ensure even cooking and prevent burning. (A toaster oven will do just fine.) Allow the nuts to cool slightly and flake off the skins. Stash away 11 nuts for garnish later. Reduce the oven heat to 300°F.

3. Grind the hazelnuts in a food processor or blender to a fine powder, but do not overgrind or you'll have an unusable paste. Add the granulated sugar and cornstarch to the nuts in the food processor and sift together with a couple of quick bursts. Reserve.

4. In a large stainless-steel mixing bowl, whip the egg whites for about 30 seconds or until frothy but not yet holding a peak. Add the powdered sugar and continue to whip until firm. Gently but thoroughly fold the ground-nut mixture into the meringue.

5. Immediately place an 8-inch flan ring, to serve as a mold, on one of the parchment-covered baking sheets. Spread an even ⅜-inch layer of meringue within it. Carefully lift away the flan ring and make 2 more identical meringue circles.

6. Bake the meringues in the oven for 1 hour. Remove from the oven and allow to cool to room temperature.

MAKING THE CHOCOLATE BUTTERCREAM

7. Melt the bittersweet chocolate with 3 tablespoons water in a small saucepan. Allow to cool to approximately body temperature and reserve.

8. Dissolve the sugar in ½ cup water in a small saucepan and bring to a boil over moderate heat. Cook until thread (230° to 234° F.)—the first stage after syrup when a droplet just begins to leave a thread.

9. While the sugar is cooking, place the eggs in the bowl of an electric mixer with the whip attached. Cut the butter into small pieces and have at the ready.

10. When the sugar gets to the thread stage, remove it from the heat. Immediately start beating the 2 eggs at full speed and, while beating, pour in the hot sugar—careful: the sugar is very hot. Continue beating until the mixture is light, fluffy, and only slightly warm—about body temperature.

11. While still beating, add the softened butter, bit by bit, and continue beating until the mixture is smooth and fluffy.

12. Still beating, pour in the melted—not hot, just body temperature—chocolate. Mix well and refrigerate. Because it will get too hard to pipe from a pastry bag, rewhip the buttercream to the perfect texture when ready to assemble cake.

MAKING THE RUM WHIPPED CREAM

13. Whip the cream with the sugar and rum until it holds a firm peak. Reserve in the refrigerator.

ASSEMBLING THE GÂTEAU

14. Fit the pastry bag with a medium star tip and fill it with buttercream.

15. Cut an 8-inch circle out of corrugated cardboard and squeeze a dab of buttercream, as cement, in the middle of it. Top with one of the 3 meringue circles (save the prettiest circle for the top layer).

16. Pipe 1½-inch-tall rosettes—side by side and touching each other—all the way around the outside edge of the meringue circle. Fill the center of this ring with half the rum whipped cream.

17. Top with the second layer of meringue and press down gently to seal it, taking care not to crack it.

18. Make another ring of buttercream rosettes on the second layer and fill with the remaining whipped cream.

19. Top with the final, prettiest meringue circle. Again press gently to seal it. Pipe 8 or 10 rosettes (one per portion) around the edge of the cake, finishing with one in the center. Garnish each rosette with a reserved roasted hazelnut and sprinkle the top with powdered sugar.

20. Refrigerate at least 3 to 4 hours before slicing to firm up the buttercream and allow the meringue to become tender.

Gâteau Marjolaine

SERVES 12

Fernand Point, who died in 1955, was the first major French *chef propriétaire*—that is, the first renowned chef to own his own restaurant and make it a "chef's restaurant," where everything from the style of the service to the decor is subservient to the chef's philosophy of good food. Point was mentor to Paul Bocuse and Jean Troisgros, and much in contemporary French cuisine reflects his genius.

The marjolaine offered here is his signature cake. I have seen many versions, but this is as close to his unique way of making it as I can determine—thin layers of hazelnut sponge cake with alternating fillings of whipped crème fraîche, whipped ganache, and praline buttercream. Beyond rich. You'll find it serves 12 because even the tiniest slice will induce guilt.

HAZELNUT SPONGE

¾ cup granulated sugar, plus more for baking sheet

1½ cups hazelnuts (filberts)

4½ tablespoons flour

6 egg whites

1 heaping teaspoon powdered sugar

WHIPPED GANACHE

8 ounces bittersweet chocolate

1¼ cups heavy cream

WHIPPED CRÈME FRAÎCHE

1 cup crème fraîche (page 55)

½ cup heavy cream

PRALINE BUTTERCREAM

½ cup hazelnuts (filberts)

⅔ cup plus ½ cup granulated sugar

2 large eggs

3¾ sticks unsalted butter, softened

RASPBERRY SAUCE

1 pint fresh raspberries

⅔ cup granulated sugar

OTHER GARNISHES

8 ounces bittersweet chocolate

Unsweetened cocoa powder

Special Equipment
18-by-18-inch baking sheet
Additional small baking sheet

MAKING THE HAZELNUT SPONGE

1. Preheat the oven to 375°F.

2. Cut a piece of parchment paper to fit the baking sheet exactly, saving the excess paper for decoration stencils. Lightly but completely butter the paper, then sprinkle the entire surface with a layer of granulated sugar and tip off the excess. Place the paper on the baking sheet.

3. Roast the hazelnuts in the oven for 10 to 12 minutes, until the skins crack and the inside turns light golden brown. Peel then grind in a food processor or coffee grinder. Mix the hazelnuts with the granulated sugar and flour. Reserve.

4. Whip the egg whites in a clean, dry bowl until foamy and doubled in volume but not yet stiff. Add the powdered sugar and continue whipping until the whites hold a firm but not hard peak. Do not overbeat. Gently but thoroughly fold in the hazelnut mixture.

5. Spread a thin even layer of this batter to within ½ inch of the edge of the parchment paper. Bake approximately 15 minutes or until golden brown and set. Remove and let cool.

MAKING THE WHIPPED GANACHE

6. Over a double boiler or bain-marie (see box, page 175), heat the bittersweet chocolate with the cream until the chocolate is melted and warm, not hot. Remove from the heat and allow to cool, stirring frequently for uniform cooling.

7. When the mixture is cool and just begins to stiffen, whip (using an electric beater, or a whisk if you're energetic) to lighten the mixture until it holds a peak. Reserve at room temperature, taking care

not to let it get so cool it hardens and becomes unspreadable.

WHIPPING THE CRÈME FRAÎCHE

8. Mix together the crème fraîche and heavy cream. Whip until it holds a firm peak—it will be somewhat heavier than plain whipped cream. Reserve in the refrigerator.

MAKING THE PRALINE BUTTERCREAM

9. Measure the hazelnuts and keep handy. Cover a small baking sheet with aluminum foil.

10. Put the ½ cup sugar (no water) in a small saucepan and place over moderate heat. Cook, stirring constantly with a wooden spoon to dissolve any lumps, until the sugar just begins to caramelize. Stir in the whole hazelnuts and cook about another 30 seconds until a medium but not dark caramel color is reached. Immediately pour onto the foil-covered cookie sheet to cool and harden—say 15 minutes.

11. While the praline is cooling, dissolve the remaining ⅔ cup sugar in ½ cup water in a small saucepan and bring to a boil over moderate heat. Cook until you reach thread (230° to 234°F.)—the first stage after syrup, when a droplet just begins to leave a thread.

12. Break the now-hardened praline into smaller chunks and grind to a coarse consistency in a food processor. Reserve.

13. Meanwhile, ready the eggs and butter: Place the eggs in the bowl of an electric mixer with the whip attached; cut the softened butter into small pieces and reserve.

14. When the sugar reaches the thread stage, remove it from the heat and immediately start beating the eggs at full speed in the mixer. While beating, pour in the hot sugar—carefully for few things are hotter than cooked sugar—and continue beating until the mixture is light, fluffy, and only slightly warm. (If you get hard chunks of sugar while beating, you have, alas, over-cooked the sugar. Start over at Step 11.)

15. While still beating, add the butter, bit by bit, and beat until the mixture is smooth and fluffy.

16. Add the ground praline—the caramelized hazelnuts—and mix well. Reserve in a cool place but do not allow it to become too hard to spread.

PREPARING THE RASPBERRY SAUCE AND CHOCOLATE GARNISH

17. Purée the raspberries with ⅔ cup sugar in a food processor or blender. Strain and reserve.

18. Coarsely grind the bittersweet chocolate in a food processor. (Do not overgrind lest the blade melt the chocolate.) Reserve.

ASSEMBLING THE CAKE (SEE NOTE)

19. Cut the large hazelnut sponge into three strips, each 13 by 6 inches. Carefully turn over one of them and peel away the parchment paper.

20. Cut a 12-by-5-inch piece of corrugated cardboard. Center the cake strip over the cardboard. (In the end we will trim away the ½-inch overhang.)

21. Spread the praline buttercream in an even ¾-inch layer over the strip of cake.

22. Invert a second layer of cake on the buttercream layer and peel away the parchment. Spread with an even ¾-inch layer of whipped ganache.

23. Invert the last layer of cake on the ganache and peel away the parchment. Spread with an even ¾-inch layer of whipped crème fraîche, leaving the top as smooth as possible—this is the top of the cake.

24. Refrigerate for at least 30 minutes, allowing the creams to set.

25. Neatly trim off ½ inch all around (flush with the cardboard underneath), using a wet knife rinsed under hot running water after each cut.

26. Coat the 4 sides of the cake—but not the top—with the coarsely ground chocolate. Use your hands but work quickly so the chocolate doesn't melt.

27. To decorate the top, cut a 1-inch-wide strip of parchment paper or waxed paper a couple of inches longer than the cake and lay it down the middle of the cake. Using a sifter or strainer, generously sprinkle the top surface with cocoa powder. Carefully lift away the paper ribbon, leaving a white racing stripe.

28. Mirror dessert plates with raspberry sauce. Top with thin slices of marjolaine. Serve.

Note It's important that the three creams be at the right consistency—firm enough to support the other layers, yet soft enough to spread. In hot weather you may even want to refrigerate the cake for 15 minutes or so after adding each new layer of cream to let it firm up.

Hot Pear Feuilleté

SERVES 8

This is a killer dessert. A little involved, but rich, extravagant, unique. Actually, it's beyond rich: The hot, buttery puff pastry, the smooth pastry cream, and the caramelized sugar on the pear are as calorie-laden as can be—but still the taste is light. It's a performance dish, too—buy a little $15 blowtorch at Sears and amaze your friends but try not to set their hair on fire.

---

2 pounds puff pastry (you can buy it at your bakery)

I egg, lightly beaten, for egg wash

PASTRY CREAM

I cup milk

2 drops vanilla extract

4 egg yolks

½ cup sugar

2 tablespoons flour

¾ cup heavy cream

I ounce good pear eau-de-vie (the brandy, *not* the liqueur)

4 small very ripe pears

Sugar for caramelizing pears

Special Equipment Blowtorch (such as Bernz-o-Matic)

MAKING THE PUFF PASTRY

1. Preheat the oven to 325°F.

2. Roll out the puff pastry into a sheet 3/16 inch thick. Lay it on a baking sheet and place in the freezer for 15 to 20 minutes.

3. Remove the pastry from the freezer and, with the point of a sharp paring knife, cut out 8 pear shapes about half again as large as the pears you'll be using. Make the cuts as clean-edged as possible.

4. Mix the egg for the egg wash. *Brushing with a pastry brush from the center toward the edges, cover just the top surface of the pastries with the egg wash, not allowing any to drip down the sides. If you do gum up the sides, your pastries won't rise properly.*

5. Bake in the oven for a total of 1¼ to 1½ hours, but about halfway through—at 45 minutes—cut the pastries horizontally in half and open them up so that the layers on the inside will cook to a crisp golden brown. Reserve.

MAKING THE PASTRY CREAM

6. Bring the milk with the vanilla to a boil.

7. Mix the egg yolks, sugar, and flour in a large mixing bowl.

8. Add the hot milk, mix well, return the mixture to the pan, and cook, stirring constantly, until it comes to a boil and for 30 seconds more. The pastry cream should now be very thick but smooth. Pour it into a mixing bowl and set aside to cool.

9. Once the pastry cream is cool, whip the cream until it holds a firm peak.

10. Add the pear brandy to the

cooled pastry cream and whisk vigorously to loosen the mixture. Carefully fold the whipped cream into the pastry cream. Reserve.

BLOWTORCHING AND FINAL ASSEMBLY

11. Preheat the oven to 350°F.

12. Peel the pears, cut lengthwise in half, and remove the cores. Lay the pear halves flat side down and cut crosswise into ⅛-inch slices. Tilt the slices and spread them out slightly like falling dominoes.

13. Using a spatula, carefully place the sliced pear halves on a buttered sheet of aluminum foil on your work surface. *Heap 2 to 3 generous tablespoons of sugar over each pear half.*

14. Place the baked pastries in the oven to warm. Make sure your pastry cream is handy.

15. Using the blowtorch, caramelize the sugar on top of the pear halves—it will take no longer than 15 to 20 seconds per pear. If necessary, add more sugar during the torching for an even coating.

16. Remove the pastries from the oven and place the bottom halves on dessert plates. Smother with generous spoonfuls of pastry cream. Top with the other halves of puff pastry. Crown each pastry with a just-caramelized pear half. Serve immediately.

Gâteau Concorde

SERVES 8 TO 12

Without a doubt, this is the most popular dessert in the restaurant, year in and year out. If I didn't include the recipe in this book, my customers would kill me. They ask for it all the time. Its appeal is that it is rich enough to satisfy the most crazed chocoholic, yet it's still deceptively light—it melts in the mouth.

I should acknowledge that I borrowed the original recipe from my friend Michel Richard, chef of Citrus, who brought it from Gaston Lenôtre, the most famous pastry chef in France. I've adapted the recipe to my taste over the years.

Advice: The key to success with this recipe, as with most recipes, is first to read the recipe all the way through, think it out, and organize all your materials before you start cooking.

MERINGUE

10 egg whites

2⅛ cups plus 5 tablespoons powdered sugar

1½ cups granulated sugar

10 tablespoons unsweetened cocoa powder

Desserts

213

¾ cup sugar

8 egg yolks

13½ ounces bittersweet chocolate, melted

2 cups heavy cream

Sprinkle of powdered sugar

Special Equipment
Large pastry bag with ⅝-inch (no. 8) plain round tip
3 baking sheets

ORGANIZING THE INGREDIENTS

1. Preheat the oven to just under 200°F.

2. Weigh the chocolate for the mousse, break it into small pieces, and put it in a pan to melt in the barely warm oven. Don't hurry it, let it melt for 5 to 10 minutes until it's just the temperature of a warm bath.

3. Carefully separate 10 egg whites for the meringue and reserve 8 of the yolks for the mousse.

4. Measure out and reserve separately:

    —5 tablespoons powdered sugar
    —1⅓ cups granulated sugar
    —1⅓ cups powdered sugar sifted with 10 tablespoons cocoa powder

5. Cut 3 pieces of parchment paper to fit the cookie sheets. On one piece draw two 8-inch circles. On a second piece, draw a third 8-inch circle at one end, leaving the other end blank.

6. Remove the melted chocolate from the oven and reserve in a warm place.

7. Increase the oven heat to 300°F. Fit the pastry bag with the plain round tip.

MAKING THE MERINGUE

8. In the clean, dry bowl of an electric mixer, beat the egg whites until they are fluffy and barely hold a soft peak. Add the 5 tablespoons powdered sugar and continue to beat until very firm. Then add the 1⅓ cups granulated sugar and beat for another 10 seconds.

9. Remove the bowl from the machine. Quickly and gently fold in the powdered sugar sifted with the cocoa, using a rubber spatula.

10. Fill the pastry bag about two-thirds full with the meringue (better to refill it than to struggle with an overfilled bag). Starting at the center and spiraling outward, pipe out three 8-inch disks on the circles on the parchment paper.

11. Using all remaining space on the second cookie sheet and all of the third unused cookie sheet, pipe out straight lines of the meringue the whole length of the sheet, separated by about ½ inch.

12. Bake for 1 hour. The meringue will be dry and brittle. Remove from the oven and let cool to room temperature.

MAKING THE MOUSSE

13. While the meringue is baking, make your sugar syrup: Put the sugar and 1 cup water in a saucepan and stir to dissolve. Allow to boil for 1 minute. Remove from the heat.

14. In a clean mixing bowl, start to beat the egg yolks at medium speed. While mixing, add just 1 cup of the hot sugar syrup. Continue beating at full speed for 3 to 4 minutes until the mixture has cooled to about body temperature (lukewarm).

15. Remove the bowl from the mixer and stir in the warm melted chocolate with a rubber spatula. Refrigerate for about 20 minutes until the mixture begins to jell and thicken but don't let it get hard.

16. Whip the cream until stiff and fold it into the cooled chocolate mixture. Refrigerate for at least another hour or until set.

ASSEMBLING THE CAKE

17. Cut a 9-inch circle from corrugated cardboard. Using a dab of mousse as glue, center one of the meringue circles on the cardboard circle.

18. Gently spread a good third of the chilled mousse in an even layer over the meringue. Do not stir or overwork the mousse, or it will forever lose its body.

19. Top with a second disk, this one with the smooth side up, and spread with another third of the mousse. Add the third disk, smooth side up. Fill in and smooth the sides and top of the cake with the remaining mousse.

20. Break the meringue sticks into uneven lengths about an inch taller than the cake. Stand them side by side around the entire cake. Break the remaining meringue into shorter uneven lengths and pile them randomly but prettily atop the cake. Sprinkle with powdered sugar.

21. Refrigerate at least 2 hours before attempting to cut and serve.

Chocolate Hazelnut Cookies

MAKES 2 DOZEN

This is a traditional Viennese cookie, a very simple recipe, no more complicated than pound cake—equal quarter-pound parts of the four ingredients. The only trick is cooking them long and gently like a meringue, so that they dry out sufficiently—ideally overnight. They are irresistible because of the roasted hazelnuts. You'll find them calling to you in the middle of the night. An ice cream sandwich made with them will slay you.

1 cup hazelnuts (filberts)

4 ounces bittersweet chocolate

¼ cup granulated sugar

2 tablespoons flour

8 tablespoons (1 stick) unsalted butter

Powdered sugar or 2 ounces white chocolate, melted, for decorating

1. Preheat the oven to 350°F.
2. Roast the hazelnuts until light golden brown—approximately 10 to 12 minutes. Flake off the charred skins and grind the peeled nuts in a food processor to a fine paste.
3. Melt the chocolate in the top of a double boiler.

4. In the bowl of an electric mixer, cream the hazelnut paste, sugar, flour, and butter together until smooth. Still mixing, add the melted chocolate and mix well. Refrigerate until firm.

5. Preheat the oven to 250°F. Line 2 baking sheets with parchment paper.

6. Form the chilled dough into balls approximately 1 inch in diameter and place them on the baking sheets 2 inches apart. Bake for 10 minutes, then reduce the heat to 200°F. and leave cookies inside for 12 hours, or overnight.

7. When the cookies are done, let them cool to room temperature. Decorate them with a sprinkle of powdered sugar or a thin zigzag or spiral of melted white chocolate piped from a paper cornet. Eat.

Pecan Wafers

MAKES ABOUT 2 DOZEN

These are perfect accompaniments to sorbets. They are a hybrid sugar cookie—just as simple to make, but with the brown sugar and the pecans, a lot tastier. Make the dough well in advance, keep it in the refrigerator or freezer, and slice and bake when ready. They are at their best straight out of the oven.

1 cup pastry flour

¾ cup plus 2 tablespoons granulated sugar

8 tablespoons (1 stick) unsalted butter

Drop of vanilla extract

Pinch of salt

1 egg

3 tablespoons finely chopped pecans

3 tablespoons brown sugar

1. Mix together the flour, sugar, butter, vanilla, and salt. Add the egg and continue mixing just until smooth.

2. Roll the dough into a long sausage approximately 1½ inches in diameter. Wrap tightly in plastic wrap and refrigerate until hard.

3. Preheat the oven to 350°F.

4. Mix together the pecans and brown sugar in a small bowl. Slice ¼-inch-thick circles of dough and press one side into the pecan mixture. Place on a buttered or papered cookie sheet and flatten a bit with your fingertips. Bake for 8 to 10 minutes, until golden brown around the edge. Remove from the oven and cool on a rack.

Chocolate Peppermint Truffles

MAKES 3 DOZEN

This bite-sized chocolate candy is as common in France as the Hershey bar in the United States. Truffle candies earned their name not from any truffle in the ingredients but from their resemblance to the dark knobby fungus. Nowadays truffles are made round or square, white or dark, soft or hard. This recipe offers a choice of two different forms—the traditional knobby candy and the bonbon—and while not hard to do, it does take a little time. Chocolate works best when not rushed.

¾ cup heavy cream

14 ounces good dark bittersweet chocolate

3 tablespoons peppermint schnapps

2 tablespoons unsalted butter

2 teaspoons safflower or other unflavored vegetable oil if making traditional truffles

¼ cup unsweetened cocoa powder if making traditional truffles

Special Equipment
Foil cups if making bonbons
Pastry bag with small round tip if making bonbons

1. Put the cream on to boil in a small saucepan.

2. In the meantime, cut 8 ounces of the chocolate into small pieces. When the cream comes to a boil, add the chocolate, cover tightly, and allow to rest off the heat for 3 or 4 minutes while the chocolate melts.

3. Stir the chocolate and cream until smooth. Stir in the peppermint schnapps and the butter. Allow to sit and cool until very thick but not hard—an hour or so.

4. With an electric mixer, whip the ganache—the cream and chocolate mixture—at full speed until it is light and fluffy and has increased in volume by half to two-thirds. But do not overwhip.

MAKING TRADITIONAL TRUFFLES — VARIATION 1

5. Chill the whipped truffle cream in the refrigerator until hard—a good hour.

6. Melt the remaining 6 ounces chocolate with the vegetable oil in the top of a double boiler. Sift the cocoa powder into a cake pan, round or square, it matters not.

7. Scoop out balls of hardened truffle cream, using a melon baller dipped in warm water between scoops. Quickly dip or roll each ball in the melted chocolate coating, then drop it into the sifted cocoa powder and swirl it around to coat well.

8. Store in the refrigerator until 15 to 30 minutes before serving. At room temperature the chocolate coating will be hard but the centers soft.

MAKING BONBONS IN FOIL CUPS — VARIATION 2

5. Melt the remaining 6 ounces chocolate in the top of a double boiler but do not add the vegetable oil.

6. Spoon a little melted chocolate into a bonbon cup, tilt it all around, coating the entire inside of the foil, and pour out the excess chocolate. Repeat with all the cups. Reserve the rest of the chocolate for the tops.

7. Fit the pastry bag with the small round tip and fill the bag with the room-temperature whipped truffle cream. Pipe the cream into the center of each bonbon cup to within 1/8 inch of the top.

8. Fill the top 1/8 inch of each cup with a little more melted chocolate to seal in the filling. Store in the refrigerator until 15 to 30 minutes before serving.

Index

K

knives, 15–16

L

lamb:
  leg of, with roasted garlic sauce, 119–20
  loin with herbs, grilled, 123
  rack of, with Pommery mustard, 112
  saddle of, with Cabernet and shallots, 113–14
leek(s):
  baby, with tomato and olive oil, 43–44
  whitefish with truffle and, 81–82
Lenôtre, Gaston, 213
lettuce, salmon with Champagne sauce and, 88
lime mint sorbet, 179
liver:
  duck, mousse with Calvados, 61–62
  see also calves' liver; foie gras
lobster:
  angel hair fisherman's style, 159
  cracking, 84
  cream sauce, 163
  fumet, 29
  and pigeon with Cabernet sauce, 152–53
  pregnant female, 29
  salad Chinoise, 40
  seafood ravioli, 162–64
  spinach soup, 26
  and truffle mousseline, turbot with, 99–100
  with turnips and Pernod, 84–85
lotte (angler or monkfish):
  saddle of, roasted with oyster mushrooms, 86–87
  scaloppini with artichoke hearts, 102
louvar, with roasted red bell pepper sauce, 103
Lucullus, Lucius, 74

M

marinade, honey and mustard, 125
marinated chanterelle salad, 42–43
marjolaine, gâteau, 209–11

mayonnaise, lemon and olive oil, 69–70
meats, 107–25
  calves' liver sautéed with Zante currants, 121
  calves' liver with shallots and gherkins, 122
  fillet of veal with paprika, 118–19
  grilled lamb loin with herbs, 123
  grilled pork tenderloin with honey and mustard, 125
  leg of lamb with roasted garlic sauce, 119–20
  rack of lamb with Pommery mustard, 112
  red, resting after cooking, 112
  saddle of lamb with Cabernet and shallots, 113–14
  state-of-the-art veal stock, 109–10
  testing for doneness, 120
  veal chops with artichoke mousseline, 117
  veal sweetbreads with port and green peppercorns, 114–15
  veal sweetbreads with shallots and sherry wine vinegar, 116
  venison with cracked black peppercorns, 111
  venison with pears and red wine, 124
  warm roast beef and potato salad, 49–50
Mère Blanc, La, 138
meringue:
  chocolate, 213, 214
  copper bowls for, 192
  hazelnut, 207–8
mint:
  chocolate ice cream, 184–85
  lime sorbet, 179
  see also peppermint
mise en place concept, 13–14
miso dressing, tuna and octopus fan with, 75
mixers, five-quart, 17–18
monkfish, *see* lotte
morels, 70
  artichoke hearts with, 69–70
  roasted rabbit saddle with, 149–50
  stuffed, 65–66
mousse:
  chocolate, 202, 203, 214–15
  chocolate pots au crème, 177–78
  duck liver, with Calvados, 61–62
  smoked salmon, 77

Index
∎
231

Index
■
233

W

wafers, pecan, 216–17
walnut torte, 205–6
warm roast beef and potato salad, 49–50
whipped cream, rum, 207, 208
whitefish:
    with leek and truffle, 81–82
    with tomato and green peppercorns, 105
wine:
    Sauternes, braised endive and asparagus with, 68
    see also Cabernet; red wine

Z

Zante currants, calves' liver sautéed with, 121
zests, citrus, 91
    three, sturgeon with, 98
zigzag, 202–4
Zinfandel sorbet, 181
zucchini, broiled John Dory with, 82–83

Liquid and Dry Measure Equivalencies

CUSTOMARY	METRIC
¼ teaspoon	1.25 milliliters
½ teaspoon	2.5 milliliters
1 teaspoon	5 milliliters
1 tablespoon	15 milliliters
1 fluid ounce	30 milliliters
¼ cup	60 milliliters
⅓ cup	80 milliliters
½ cup	120 milliliters
1 cup	240 milliliters
1 pint (2 cups)	480 milliliters
1 quart (4 cups. 32 ounces)	960 milliliters (.96 liters)
1 gallon (4 quarts)	3.84 liters
1 ounce (by weight)	28 grams
¼ pound (4 ounces)	114 grams
1 pound (16 ounces)	454 grams
2.2 pounds	1 kilogram (1000) grams

Oven Temperature Equivalencies

DESCRIPTION	°FAHRENHEIT	°CELSIUS
Cool	200	90
Very slow	250	120
Slow	300–325	150–160
Moderately slow	325–350	160–180
Moderate	350–375	180–190
Moderately hot	375–400	190–200
Hot	400–450	200–230
Very hot	450–500	230–260